Hong Kong's Legislature under China's Sovereignty

# Chinese and Comparative Law Series



VOLUME 3

The titles published in this series are listed at *brill.com/ccls*

# Hong Kong's Legislature under China's Sovereignty

*1998–2013*

*By*

Gu Yu

BRILL
NIJHOFF

LEIDEN | BOSTON

Library of Congress Cataloging-in-Publication Data

Yu, Gu, 1981- author.
Hong Kong's legislature under China's sovereignty 1998-2013 / by Gu Yu.
pages cm. -- (Chinese and comparative law series ; volume 3)
Includes bibliographical references and index.
ISBN 978-90-04-27790-8 (hardback : alk. paper) -- ISBN 978-90-04-27628-4 (e-book) 1. Hong Kong (China). Legislative Council. 2. Legislative bodies--China--Hong Kong. 3. Hong Kong (China)--Politics and government--1997- I. Title.

KNQ9348.3.Y84 2015
328.5125--dc23

2014049193

This publication has been typeset in the multilingual "Brill" typeface. With over 5,100 characters covering Latin, IPA, Greek, and Cyrillic, this typeface is especially suitable for use in the humanities. For more information, please see www.brill.com/brill-typeface.

ISSN 2213-4875
ISBN 978-90-04-27790-8 (hardback)
ISBN 978-90-04-27628-4 (e-book)



This book is printed on acid-free paper.

*In memory of my sister, qiqi*
*Dedicated to my parents, Gu Kaike and Xu Xuejun*
*and*
*my husband Clement*

# Contents

**Foreword** XI
**Acknowledgements** XIII
**List of Tables and Figures** XIV
**List of Cases** XVII
**List of Rulings of Presidents of the Legislative Council** XVIII
**List of Abbreviations** XX

1 **Assessing The Legislative Council**
*Autonomy and Performance* 1
Introduction 1
Functions of Legislatures: Do Legislatures Exist to Make Law? 6
Autonomy of Legislatures 9
Conclusion 14

2 **External Environment and Internal Characteristics of Legco's Autonomy** 17
Autonomy of the Pre-1997 Legco 17
*Separation from the Executive* 17
*Administrative and Financial Autonomy* 18
*Committee Autonomy* 19
*Political Parties of Legco in the Colonial Period* 20
*Legco in 1997* 21
Autonomy of Post-1998 Legco 22
*External Environment* 23
*Internal Characteristics: Rules, Committee Autonomy, Administrative Autonomy and Financial Autonomy* 34
Conclusion 41

3 **Scrutiny of Legislation** 43
Private Member's Bill Under Article 74 of Basic Law 43
*Decline of Private member's Bills* 44
*President's Rulings on Private member's Bills* 45
*Summaries* 51
Scrutiny of Bills: Bills Committees 52
*Bills Scrutinised by Bills Committees* 53
*Legislators' Participation in BCs* 55
*Deliberation in BCs* 57

*Case Study: Bills Committee on the Interception of Communications and Surveillance Bill* 59
*Summaries* 65
Scrutiny of Bills: Members' Committee Stage Amendments to Government Bills 66
*Restrictions on the Introduction of Members' CSAs* 66
*Introduction of Members' CSAs* 71
*Determinants of Members' CSAs* 73
*Filibuster: An Unusual Procedural Weapon* 82
*Summaries* 87
Study of Several Bills: Government's Defeats 88
*National Security (Legislative Provisions) Bill* 88
*Government's Defeat in Race Discrimination Bill* 96
Scrutiny of Subsidiary Legislation 98
*Results of Subsidiary Legislation* 99
*Negative Vetting or Positive Vetting* 101
*Case Study: Country Parks (Designation) (Consolidation) (Amendment) Order 2010* 105
*Summaries* 108
Conclusion 108

4 **Scrutiny of Public Finance** 110
Institutional Framework for Financial Scrutiny by Legco 112
*Legco's Power to Amend and Approve Public Expenditure* 112
*Restrictions of 'Public Expenditure' and 'Charging Effect'* 114
*Ex ante Scrutiny*: Control over Budget and Public Expenditure 116
*Examination of Budget Proposals* 116
*Examination of Other Financial Proposals* 127
*Collapsed Levies* 129
*Means of Scrutinising Budget and Taxation Issues* 133
*Ex post Scrutiny*: The Public Accounts Committee 134
*Objectives of the PAC* 135
*Relation between Audit Commission and PAC* 136
*Composition of the PAC* 137
*PAC Scrutiny of Public Expenditure* 138
*Impact of the PAC* 147
Expenditure Without Legco Approval 148
Conclusion 151

5 **Motions Without Legislative Effect** 153
Restrictions on Moving a Motion or Amendment to a Motion 154
Determinants of Result of Members' Motions 160
*Introduction of Motions* 162
*Separate Voting Mechanism* 164
*Political Orientation and the Nature of the Issues* 166
*Government's Response to Successful Motions* 168
No Confidence Motions 170
*No Confidence Motions in Early Days of the* HKSAR 172
*Recent Development of no Confidence Motions* 175
*Propriety of Introducing a No Confidence Motion* 177
Motion for Adjournment of The Council 179
Conclusion 183

6 **Questions** 185
Notice and Number of Questions 186
Content of Questions 186
Questions to the Government 190
Chief Executive's Question-and-Answer Session 193
Conclusion 195

7 **Investigation Power**
***Legislative Council (Powers And Privileges) Ordinance*** 197
Drafting History of the 1985 Legislative Council (Powers and Privileges) Ordinance 197
How Legco Uses its Investigation Power Under the PPO 200
Significance Of Investigation Power Under The PPO 205
Challenges To The PPO: Cheng Kar Shun Case 208
Conclusion 213

8 **Conclusion** 215
Level of Autonomy 215
*External Environment* 215
*Internal Characteristics* 218
*Autonomy of Legco* 221
Actual Impact of Legco 221
*Interaction Pattern* 222
*Trends in Legco's Actual Impact* 223
Strategy Shift and New Rule After 2012 224

*Beijing's New Strategy and Its Impact* 224
*Rule of Leung Chun Ying* 226

**Bibliography** 231
Articles and Books 231
Selected Committee Minutes, Reports and Factsheets of Legco and Government Documents 236
Internet Sources 239

**Index** 241

# Foreword

The political evolution of Hong Kong from a British colony to a Special Administrative Region of the People's Republic of China (PRC) is a rare and interesting phenomenon in the history of colonialism and imperialism. From the Chinese point of view, the cessation of Hong Kong Island by the Qing Emperor to the British Empire in 1842 after China's defeat in the 'Opium War' was the beginning of modern China's history of oppression and humiliation by Western powers. The return of Hong Kong to China in 1997 was thus of great symbolic and psychological importance to the Chinese nation and its people, and was part and parcel of the project of the 'great revival' (weida fuxing 偉大復興) of Chinese civilization.

The reunification of Hong Kong with the Chinese mainland was not a process of simple absorption of the former colony by the motherland, or the simple substitution of an official from mainland China appointed by the Beijing government for the governor of colonial Hong Kong appointed by London. Instead, the reunification was achieved on the basis of the concepts of 'One Country, Two Systems' and 'Hong Kong people ruling Hong Kong' developed by the late Chinese statesman Deng Xiaoping and enshrined in the Sino-British Joint Declaration on Hong Kong's future signed in 1984. Hong Kong was to retain its pre-existing capitalism, including its legal and social systems, civil liberties and way of life, and the government of Hong Kong was to be staffed by Hong Kong people. This experiment in 'One Country, Two Systems' began in 1997.

One of the major challenges faced by Hong Kong since the 1997 handover was the development of a political system that is appropriate for Hong Kong as a Special Administrative Region (HKSAR) of the PRC. Before the Joint Declaration of 1984, Hong Kong had a reasonably sound legal system based on English common law, but it did not enjoy any democracy in terms of the political rights of the people to elect their government and legislators. Since the mid-1980s, the colonial government started to move Hong Kong towards 'representative government' by introducing elected elements into its Legislative Council. The project of democratization continued after 1997 on the basis of the Hong Kong Basic Law—the constitutional instrument enacted by the Chinese National People's Congress in 1990 for the governance of the HKSAR.

The present book is an in-depth study of the nature and operation of the constitutional and political system of the HKSAR as it has evolved since 1997, particularly from the perspective of its legislature and the relationship between the legislature and the executive branch of government.

It has often been said by officials of the Central Government of the PRC and of the HKSAR Government, by mainland scholars of the Hong Kong Basic Law, and even by some Hong Kong judges in their judgments, that the design of the HKSAR constitutional and political system is 'executive-led'. On the basis of a thorough study and analysis of the data on the actual operation of the Legislative Council of the HKSAR since 1997, including the exercise of its powers and functions of legislation, financial control and scrutiny of the administration, this book shows that in practice there is a significant degree of sharing of power between the executive branch of the HKSAR government and the legislature. The author demonstrates with abundant evidence that despite the formal restrictions on the power of legislators stipulated in the Basic Law, the power of the Legislative Council to veto any legislative or financial spending proposal put forward by the Government enables it to bargain effectively with Government officials and secure the outcomes it desires.

The most significant contribution of the book lies in its in-depth empirical and statistical study of how this power of veto and of participation in deciding matters of law and public expenditure has been exercised by the Legislative Council for a period of fifteen years. It will enable the community of scholars of Hong Kong, and members of the public in Hong Kong, to better understand the real nature of Hong Kong's constitutional and political system as one in which power-sharing between the executive and legislative branches of government prevails over and overrides the original legislative intent, if any, of establishing an 'executive-led' government. This finding is, I believe, of far-reaching significance for the study of the government and politics of the HKSAR.

*Professor Albert H.Y. Chen*
Chan Professor of Constitutional Law
University of Hong Kong
8 August 2014

# Acknowledgements

This book originates in my doctoral thesis. I wish to express my deep gratitude to Professor Albert Hung-yee Chen, my doctoral supervisor at The University of Hong Kong. Professor Chen has given careful guidance to me on research methods. He has also kindly helped to facilitate my interviews with legislators. This book could not have been completed without his advice and encouragement.

I would like to thank the following Legislative Councillors who have kindly accepted my interview requests (names in alphabetical order):

Mrs Rita FAN HSU Lai-tai
Mr Albert HO Chun-yan
Ms Emily LAU Wai-hing
Mr LEE Cheuk-yan
Mr TAM Yiu-chung
Mr James TO Kun-sun
Mr Ronny TONG Ka-wah
Mr Jasper TSANG Yok-sing

I am especially grateful to Professor Richard Cullen for his kind help and generous comments on my study. I also wish to thank Professor Sonny Lo and Mr Benny Tai for their precious comments on the original thesis. I benefit enormously from Professor Lo's critical comments from the perspective of political science.

My special thanks also go to Professor Anne Cheung for her enthusiastic support and encouragement. I appreciate of Professor Fu Hualing's kind help with my research and the publication of this book.

I wish to thank my friend, Dr Jiang Qin for his helpful advice regarding quantitative analysis. I appreciate the help of Dr Karen Lee and Dr Yang Xiaonan in offering useful materials and enlightening suggestions.

I would like to extend my gratitude to Ms Ingeborg van der Laan from Brill for her patience and consideration.

Above all, I must thank my family who give me love and wholehearted support. I should like to record my great debt of gratitude to my parents and Clement's parents. I wish to express my special appreciation to my brother-in-law, Mr Li Tie, for his firm support.

I am most grateful to Clement for his love, support and encouragement.

Of course, I take complete responsibility for all the statements and views expressed in this book.

# List of Tables and Figures

## Tables


1.1 Professor Sisson's indices of institutional autonomy 11
1.2 External environment for Legco's autonomy 13
1.3 Internal characteristics of Legco's autonomy 15
2.1 Political orientation of Legco members, 1998–2016 28
2.2 Proportion of panel chairs without legislative experience in the first session of term 41
3.1 Result of bills introduced by members, 1998–2013 45
3.2 President's rulings on public bills introduced by members, 1998–2013 47
3.3 Proportion of bills committees that completed their work, 1998–2012 54
3.4 Proportion of bills scrutinised by Bills Committees, 1998–2012 54
3.5 Bills Committees and government amendments, 1998–2012 58
3.6 President Rita Fan's rulings on members' CSAs, 1998–2008 67
3.7 President Jasper Tsang's rulings on members' CSAs, 2008–2012 68
3.8 Members' CSAs by sponsors' constituencies, 1998–2012 71
3.9 Members' CSAs by sponsors' political orientation, 1998–2012 73
3.10 Result of members' CSAs to government bills, 1998–2012 74
3.11 Determinants of unsuccessful CSAs, 1998–2012 75
3.12 Proportion of CSAs negatived by separate voting mechanism, 1998–2012 75
3.13 Members' CSAs negatived by different constituencies under the SVM controlling for sponsors' political orientation, 1998–2012 76
3.14 Members' CSAs negatived by different constituencies under the SVM controlling for the nature of the issues, 1998–2012 77
3.15 Voting result in FCs by the nature of the issues controlling for sponsors' political orientation, 1998–2012 78
3.16 Voting result in GCs by the nature of the issues controlling for sponsors' political orientation, 1998–2012 79
3.17 Voting behaviour of the major political groups on members' CSAs in selected years 81
3.18 Division over members' CSAs in various camps by the nature of the issues in selected years 82
3.19 Result of subsidiary legislation under positive vetting procedure, 1998–2013 100
3.20 Result of subsidiary legislation under negative vetting procedure, 1998–2013 101

3.21 Result of amendments to subsidiary legislation under negative vetting procedure, 1998–2013 102
3.22 Votes required to make subsidiary legislation effective under different vetting procedures, 1998–2012 102
4.1 Restriction on members' power to move financial initiatives or amendments to financial proposals 114
4.2 Time spent on the examination of the estimates of expenditure, 1998–2013 118
4.3 Articles containing 'eight-party coalition/八黨聯盟' in Hong Kong Newspapers, 1998–2010 123
4.4 Eight-party consensus on the 2001–02 budget proposals and government response 124
4.5 Results of non-budget financial proposals, 1998–2013 128
4.6 Proportions of non-budget financial proposals with recommendation of subcommittees, 1998–2013 129
4.7 Political orientation of PAC members, 1998–2013 138
4.8 Public hearings held by PAC, 1998–2013 139
4.9 The average number of public hearings per subject, 1998–2013 140
5.1 President's rulings on members' motion or amendments relating to the NPCSC and CPG 157
5.2 Result of motions moved by members, 1998–2013 161
5.3 Amendments to members' motions, 1998–2013 161
5.4 Passed members' motions, 1998–2013 161
5.5 Members' motions by the sponsors' constituencies, 1998–2013 162
5.6 Members' motions by the nature of the issues controlling for the sponsors' constituencies, 1998–2013 163
5.7 Proportion of motions negatived by SVM of negatived motions, 1998–2013 165
5.8 Motions negatived by FCs by the nature of the issues controlling for the sponsors' political orientation, 1998–2013 165
5.9 Motions negatived by GCs by the nature of the issues controlling for the sponsors' political orientation under SVM, 1998–2013 166
5.10 Pass rate of members' motions by the nature of the issues controlling for the sponsors' political orientation, 1998–2013 167
5.11 No confidence motions moved at Legco's Plenary Meetings, 1998–2013 172
5.12 Result of motions for adjournment debate, 1998–2013 181
6.1 Restrictions on content of questions 187
6.2 Number of questions per session, 1998–2013 191
6.3 Top six policy bureaux in selected sessions 192
6.4 CE's question-and-answer sessions, 1998–2013 194
7.1 Select committees/subcommittees carrying out investigation function, 1998–2013 203

## Figures

2.1 Chairmanship of Legco panels (excluding Deputy Chairmanship), 1998–2013 40
3.1 Membership of Bills Committees, 1998–2012 56
3.2 Proportion of democrats in FCs and proportion of the CSAs moved by them, 1998–2012 72
4.1 Questions and requests raised by members of the Finance Committee, 1998–2013 117
7.1 Motions/resolutions invoking the PPO, 1985–2013 201

# List of Cases

*Cheng Kar Shun and Leung Chi Kin v the Honourable Li Fung Ying and Others* [2009] HKEC 1587 25
*Julita F Raza and Others v Chief Executive in Council and Others* [2005] 3 HKLRD 561 132
*Koo Sze Yiu & Anor v Chief Executive of the HKSAR* [2006] 3 HKLRD 455 60
*Leung Kwok Hung & Anor v Chief Executive of the HKSAR* [2006] HKEC 239 59
*Leung Kwok Hung v The President of the Legislative Council of the Hong Kong Special Administrative Region* [2012] 3 HKLRD 470 84
*Leung Kwok Hung v The President of the Legislative Council of the Hong Kong Special Administrative Region* [2014] HKEC 1604 84
*Leung Kwok Hung v The President of the Legislative Council of the Hong Kong Special Administrative Region and Another* [2007] 1 HKLRD 387 115
*Ng Ka Ling v Director of Immigration* (1999) 2 HKCFAR 4 210
*Director of Immigration v Chong Fung Yuen* (2001) 4 HKCFAR 211 210

# List of Rulings of Presidents of the Legislative Council


Ruling on Amendment Proposed by Hon LEE Cheuk-yan (14 May 2004) 155

Ruling on Amendment Proposed by Hon Chan Wai Yip (17 June 2009) 159

Ruling on Amendments Proposed by Dr Hon YEUNG Sum (9 December 2003) 156

Ruling on Amendments Proposed by Hon Martin LEE Chu-ming (30 April 2004) 155

Ruling on Closing the Joint Debate at the Committee stage of the Legislative Council (Amendment) Bill 2012 (22 May 2012) 83

Ruling on Committee Stage Amendment to Legislative Council (Amendment) Bill 2007 Proposed by Hon Sin Chung Kai (17 April 2008) 71

Ruling on Committee Stage Amendments Proposed by 14 Members to the Appropriation Bill 2014 (27 April 2014) 86

Ruling on Committee Stage Amendments to the Buildings (Amendment) Bill 2010 Proposed by Hon Kam Nai-wai (27 June 2011) 70

Ruling on Employment (Amendment) (No. 2) Bill 2001 Proposed by Hon CHAN Kwok-keung, Hon LI Fung-ying, JP and Hon LEUNG Fu-wah, MH, JP (14 March 2002) 50

Ruling on Forests and Countryside (Amendment) Bill 2006 proposed by Hon CHOY So-yuk (18 January 2007) 49

Ruling on Hon CHAN Kwok-keung's Proposed Legal Aid (Amendment) Bill 2000 (29 June 2000) 50

Ruling on Hon Cyd HO's Proposed Amendment to Clause 59 (concerning the Functions of District Councils) in the District Councils Bill (8 March 1999) 70

Ruling on Hon Ronny TONG Ka-wah's Proposed Amendment to Hon CHAN Kam-lam's Amendment to the Motion on 'Introducing Legislative Amendments to Open Up Community Radio Stations' to Be Moved by Hon James TO Kun-sun at the Council Meeting of 23 January 2008 (22 January 2008) 156

Ruling on Legislative Council (Amendment) Bill 1997 (14 November 1997) 51

Ruling on Motions Relating to the Scrutiny of the National Security (Legislative Provisions) Bill Proposed by Hon Albert HO Chun-yan for the Legislative Council Meeting on 21 May 2003 (5 May 2003) 155

Ruling on Professional Accountants (Amendment) Bill 2004 Proposed by Dr Hon Eric LI Ka-cheung (4 March 2004) 48

Ruling on Proposed Resolution to Repeal the Country Parks (Designation) (Consolidation) (Amendment) Order 2010 Proposed by Hon Tanya CHAN (7 October 2010) 106, 217

Ruling on Proposed Resolutions to Amend the Employees Retraining Ordinance (Amendment of Schedule 3) (No. 2) Notice 2008 Proposed by Hon Mrs Regina IP LAU Suk-yee and Hon LEE Wing-tat (8 December 2008) 132
Ruling on the Amendment Proposed by Hon LEUNG Kwok-hung (21 January 2008) 156
Ruling on the Amendments Proposed to the Legislative Council Bill by the Hon Andrew Wong (24 September 1997) 70
Ruling on the Amendments Proposed to the Legislative Council Bill by the Hon K.K. Fung (25 September 1997) 70
Ruling on the Application for Moving a Motion for the Adjournment of the Council by Hon LEUNG Kwok-hung (11 December 2012) 182
Ruling on the Application for Moving a Motion for the Adjournment of the Council by Hon LEUNG Kwok-hung (22 January 2010) 181
Ruling on the Application for Moving a Motion for the Adjournment of the Council by Hon LEUNG Kwok-hung (29 January 2013) 182
Ruling on the Charging Effect of Hon LEUNG Yiu-chung's Amendment to the Holidays (Amendment) Bill 1998 (23 July 1998) 69
Ruling on the Committee Stage Amendments to Chief Executive Election and Legislative Council Election (Miscellaneous Amendments) Bill 2006 proposed by Dr Hon Yeung Sum and Hon James Tien Pei Chun (4 May 2006) 71
Ruling on the Committee Stage Amendments to Chief Executive Election Bill proposed by Hon Martin Lee Chu Ming (5 July 2001) 70
Ruling on the Employment (Amendment) (No. 2) Bill 1998 Proposed by the Hon. LEE Cheuk-yan (19 July 1999) 50
Ruling on the Employment (Amendment) Bill 1999 proposed by Hon. Andrew CHENG Kar-foo (16 July 1999) 44
Ruling on the Fair Competition Bill Proposed by Hon Fred LI and Hon SIN Chung-kai (12 February 2001) 50
Ruling on the Holiday (1999) Bill Proposed by the Hon LEUNG Yiu-chung (15 September 1999) 47
Ruling on the Labour Relations (Right to Representation, Consultation and Collective Bargaining) Bill (19 July 1999) 46
Ruling on the Labour Relations (Right to Representation, Consultation and Collective Bargaining) Bill Proposed by the Hon. LEE Cheuk-yan (19 July 1999) 114
Ruling on the Medical Registration (Amendment) Bill 2010 Proposed by Councillor Leung Ka Lau (25 June 2010) 48
Rulings on the Committee Stage Amendments proposed by Members to Legislative Council (Amendment) Bill 1999 (12 July 1999) 70
The President's Ruling on Albert HO Chun-yan's Application for Moving a Motion for the Adjournment of the Council (14 June 2011) 180

# List of Abbreviations

| | |
|---|---|
| ADPL | Association for Democracy and People's Livelihood |
| BC | The Bills Committee |
| BG | Breakfast Group |
| BLDC | The Basic Law Drafting Committee |
| CE | The Chief Executive |
| CFA | The Court of Final Appeal |
| CFI | The Court of First Instance |
| CP | Civic Party |
| CPG | The Central People's Government |
| CRC | The Co-operative Resource Centre |
| CSA | Committee Stage Amendment |
| CTU | Hong Kong Confederation of Trade Unions |
| DAB | The Democratic Alliance for the Betterment and Progress of Hong Kong |
| DP | The Democratic Party |
| EC | The Election Committee |
| ES | Economic Synergy |
| Exco | The Executive Council of Hong Kong |
| FCS | The Functional Constituencies |
| FLU | The Federation of Hong Kong and Kowloon Labour Unions |
| FS | The Financial Secretary |
| FTU | The Hong Kong Federation of Trade Unions |
| GCS | The Geographical Constituencies |
| HKPA | Hong Kong Progressive Alliance |
| HKSAR | The Hong Kong Special Administrative Region |
| Legco | The Legislative Council of Hong Kong |
| LOCPG | The Liaison Office of the Central People's Government |
| LP | The Liberal Party |
| LSD | League of Social Democrats |
| NPCSC | The Standing Committee of National People's Congress |
| NPP | New People's Party |
| NWSC | Neighbourhood and Worker's Service Centre |
| OMELCO | The Office of Members of the Executive and Legislative Councils |
| OMLEGCO | The Office of the non-government members of the Legislative Council |
| PAC | The Public Accounts Committee |
| PC | The Preparatory Committee |
| PLC | The Provisional Legislative Council |

| | |
|---|---|
| PP | People Power |
| PPO | The Legislative Council (Powers and Privileges) Ordinance |
| PRC | The People's Republic of China |
| PWC | The Preliminary Work Committee |
| PWSC | The Public Woks Subcommittee of the Finance Committee |
| RoP | The Rules of Procedure of the Legislative Council |
| SVM | The Separate Voting Mechanism |
| UDHK | The United Democrats of Hong Kong |
| UMELCO | The Office of the Unofficial Members of the Executive and Legislative Councils |

CHAPTER 1

# Assessing the Legislative Council

*Autonomy and Performance*

## Introduction

The reunification of Hong Kong with the People's Republic of China (PRC) in 1997 has brought about 'a shift in the *Grundnorm*', a move from the validity of the constitutional foundation formed by the Letters Patent and the Royal Instructions to that of the Constitution of the PRC.[1] The previous constitutional structure was substituted by one based on the Basic Law of the Hong Kong Special Administrative Region (HKSAR) and the Constitution of the PRC. The Basic Law provides an intricate design for the separation of powers, along with checks and balances. The government is split into three branches: the executive branch, responsible for implementing laws and policies; the legislature, responsible for enacting laws and controlling taxation and public expenditure; and the judiciary, responsible for interpreting laws and adjudicating on disputes put before it. Various powers are granted to the executive authorities and the legislature respectively to achieve a counterbalance. For instance, the legislature has the power to impeach the Chief Executive (CE), whilst the CE has the power to dissolve the legislature.[2] The legislature's power to pass or amend legislation is counteracted by the executive's monopoly of initiation and the CE's power to withhold legislation that has been passed.[3]

As Professor Yash Ghai points out, the political structure under the Basic Law is designed to achieve some particular political objectives, principally the overall control over Hong Kong's policy and politics by the Central Authorities.[4] Various mechanisms are intended to secure this objective, such as control over the selection of the CE and preserving the Functional Constituencies (FCs) in the legislature to protect the interests of the business class and professionals.[5] To secure the position of the prevailing conservatives, it therefore becomes

1 Albert H.Y. Chen, 'The Provisional Legislative Council of the SAR', *Hong Kong Law Journal*, 27/1 (1997) 10–11.

2 Basic Law, Article 73(9), Article 50.

3 Basic Law, Article 48(3).

4 Yash Ghai, *Hong Kong's New Constitutional Order: The Resumption of Chinese Sovereignty and the Basic Law* (2nd edn., Hong Kong: Hong Kong University Press, 1999), 288.

5 Ibid., 288–289.

 | DOI 10.1163/9789004276284_002

necessary to slow the development of democratisation and party politics.[6] This governing mentality applied to Hong Kong's political structure is usually called executive dominance or an executive-led philosophy, underlining the dominance of the executive over the legislature in addition to their 'cooperation' and weakening the supervisory role of the legislature over the executive.

An 'executive-led' government is considered essential to having Beijing's views embedded in Hong Kong's political structure, requiring a strong CE who is substantively appointed by and loyal to the Central People's Government (CPG).[7] In its 2004 Decision on the Selection of the CE in 2007 and the Formation of the Legislative Council (Legco) in 2008 (2004 Decision hereinafter), the Standing Committee of the National People's Congress (NPCSC) announced that 'Any changes relating to the methods for selecting the CE and for forming the Legco...shall conform to principles such as...being conducive to the effective operation of the executive-led system'. In 2007, Mr Wu Bangguo, then Chairman of the NPCSC, stressed in a speech at a conference to mark the 10th anniversary of the implementation of the Basic Law that 'the biggest feature of the political structure of the HKSAR is that it is executive-led'.[8] Professor Lau Siu Kai, a former Head of the Central Policy Unit that provides advice on policy matters to the CE, the Chief Secretary for Administration and the Financial Secretary, points out that an executive-led political system is 'a core component' of the 'one country, two systems' (OCTS) policy.[9]

However, the system designed under the Basic Law does not necessarily produce the outcomes expected, not just because of inherent contradictions in the Basic Law,[10] but also the institutional autonomy of the legislature that encourages competition with the executive branch and fosters party politics through popularly elected constituencies.

First, despite the objectives of cooperation and executive dominance, the political structure under the Basic Law is more likely to produce deadlock or impasse. The HKSAR must accommodate multi-level institutional actors in its governance system and democratic development, including the CPG, the CE (representing the political executive) and Legco. Given the incomplete

---

6 Ibid., 289.

7 Albert H.Y. Chen, 'The Constitutional Controversy of Spring 2004', *Hong Kong Law Journal*, 34 (2004) 224.

8 The full text is available at *Ta Kung Pao*, 7 June 2007, A05.

9 Siu Kai Lau, 'In Search of a New Political Order', in Yue Man Yeung (ed.), *The First Decade: The Hong Kong SAR in Retrospective and Introspective Perspectives* (Hong Kong: Chinese University Press, 2007), 145.

10 Ghai (n 4), 292.

constitutional powers of the HKSAR, the relationship between the executive and the legislature depends on more variables than in a nation state. The fundamental power to amend the constitution (Basic Law) rests with the NPC, whilst the CE and Legco have only limited roles in proposing amendments to the Basic Law.[11] In respect of emergency power, whilst the CE in consultation with the Executive Council (Exco) has the power to 'make regulations on occasions of emergency or public danger',[12] the NPCSC may 'decide that the HKSAR is in a state of emergency' according to Article 18 of the Basic Law. The NPCSC's 2004 Decision essentially placed the power to initiate changes in the political system of the HKSAR with the NPCSC.[13] This Decision clearly conveyed the message that Hong Kong is incapable of independently determining the pace of development of its constitutional reform and essentially prolonged Hong Kong's transition to democracy.[14] However, given that the semi-democratic nature of Legco will be maintained at least until 2020, slowing the move towards universal suffrage consolidates Legco's temporary advantage over the CE in having a public mandate. Selected by a committee of 800 members (1200 members since 2012), the CE would find it difficult to counter the strong public opinion represented by Legco, which is particularly evident when the government is promoting unpopular public policy. This intricate political structure may bring about an unstable and weak governance system. The CPG and its representatives in Hong Kong may then intervene to achieve a powerful CE and an executive-led government, leading to controversy over the extent of the HKSAR's autonomy. With some fundamental powers resting with the NPC, both the executive and the legislature may not be strong enough.

---

11 See Article 159 of the Basic Law (adopted by the National People's Congress on 4 April 1990, effective 1 July 1997): 'The power of amendment of this Law shall be vested in the National People's Congress. The power to propose bills for amendments to this Law shall be vested in the Standing Committee of the National People's Congress, the State Council and the Hong Kong Special Administrative Region. Amendment bills from the Hong Kong Special Administrative Region shall be submitted to the National People's Congress by the delegation of the Region to the National People's Congress after obtaining the consent of two-thirds of the deputies of the Region to the National People's Congress, two-thirds of all the members of the Legislative Council of the Region, and the Chief Executive of the Region'.

12 Emergency Regulations Ordinance, Cap 241, s 2.

13 Chen (n 7), 218.

14 For the challenge of a 'protracted transition' to democracy, see Ngok Ma, 'Democratic Development in Hong Kong: A Decade of Lost Opportunities', in Joseph Y.S. Cheng (ed.), *The Hong Kong Special Administrative Region in Its First Decade* (Hong Kong: City University of Hong Kong Press, 2007), 72.

In addition, the distribution of constitutional powers between the executive and Legco does not permit complete dominance of one over the other. Researchers attempting to classify the form of government of the HKSAR as presidentialism, semi-presidentialism or a hybrid system may be aware of the incomplete constitutional powers of the Hong Kong government as a local government.[15] It appears that the intention of the Basic Law is to build up a powerful CE and a legislature with essential functions and powers that a modern legislature usually has. After all, the government's accountability to Legco has been recognised in the Sino-British Joint Declaration signed between the British government and the government of the PRC on 19 December 1984.[16] Whilst the executive possesses the advantage of pre-emption on many occasions, especially at the initiation stage of the legislative process, article 73 of the Basic Law provides genuine powers for Legco to enact, amend or repeal laws, to approve budgets and to supervise the executive. The Basic Law also includes such provisions as article 73(10) that empowers Legco to summon persons to testify or give evidence. These functions and powers may counteract those of the executive-led government, if used skilfully.

Second, Legco's institutional autonomy deserves careful consideration when observing its capacity to provide checks and balances to the executive. As a measure of the level of institutionalisation, autonomy, to quote Professor Huntington, refers to 'the extent to which political organisation and procedures exist independently of other social groupings and methods of

15 On a hybrid system, Professor Richard Cullen argues that the HKSAR has 'a hybrid system—part presidential, part parliamentary and embedded in a colonial tradition', see Richard Cullen, Antonietta Wong, and Civic Exchange, *The Foundations of the Hong Kong Revenue Regime* (Hong Kong: Civic Exchange, 2008), 8; on a system similar to presidentialism, see Professor Ma Ngok's arguments that the political system of the HKSAR is similar to a presidentialism, with the mutual independence of the CE and the Legco which have their own sources of legitimacy respectively, Ngok Ma, 'Executive-Legislative Relations: Assessing Legislative Influence in an Executive-Dominant System', in Siu Kai Lau (ed.), *The First Tung Chee-Hwa Administration: The First Five Years of the Hong Kong Special Administrative Region* (Hong Kong: The Chinese University Press, 2002), 353; on semi-presidentialism, see Benny Tai, '半總統制可解行政與立法困局 (Semi-Presidentialism Can Break the Deadlock between the Executive and the Legislature)', *Hong Kong Economic Journal*, 30 November 2012, A25.

16 See Joint Declaration of the Government of the United Kingdom of Great Britain and Northern Ireland and the Government of the People's Republic of China on the Question of Hong Kong (signed 19 December 1984, ratified 27 May 1985) Cap 2301, Annex I: Elaboration by the Government of the People's Republic of China of Its Basic Policies Regarding Hong Kong, Section I: Constitution.

behaviour'.[17] Professor Polsby defines institutional autonomy in terms of the 'difficulty of entry and internal recruitment of leadership'.[18] Couderc points out that the autonomy of legislature is first defined as its 'non-dependence and non-subordination' in relation to the executive, which is often recognised in constitutions by means of 'separation of powers'.[19] The extent of legislature's autonomy is examined in terms of institutional power (autonomy in drawing up and applying procedures), administration (internal organisation and parliamentary authority and control over parliamentary staff) and finances (budgets).[20] Of these, administrative and financial autonomy is 'a necessary condition for the full exercise of its powers by a Parliament'.[21] The extent of its autonomy determines whether the legislature is able to freely 'exercise the competence with which it is invested by the Constitution'.[22]

Whilst constitutional powers determine the fundamental context within which a legislature operates, the institutional powers and internal autonomy of a legislature determine the way in which the legislature exercises those powers. Legco of the HKSAR is a continuation of Legco in the colonial period in terms of organisational structure and rules regulating its internal business. It draws up its own procedures and determines the internal practice of committees. Given that its sources of legitimacy are different to those of the CE, Legco will inevitably compete and conflict with the executive and attempt to use its powers and procedural weapons to extend its own influence over the policy-making process. This occurrence is expected, to some extent, to compensate for the absence of initiation power and other constitutional restrictions on Legco. The introduction of the notion of legislative autonomy through attaching importance to its independence provides a new perspective for assessing the potential of Hong Kong's Legco, which contributes to characterising the trend in Legco's influence and partly explaining the alleged executive-led system malfunctions in Hong Kong's political structure.

---

17 Richard Sisson, 'Comparative Legislative Institutionalization: A Theoretical Exploration', in Allen Kornberg (ed.), *Legislatures in Comparative Perspective* (New York: David McKay Company, Inc., 1973), 21.

18 Ibid., 23.

19 Michel Couderc, 'The Administrative and Financial Autonomy of Parliamentary Assemblies' (web document) (Association of Secretary Generals of Parliament, 1998), <http://www.asgp.info/Resources/Data/Documents/CVCNKQUEFMEUUCJWPENOSNADTHSKQJ.pdf>, accessed 1 June 2014, 15.

20 Ibid., 18.

21 Ibid., 16.

22 Ibid., 17.

From the preceding discussion, Legco's role in Hong Kong's political system and its relationship with the executive depend on several determinants: interplay between the multi-level institutional actors, which increases the complexity of Hong Kong's political structure; the alleged executive-led government, which is intended to counteract the supervisory function of Legco; and the development of Legco's autonomy, which is expected to help unveil more about what Legco can do. Although many legislatures world-wide are a 'core feature of democratic states',[23] how Legco rises to the challenge brought about by the increasing demand for democratisation in Hong Kong society clashing with the protracted move to universal suffrage deserves particular attention.

This book begins by discussing the potential of Legco when fulfilling its constitutional role, and devises indicators that determine or change institutional arrangements for Legco's autonomy, in particular its independence in relation to the executive. It constitutes a basic framework for exploring the actual effect of Legco, which must rely on empirical data on Legco's major activities or functions, including legislation, financial control and supervision of the executive branch. These functions are typically the major means by which a legislature can intervene and make changes in the policy-making process.

## Functions of Legislatures: Do Legislatures Exist to Make Law?

The first question we need to address is what a legislature can do if it is unable to propose bills. Legco of the HKSAR is a case in point. Article 74 and Annex II of the Basic Law impose far-reaching restrictions on Legco's powers. Article 74 reads as follows.

> Members of the Legislative Council of the Hong Kong Special Administrative Region may introduce bills in accordance with the provisions of this Law and legal procedures. Bills which do not relate to public expenditure or political structure or the operation of the government may be introduced individually or jointly by members of the Council. The written consent of the Chief Executive shall be required before bills relating to government policies are introduced.

23 David M. Olson and Philip Norton, 'Legislatures in Democratic Transition', in David M. Olson and Philip Norton (eds.), *The New Parliaments of Central and Eastern Europe* (London; Portland, Ore.: Frank Cass, 1996), 1.

Further, Section II of Annex II stipulates the method for the passage of Legco members' initiatives.

> The passage of motions, bills or amendments to government bills introduced by individual members of the Legislative Council shall require a simple majority vote of each of the two groups of members present: members returned by functional constituencies and those returned by geographical constituencies through direct elections and by the Election Committee.

The former provision essentially deprives Legco members of the power to propose public bills and the latter, namely, the Separate Voting Mechanism (SVM), makes the passage of bills and motions introduced by Legco members more difficult than government bills. As FCs are often considered to be close to the government, to a large extent this mechanism is designed to vest FCs with the power to veto Legco members' initiatives. Both provisions are new restrictions that did not exist in the colonial era, intended to place executive dominance over the legislative agenda. Thus, the major role of Legco is restricted to passive 'scrutiny and review of governmental proposals'.[24] Many pessimistic predictions about Legco's powerlessness originate from such constitutional constraints on Legco's initiation power.[25] However, the effect of Article 74 of the Basic Law is not self-evident.

When considering what Legco can do, we start with 'a fundamental misunderstanding' as described by Professor Blondel. He points out that 'a fundamental misunderstanding' of the functions of legislatures is demonstrated by seventeenth-century theorists such as Locke and Montesquieu: 'the function of legislatures is to make laws' and, as representative bodies, they would promote liberty and later democracy.[26] Professor Mezey notes that institutions that were called legislatures in some countries 'could not be considered law-making bodies.[27] A clear choice is thus put before scholars: abandoning law making as a necessary characteristic of a legislature, or excluding certain institutions from being classified as legislatures.[28] By examining possible activities of legislatures and their members, Mezey refers to a legislature as 'a flexible institution capable of performing several different functions within a political

24 Ghai (n 4), 282.

25 See Ghai (n 4), 301; Percy Luen-Tim Lui, 'The Legislature', in Lam Wai-Man et al. (eds.), *Contemporary Hong Kong Politics: Governance in the Post-1997 Era* (Hong Kong: Hong Kong University Press, 2007), 48.

26 J. Blondel, *Comparative Legislatures* (Englewood Cliffs, N.J.: Prentice-Hall, 1973), 4–5.

27 Michael L. Mezey, *Comparative Legislatures* (Durham, N.C.: Duke University Press, 1979), 3.

28 Ibid., 3–4.

system'.[29] Professor Norton asserts that 'there is more to legislatures than law-making'.[30]

The functions of legislatures, in the view of Professor Packenham, are the consequences of legislative activity for the political system.[31] Packenham provides eleven functions grouped into three categories: legitimation; recruitment, socialisation and training; and the decisional or influence function.[32] The list of functions is regarded as 'providing the most extensive delineation of functions' by Norton who reworks Packenham's list by adding the category 'seeking redress for a grievance' and removing the ranking of functions.[33] Another way in which to view the functions of legislatures is Mezey's 'activity package': policy-making activities, representation activities and system-maintenance activities.[34] Legislatures that have little role in initiating policies may still perform a deliberative function.[35] The terms of 'law making' and 'policy making' are absent from Carey's list of five jobs that democratic legislatures aim to carry out: representation, deliberation, information, decisiveness and checks.[36] Despite their different perspectives, all of these approaches remove the law-making function, particularly initiation power, from the tasks to be performed by legislatures and adopt a broader view of the role of legislatures in political structures. Accordingly, a legislature may perform only some of these functions, and the order in which they are ranked in terms of importance depends on particular constitutional structure and political environment in which the legislature operates.

Scholars further revise the law-making function by dividing up the stages of the legislative process. Reworking Professor Mezey's classic definition of legislatures, Professor Norton introduces a new, complementary variable: legislative capacity to formulate or substitute policy. This capacity applies to the early

29 Ibid., 12.

30 Philip Norton, *Parliament in British Politics* (Contemporary Political Studies Series; Houndmills, Basingstoke, Hampshire; New York: Palgrave Macmillan, 2005), 4.

31 Robert A. Packenham, 'Legislatures and Political Development', in Allan Kornberg, Lloyd D. Musolf, and American Society for Public Administration Comparative Administration Group (eds.), *Legislatures in Developmental Perspective* (Comparative administration Group series; Durham, N.C.: Duke University Press, 1970), 522.

32 Ibid., 527–536.

33 Norton (n 30), 10–11.

34 Mezey (n 27), 7–11.

35 Norton (n 30), 7.

36 John M. Carey, 'Legislative Organization', in R.A.W. Rhodes, Sarah A. Binder, and Bert A. Rockman (eds.), *The Oxford Handbook of Political Institutions* (Oxford; New York: Oxford University Press, 2006), 431.

stage of the legislative process, whereas legislatures may exercise influence at other, 'later stages'.[37] Control by the legislature over the early stage, namely initiation, is no longer a necessary condition for a strong legislature. As Cox and Morgenstern argue, 'an important role in the legislative process does not always require proactive powers—the ability to initiate legislation and set the agenda', but 'stem from the ability to shape or kill executive proposals'.[38]

These arguments in the comparative study of legislatures have vital significance for research on Hong Kong's Legco. An unexpected outcome might be a greater focus on supervision functions and committee work, in particular Bill Committees and panels.[39] By adopting a broader perspective on the functions of legislatures, Legco is not necessarily weak because it may still perform a deliberative function and exercise oversight over the executive, to constrain the executive and press for changes in public policy. Even when focusing only on legislative power, 'anticipated reactions' may become a flexible bargaining model, as stated by Professor Mezey:

> Private discussions between the government and its supporters in the legislature may lead the government to modify its proposals before submission to the legislature in order to mollify party dissidents... Anticipated opposition in the legislature may lead the government to postpone a potentially controversial proposal until the climate of opinion is more favorable, or it may lead it to phrase its proposals in such a way as to ameliorate anticipated objections. Thus all government proposals appear to pass the legislature unopposed and unamended simply because the government avoids introducing those things which may provoke legislative resistance, or because it has acceded to changes privately.[40]

### Autonomy of Legislatures

The extent of autonomy is one measure of the level of institutionalisation. In Professor Richard Sisson's 1973 article on the theoretical exploration of

37 Philip Norton, 'Parliament and Policy in Britain: The House of Commons as a Policy Influencer', *Teaching Politics*, 13/2 (1984) 201.

38 Gary W. Cox and Scott Morgenstern, 'Latin America's Reactive Assemblies and Proactive Presidents', *Comparative Politics*, 33 (2001) 172.

39 Ngok Ma, 香港政治：發展歷程與核心課題 (*Hong Kong Politics: Development Process and Key Issues*) (Hong Kong: Hong Kong Institute of Asia-Pacific Studies, 2010), 92.

40 Mezey (n 27), 26.

legislative institutionalisation, institutionalisation refers to 'the existence and persistence of valued rules, procedures and patterns of behaviour which enable the accommodation of new configurations of political claimants and/ or demands within a given organisation'.[41] Based on Professors Huntington and Polsby's research on autonomy, Sisson devises variables for autonomy that are considered to be sub-indices of structural indices of legislative institutionalisation. As the process of institutionalisation requires explanation of the relationship and the interaction between the relevant institutions on the one hand, and the implications of such interaction to the internal structure of the institution on the other,[42] the extent of autonomy is examined on two levels: external and internal. The external environment is a prerequisite for internal autonomy, whilst internal autonomy secures the maintenance of institutional boundaries.[43]

As Table 1.1 shows, there are four measures for institutional autonomy of the legislature from the perspective of the external environment: boundary differentiation and maintenance; constitutional stipulation power; policy/specific control; and pluralisation of social representation. The internal indices focus on selection of leaders and formal elites, appearing to accept Polsby's argument regarding 'difficulty of entry and internal recruitment of leadership'.[44]

Sisson's indices attach greater importance to the external perspective of institutional autonomy, emphasising the independent character of the legislature in relation to other institutions and its necessary constitutional role. By contrast, based on the practice of 52 assemblies,[45] Couderc's report highlights the internal dimension, including autonomy in drawing up and applying rules, autonomy in determining its form of organisation and financial autonomy.[46]

Given the significance to the legislature of organisational structure and rules,[47] Mattson and Strom focus on parliamentary committees, considered to be a 'microcosm' of the full legislature.[48] 'The larger the number of committees and the greater the part they play in the legislative process, the higher the

41 Sisson (n 17), 24.

42 Ibid.

43 Ibid.

44 Ibid., 23.

45 Couderc (n 19), 15.

46 Ibid.

47 Ingvar Mattson and Kaare Strom, 'Parliamentary Committees', in Herbert Döring (ed.), *Parliaments and Majority Rule in Western Europe* (Frankfurt/Main; Campus Verlag; New York: St. Martin's Press, 1995), 256.

48 Ibid., 249.

TABLE 1.1 *Professor Sisson's indices of institutional autonomy*

| | Indices | Variables |
|---|---|---|
| External environment | Boundary differentiation and maintenance: independence of legislative institutions from external institutions | a. Difficulty of entry;<br>b. Continuity of institutional membership. |
| | Institutional/generic control: constitutional stipulations | a. Budget control;<br>b. Power of appointment;<br>c. Legislative self-government;<br>d. Participation in the determination of rules fundamental to the constitutive system. |
| | Policy/specific control | Effective participation in:<br>a. Setting of public goals;<br>b. Creation of the means for their achievement;<br>c. Policy execution, whether direct or through review and appraisal. |
| Internal | Pluralisation of social representation<br>Recruitment to strategic positions of institutional authority<br>Constraints on external participation in the selection of formal elites | |

SOURCE: AN ADAPTATION OF PROFESSOR SISSON'S TABLE 1.1, IN RICHARD SISSON, 'COMPARATIVE LEGISLATIVE INSTITUTIONALIZATION: A THEORETICAL EXPLORATION', IN ALLEN KORNBERG (ED.), *LEGISLATURES IN COMPARATIVE PERSPECTIVE* (NEW YORK: DAVID MCKAY, 1973), 25–26.

potential output of parliament'.[49] To develop specialisation and perform functions within their jurisdictions, parliamentary committees need to be autonomous and to enjoy some institutional privileges.[50] Regarding committee autonomy, committees first 'have a very independent role in the policy-making process', given that committee members can determine policy within their jurisdiction; second, can develop expertise and acquire information, including

49 Ibid., 251.
50 Ibid., 253.

summoning witnesses and demanding documents; and third, are regarded as extensions of majority parties.[51]

Mattson and Strom therefore establish the key features of autonomous committees that are able to create efficiency and enhance legislative impact. The article of Carey and others also points out that a 'stable and specialized' committee system is necessary for autonomy of the legislature.[52]

Based on the abovementioned literature, this study defines legislature's autonomy as the extent to which a legislative institution can determine its own organisation, procedures and business and make independent and informed decisions when performing various constitutional functions. A higher level of autonomy usually means that there is more capacity to achieve policy goals. The indicators are grouped under each perspective as follows:[53]

(1) External environment:
   a. Separate institution from the executive;
   b. Constraints from external institutions, e.g. party control and courts;
   c. Constitutional powers and role in the policy-making process, financial scrutiny and supervision of the executive;
   d. Representation of social stratification;
   e. General public support and channels for communication with the public.

(2) Internal characteristics:
   a. Exclusive authority over internal rules and procedures;
   b. Agenda control;
   c. Committee autonomy;
   d. Leadership selection;
   e. Administrative and financial autonomy, and research support.

Analysis of legislative autonomy provides the 'original' picture of constitutional powers and institutional capacity and the context within which the legislature works. Developing an effective tool to measure its potential helps to avoid ambiguous and misleading conclusions of a weak or strong legislature which often place more emphasis on Legco's constitutional powers and disregard its internal operations. Applying the indicators to Hong Kong's Legco

51 Ibid., 255, 285.

52 John M. Carey, Frantisek Formanek, and Ewa Karpowicz, 'Legislative Autonomy in New Regimes: The Czech and Polish Cases', *Legislative Studies Quarterly*, 24 (1999) 571–572.

53 This study borrows titles of two indicators for political activities of the legislature devised by Olsen and Norton, see Olson and Noton (n 23), 6.

in a comparative legislative study allows the development of a question framework to measure the level of Legco's autonomy, as shown in Table 1.2.

With respect to the external environment, the first three indicators in Table 1.2, concerning the relations between Legco and the executive, can be readily assessed given the clear separation of their powers under the Basic Law. The remaining two indicators focus on the relationships between Legco and the citizenry and require relatively complex questions to be analysed. Representation of social stratification is related to the electoral system and the distribution of political parties within Legco. Important measures are provided by the franchise basis and by political parties' organisation and policy orientation. The representation indicator is correlated with the next indicator, the level of public support and effective communication with the public. Overall, the more public support Legco has, the higher the level of its autonomy. In addition to connections with constituency electorates, institutional

TABLE 1.2 *External environment for Legco's autonomy*

| Indicators in the comparative legislative study | Question framework for the external environment for autonomy of Legco |
|---|---|
| Separate institution from the executive | Are the existence and the composition of Legco independent of the executive? |
| Constraints from external institutions | Is the operation of Legco subject to constraints exercised by any external institution? |
| Constitutional powers and role | a. Do members of Legco have the power to initiate legislation and financial proposals?<br>b. Do members of Legco have the power to amend or veto legislation and financial proposals introduced by the executive?<br>c. Does Legco have the power to hold the executive accountable? |
| Representation of social stratification | Does Legco fully represent social stratification? |
| General public support and channels for communication with the public | a. Does Legco have the general support of the public?<br>b. Does Legco have adequate channels of communication with the public? |

arrangements in Legco that provide and accommodate channels of communication between legislators and the public deserve more attention. To some extent, the development of street politics and social movements essentially demonstrates the level of representation of social stratification and whether or not there are adequate channels for Legco to communicate with the public.

For the internal characteristics, given the relatively simple character of leadership selection and administrative and financial autonomy, emphasis is placed on other indicators, particularly exclusive authority over internal rules and norms, and committee organisation and jurisdiction, as shown in Table 1.3. The notion of agenda control is used here in its simplest sense, namely the determination of the agenda of business.

The rules and norms of Legco govern the way it operates. It is therefore important to examine whether Legco can determine its internal rules and procedures for plenary and committee meetings free from external interference, and to which extent the position of the executive is considered when making such decisions. Considering the voting rule as an example, based on the electoral system comprising election by FCs and geographical constituencies (GCs) (and the Election Committee (EC) up until 2004), the SVM stipulates bicameral approval by FCs and GCs of Legco members' proposals, whilst government proposals only require a simple majority. However, according to the Rules of Procedure of Legco (RoP) and other committee rules, the SVM does not apply to voting by panels and committees, enabling legislators to enjoy more autonomy in such panels and committees. The enactment of the RoP, the rulings of its President and the decisions of committee chairs are thus important subjects for study.

The autonomy of committees may be the most important indicator for Legco's autonomy. In addition to the organisation of committee system, the effect of the executive and political parties on the autonomy of committees is given due weight because committees cannot develop efficiency and specialisation adequately if they are established only as copies of Legco that maintain the majority party control. Another indicator conducive to developing efficiency and specialisation is information acquisition, including the power of committees to summon witnesses and demand documents, as shown in Table 1.3.

## Conclusion

The HKSAR is 'very far from being an independent city-state',[54] despite its enjoyment of a high degree of autonomy. The status of Hong Kong as a city

54 Albert H.Y. Chen, 'The Basic Law and the Development of the Political System in Hong Kong', *Asia Pacific Law Review*, 15/1 (2007) 39.

TABLE 1.3 *Internal characteristics of Legco's autonomy*

| **Indicators in the comparative legislative study** | **Question framework for the internal autonomy of Legco** |
|---|---|
| Exclusive authority over internal rules and procedures | Do Legco and committee leaders have the authority to make final decisions on internal rules and procedures? |
| Agenda control | Can Legco and its committees or subgroups determine the agenda for internal business? |
| Committee organisation and jurisdictions | a. Does Legco have standing committees for the scrutiny of bills and budgets?<br>b. Does Legco have a specialised committee system?<br>c. To which extent do committee members adhere to the party line when exercising their powers?<br>d. Do committees have the power to summon witnesses and demand documents? |
| Leadership selection | Can legislators select leaders of Legco and committees free from external interference? |
| Administrative and financial autonomy, and research support | a. Can Legco manage its administrative affairs and determine its budget independent of external interference?<br>b. Does Legco have stable and proportionate research support? |

makes it necessary to consider the role of the Central Authorities and their agencies in Hong Kong, this being very often the Liaison Office of the Central People's Government (LOCPG), when observing the HKSAR's constitutional structure. The effect of the Central Authorities on Legco's role in Hong Kong's political system may be understood on two levels: on the macro level, the CPG's involvement in slowing the pace of democratisation to secure dominance of the executive over Legco, by interpretations of the Basic Law and continuing clarification of the policy of the OCTS; and on the micro level, involvement in Legco elections, leadership selection and the voting behaviour of legislators, usually through the LOCPG and other HKSAR agencies. The CPG's intervention becomes the most influential feature in Hong Kong's political structure, and the 'delicate balance' between the executive and the legislature may no longer exist following adjustments to the CPG's policy on Hong Kong.[55] A legislature that lacks the capacity to press for policy changes and provide checks to the executive does not necessarily lead to a strong executive and may be accompanied by ineffective government accountability to Legco and a crisis in the governance system. Although 'what Legco can do' does not equate to Legco's actual effect, an analysis of Legco's potential provides the context within which the variables interact and ultimately shape an actual picture of Legco's performance. Hence, it is necessary to devise indicators for measuring Legco's capacity, in particular its autonomy.

---

55 On 'delicate balance', see Ghai (n 4), 283.

CHAPTER 2

# External Environment and Internal Characteristics of Legco's Autonomy

## Autonomy of the Pre-1997 Legco

Up until 1984, Hong Kong was a British colony with 'no democracy and no elected legislators but enjoying the Rule of Law, judicial independence and a reasonable degree of civil liberties'.[1] A classic explanation of Hong Kong's political structure up to the 1970s is Professor Ambrose King's theory of 'administrative absorption of politics'. The theory depicts how the colonial government consistently absorbed the political forces, particularly the local elite, into the administrative decision-making body to achieve some level of integration of elite consensus.[2] By appointing members of the local elite to Legco, the government was able to legitimise its governance authority and manage the integration crisis.[3] However, it was limited political participation only open to those in the top level of society. In other words, it is 'an elite-consensual policy' rather than 'a mass-consensual community'.[4]

### *Separation from the Executive*

Alongside the gradual constitutional reforms initiated in the 1980s, a Legco with some of the characteristics of a modern legislature emerged. In 1984, the year the Joint Declaration to determine the future of Hong Kong was signed, Legco consisted of the Governor (as the President), three ex-officio members, 15 official members and 29 unofficial members.[5] All members were appointed by the Governor with the approval of the Secretary of State for Foreign and Commonwealth Affairs. The functions of Legco were the enactment of legislation, questioning the administration on matters of the public interest, debating questions of policy and controlling public expenditure through the Finance

1 Chen, 'The Basic Law and the Development of the Political System in Hong Kong', 20.

2 Ambrose King, 'Administrative Absorption of Politics in Hong Kong: Emphasis on the Grass Roots Level', *Asian Survey*, 15/5 (1975) 422–439.

3 Ibid., 425, 430.

4 Ibid., 427.

5 Hong Kong Government, 'Green Paper: The Further Development of Representative Government in Hong Kong' (1984) 5.

 | DOI 10.1163/9789004276284_003

Committee.[6] In 1991, directly elected members entered Legco for the first time. Elected members, comprising 18 returned by GCs and 21 by FCs, formed the majority in the 60-seat Legco.[7] Thus, the executive largely lost control of Legco.[8]

Complete separation of Legco and Exco was proposed by Governor Patten in his 1992 reform package.[9] Legco was expected to hold the executive accountable, as provided in the Joint Declaration and the Basic Law, by developing its financial and managerial autonomy and its own committee structure.[10] Legco's President would be elected by its own members, whilst the Governor, as the head of the executive, would be answerable to Legco.[11] Governor Patten subsequently implemented this package. In 1993, he handed over the presidency to a member elected from amongst the non-government members.[12] In the 1995 Legco election, all members of Legco were elected, with 30 returned by FCs, 10 by EC and 20 by GCs.[13]

The introduction of direct elections to Legco brought active democrats into Legco. They actively pushed institutional reforms to enhance Legco's institutional effect by making it more independent from the executive, improving the transparency of the meeting proceedings and instituting more mechanisms for checks on the government.[14]

### *Administrative and Financial Autonomy*

Legco gradually established an independent staff agency system and financial autonomy. In 1986, Office of the Unofficial Members of the Executive and

6 Ibid.

7 Kin-Shuen Louie and Kwok Cheung Shum (eds.), 香港選舉資料彙編 1982 年–1994 年 (*Hong Kong Electorate Facts: 1982–1994*) (Hong Kong: Hong Kong Institute of Asia-Pacific Studies, The Chinese University of Hong Kong, 1995), 173.

8 Ma, 'Executive-Legislative Relations: Assessing Legislative Influence in an Executive-Dominant System', 351.

9 Governor Christopher Francis Patten's annual address to the Legislative Council, in Hansard HK (7 October 1992), 38–49. 'Hansard HK' stands for *Official Record of Proceedings of Hong Kong Legislative Council* which has been published by the Hong Kong Legislative Council.

10 Ibid., 43.

11 Ibid., 42.

12 The Legislative Council, 'The History of the Legco' [web document], <http://www.legco.gov.hk/general/english/intro/hist_lc.htm>, accessed 20 October 2010.

13 Kathleen Cheek-Milby, *A Legislature Comes of Age: Hong Kong's Search for Influence and Identity* (Hong Kong: Oxford University Press, 1995) 5, Table 1.1.

14 Ngok Ma, *Political Development in Hong Kong: State, Political Society, and Civil Society* (Hong Kong: Hong Kong University Press, 2007), 103.

Legislative Councils (UMELCO) was renamed the Office of Members of the Executive and Legislative Councils (OMELCO). The government removed 'unofficial' from all Hong Kong ordinances through the Executive and Legislative Councils (Members) Bill.[15] Following removal of this 'inappropriate' and 'misleading' title, all members of Legco were expected to sit on the 'same' Council.[16] In 1992, in light of Governor Patten's proposals for separation of the membership of Legco and Exco, the OMELCO was renamed the Office of the non-government members of the Legislative Council (OMLEGCO), and its secretariat became an independent body which solely provided support services for legislators.[17]

The most important reform affecting the autonomy of Legco occurred in 1994 when the government introduced the Legislative Council Commission Bill, setting up an independent Legco Commission with the statutory power to 'develop financial and managerial autonomy in organising their administration and support facilities'.[18] This Bill provides the legal framework that enables Legco to recruit its own staff and determine its organisation of administration, support services and spending, separate from the executive. This reform is regarded by members as a 'milestone in the history of Hong Kong's constitutional development' in terms of underpinning an independent legislature and its secretariat.[19]

### *Committee Autonomy*

Legco's informal committee system existed until the early 1990s. In view of increasing public desire for a more open government and transparent legislative process, in 1991 Legco set up a working group to conduct an overall review of the committee structure.[20] Proposals by Councillor Ronald Arculli for a new committee structure (the Arculli model) were eventually accepted and a formalised committee structure including the House Committee and Bill Committees was established through several major amendments to the

---

15 The Chief Secretary's speech on the second reading of the Executive and Legislative Councils (Members) Bill 1987, see Hansard HK (14 October 1987), 74.

16 Sir Edward Youde's policy address in 1986, see Hansard HK (8 October 1986), 11.

17 M.J.A Cooray, 'Hong Kong's Ombudsman: The First Decade', in Institutional Ombudsman Institute and Reif L.C. (ed.), *The International Ombudsman Yearbook, Vol. 3* (The Hague: Kluwer Law International, 1999), 115.

18 The Chief Secretary's speech on the second reading of the Legislative Council Commission Bill, see Hansard HK (9 March 1994), 2702.

19 Councillor Elsie Tu's speech on the resumption of the second reading of the Legislative Council Commission Bill, see Hansard HK (30 March 1994), 3062.

20 Councillor Elsie Tu's speech on motion to amend Standing Orders of the Legislative Council, see Hansard HK (8 July 1992), 77.

Standing Orders of Legco in 1992.[21] Legco's in-house meeting was formalised as the House Committee, comprising all of the members except the Deputy President and ex-officio members. Its primary functions were to 'allocate bills to the Bills Committees', 'provide guidelines relating to practices and procedures of the Bills Committees' and 'consider other items relating to business of the Legco'.[22] After 1994, the Finance Committee no longer included government officials. All public expenditure that exceeded HK$10 million and was not included in the annual budget had to be approved by the Finance Committee.[23] The panels of the OMELCO were preserved and Legco panels were developed in parallel with the government departments. A formal committee system with statutory power was thus achieved.

### *Political Parties of Legco in the Colonial Period*

Direct election stimulated the development of political parties. In post-1991 Legco, consensus politics were gradually replaced as the central feature of the governance system by a new political culture characterised by confrontation and competition between political forces.

The announcement of the direct election for 1991 was considered to be a 'catalyst' stimulating the formation of political parties.[24] In 1990, the United Democrats of Hong Kong (UDHK) was founded by the Hong Kong Affairs Society, the Meeting Point and the Association for Democracy and People's Livelihood.[25] In 1992, the Democratic Alliance for the Betterment of Hong Kong (DAB) was founded as a result of China's determination to counter the political impact of democrats.[26] 1994 proved to be fruitful for the growth of political parties: in this year, the UDHK and the Meeting Point merged into the Democratic Party (DP), and the Cooperative Resource Centre (CRC) was transformed into the Liberal Party (LP).[27] In 1996, the Hong Kong Progressive Alliance (HKPA) was founded by a group of pro-Beijing business elites; meanwhile, the Frontier was founded by a group of democratic activists who were considered to be more aggressive than the DP.[28] These political parties or

21 Ibid.

22 Ibid.

23 Ma (n 14), 111.

24 Norman John Miners and Tuck-Hang James Tang, *The Government and Politics of Hong Kong* (5th edn., Hong Kong: Oxford University Press, 1998), 199.

25 Ibid.

26 Siu-Kai Lau and Hsin-Chi Kuan, 'Partial Democratization, "Foundation Moment" and Political Parties in Hong Kong', *The China Quarterly*, 163 (2000) 713.

27 Ma (n 14), 140.

28 Ibid.

groups actively took part in the Legco election, both in FCs and GCs. In the Legco elections of 1991 and 1995, members with a political affiliation won more than 70 per cent of the seats.[29] The 'foundation moment' of these political parties resulted in political cleavage becoming the most important way of distinguishing political parties before 1997.[30] Hence, the embryonic division between the pro-Beijing and the pro-democracy camps was revealed, in particular.

### *Legco in 1997*

As Dr Cheek-Milby points out, the post-1985 legislature did not have more policy-making power than before, but it 'matured' in exercising those powers.[31] Changes in the composition of Legco, in particular the development of political parties, were the essential determinants of a Legco that was more active in influencing public policy and performing various functions. Since 1991, political parties have become major participants in all activities of Legco.

Legco members exercised their powers and performed their functions more frequently after 1992. Following the enactment of the Legislative Council (Powers and Privileges) Ordinance (PPO) in 1985, Legco has gradually consolidated its enquiry and investigation mechanism under s 9(2) of the PPO, by asking civil servants to reveal information and give evidence in public. From 1995 to 1997, Legco experienced a more active period during which members used the summons power to investigate the wide-ranging issues that included the departure of senior civil servants, the arrangements for Legco elections, landslip disaster and labour disputes.

The introduction of private member's bills had a noticeable effect on the government and became a 'very common weapon' after 1995,[32] even though the government was still protected by Clause XXIV of the Royal Instructions, which imposed restrictions on the power of Legco members to introduce initiatives involving charges against revenue. All government bills were scrutinised by Legco via its Bill Committees and in the committee stage of the whole Council.

With regard to control over public finances, a communication mechanism was set up between the government and political parties in Legco. Before introducing budget bills, the Financial Secretary consulted individual members and parties of Legco to give them the opportunity to provide suggestions and comments. After 1994, the Financial Secretary provided a list for political

29 The author's calculation is based on Tables 5.4 and 5.5 in Ma (n 14), 106.

30 Lau and Kuan (n 26), 714.

31 Cheek-Milby (n 13), 165.

32 Ma (n 14), 109.

parties that indicated how many proposals introduced by those political parties had been accepted by the government.[33] It proved to be a popular practice for providing a record of the performance of political parties. Legco's scrutiny of public finances was clearly effective, as, each year since 1992, some government financial proposals were amended, not approved or withdrawn.[34]

In the last years of the colonial era, Legco became an active organ with the capacity to push through policy changes and achieve its goals on many occasions. The rise of the liberal and pro-democracy camp within Legco promoted reform in transparency, civil liberties and public services, for example, the introduction of the Code on Access to Information in early 1995 and the establishment of the Equal Opportunities Commission in 1996.

The remodelling of Legco since the 1980s, not only in composition but also in autonomy, created a prerequisite for a more autonomous and active Legco. In terms of institutionalisation, Legco in 1997 was ready to rise to the challenge of the coming transfer of sovereignty, including the increasing level of representation, the formal committee system, the rules and norms governing its internal procedures and the necessary administrative and financial autonomy.

## Autonomy of Post-1998 Legco

The legislature elected by the 1995 election was unable to transition to the legislative branch of the HKSAR government owing to the breakdown of Sino-British negotiations on Governor Patten's constitutional package and the abandonment by the Chinese government of the 'through train' plan. According to an NPC Decision in 1990, members of Legco in its last term before the change in sovereignty would be able to become members of the first Legco of the HKSAR if they met the requirements laid down by this Decision.[35] However, a

33 Chi-Keung Choy and Sai-Leung Lau, '九七回歸前的行政立法關係 (The Executive-Legislative Relations in Hong Kong before 1997)', *Hong Kong Journal of Social Sciences*, 8 (1996) 253.

34 See Table 5.7 in Ma (n 14), 113.

35 Para 6 of the Decision of the National People's Congress on the Method for the Formation of the First Government and the First Legislative Council of the Hong Kong Special Administrative Region (adopted on 4 April 1990) sets out: 'If the composition of the last Hong Kong Legislative Council before the establishment of the Hong Kong Special Administrative Region is in conformity with the relevant provisions of this Decision and the Basic Law of the Hong Kong Special Administrative Region, those of its members who uphold the Basic Law of the Hong Kong Special Administrative Region of the People's

Provisional Legislative Council (PLC) was instead the political legacy of the breakdown in negotiations.[36] From January 1997 to June 1998, the PLC assumed part of the functions of Legco and Legco of the first term provided for under the Basic Law was not returned until July 1998.

### *External Environment*

Different constitutional structures have different effects on legislative autonomy.[37] In Hong Kong, under the constitutional framework embedded in the Basic Law, Legco is an independent institution in relation to the executive. Given the low number of dual members of Legco and Exco following the return of sovereignty to China, the legislature and the executive of the HKSAR, returned by separate methods, are often considered to be independent of each other. Further, checks and balances laid down by the Basic Law enhances Legco's independence.

#### Constitutional Role

Regarding Legco's constitutional powers and its role, we refer to various provisions under the Basic Law. The main provision for functions of Legco is contained in Article 73 of the Basic Law as follows.

> The Legislative Council of the Hong Kong Special Administrative Region shall exercise the following powers and functions:
> (1) To enact, amend or repeal laws in accordance with the provisions of this Law and legal procedures;
> (2) To examine and approve budgets introduced by the government;
> (3) To approve taxation and public expenditure;
> (4) To receive and debate the policy addresses of the Chief Executive;
> (5) To raise questions on the work of the government;
> (6) To debate any issue concerning public interests;
> (7) To endorse the appointment and removal of the judges of the Court of Final Appeal and the Chief Judge of the High Court;

Republic of China and pledge allegiance to the Hong Kong Special Administrative Region of the People's Republic of China, and who meet the requirements set forth in the Basic Law of the Region may, upon confirmation by the Preparatory Committee, become members of the first Legislative Council of the Region'.

36 Sonny Shiu Hing Lo, 'Hong Kong's Legislative Council as a Symbol of Political Development', *Hong Kong Law Journal*, 27/2 (1997) 282.

37 Carey, Formanek, and Karpowicz, 'Legislative Autonomy in New Regimes: The Czech and Polish Cases', 572.

(8) To receive and handle complaints from Hong Kong residents;
(9) If a motion initiated jointly by one-fourth of all the members of the Legislative Council charges the Chief Executive with serious breach of law or dereliction of duty and if he or she refuses to resign, the Council may, after passing a motion for investigation, give a mandate to the Chief Justice of the Court of Final Appeal to form and chair an independent investigation committee. The committee shall be responsible for carrying out the investigation and reporting its findings to the Council. If the committee considers the evidence sufficient to substantiate such charges, the Council may pass a motion of impeachment by a two-thirds majority of all its members and report it to the Central People's Government for decision; and
(10) To summon, as required when exercising the above-mentioned powers and functions, persons concerned to testify or give evidence.

The first three functions, namely legislative power, financial control and taxation, have more binding powers, whilst the other functions exist to monitor the government without any binding power, in addition to the summons power provided in Article 73(10). It is clear that Legco possesses real power to veto bills and financial proposals (including budgets). However, considering Article 74 and Annex II concurrently, it is evident that Legco has little initiation power and that its power to amend bills and financial proposals is subject to limitations on the content and the voting procedure. Under Annex II of the Basic law, any amendment moved by a Legco member requires the approval of FCs and GCs respectively. In addition, Rules 31 and 57(6) of the RoP preserve the restriction against a 'charging effect' of Legco members' amendments or motions.

Regarding Legco's power to hold the executive accountable, Article 64 of the Basic Law provides that

> The Government of the Hong Kong Special Administrative Region must abide by the law and be accountable to the Legislative Council of the Region: it shall implement laws passed by the Council and already in force; it shall present regular policy addresses to the Council; it shall answer questions raised by members of the Council; and it shall obtain approval from the Council for taxation and public expenditure.

However, it is questionable whether Article 64 covers all aspects of the accountability of the executive to Legco. Article 73 should be considered jointly with Article 64 when examining the meaning of this accountability. The power of impeachment of the CE provided in Article 73(9) is a key feature of government accountability but is not covered by Article 64, and the final decision rests with the CPG. Whilst Articles 73(2) and 73(3) empower Legco to approve budgets and to approve taxation and public expenditure respectively, the accountability provision under Article 64 merely states that 'it [the government] shall obtain approval from the Council for taxation and public expenditure'. Budget control is usually considered to be an important means of financial accountability. In addition, as a strand of financial accountability and a long-standing practice, Legco can scrutinise the efficiency and effectiveness of public spending through the work of the Public Accounts Committee (PAC).

This complicated accountability system is likely to result in a stalemate. On the one hand, Legco lacks the necessary tools to hold the government truly accountable, e.g., by replacing the CE and principal officials through a censure motion or other means;[38] on the other hand, the CE's power to dissolve Legco under Article 50 is 'a double-edged sword',[39] as dissolving Legco may also pose a real risk of resignation to the CE if he/she cannot reach a consensus with the new Legco on the bill under dispute.

### External Constraint

To examine whether the operation of Legco is subject to intervention by any external institution, judicial review is considered first. In *Leung Kwok Hung v The President of The Legislative Council of The Hong Kong Special Administrative Region and Another* (2007),[40] the court held that Hong Kong's courts, despite having the jurisdiction over the constitutionality of the RoP, should exercise such jurisdiction 'in a restrictive manner'.[41] The case of *Cheng Kar Shun and Leung Chi Kin v the Honourable Li Fung Ying and Others* is more significant because it was the first time that the court granted permission for judicial

38 A motion for impeachment of the CE was negatived in Legco by 9 to 23 in FCs and 18 to 14 in GCs, see Hansard HK (9 January 2013), 4641.

39 Ma (n 8), 353. Article 50 of the Basic Law stipulates: 'If the Chief Executive of the Hong Kong Special Administrative Region refuses to sign a bill passed the second time by the Legislative Council, or the Legislative Council refuses to pass a budget or any other important bill introduced by the government, and if consensus still cannot be reached after consultations, the Chief Executive may dissolve the Legislative Council.

The Chief Executive must consult the Executive Council before dissolving the Legislative Council. The Chief Executive may dissolve the Legislative Council only once in each term of his or her office'.

40 *Leung Kwok Hung v The President of the Legislative Council of the Hong Kong Special Administrative Region and Another* [2007] 1 HKLRD 387.

41 Ibid., 393–394.

review of the power of Legco's committee.[42] In the case, although the court indicated its reluctance to 'impose a straitjacket on the Legislative Council as to how it may go about its business'[43] and to 'interfere with the internal working of the legislature',[44] it declared that 'the courts do have jurisdiction to intervene' where 'questions of whether Legco, in going about its business, has acted in contravention of the provisions in the Basic Law arise'.[45] Moreover, according to the court, 'the jurisdiction must be exercised with great restraint having regard to the different constitutional roles assigned under the Basic Law' to Legco, the executive and the judiciary.[46] More recently, in September 2014, the CFA made a landmark decision on *Leung Kwok Hung v The President of the Legislative Council of the Hong Kong Special Administrative Region* [2014] HKEC 1604 (discussed in Chapter 3), dealing with a constitutional issue: under what circumstances the Legco President's ruling is amenable to judicial review. In this case, the CFA applied the common law doctrine of the separation of powers and the 'non-intervention principle',[47] thereby recognising the exclusive authority of Legco in managing its own internal processes.[48] Furthermore, the court refused to regard compliance with procedural regularity in the law-making processes of a legislature as a condition of the validity of an enacted law.[49] Although the courts have the jurisdiction to determine 'the existence of a power, privilege or immunity' that Legco and its President have, they will not determine 'the occasion or the manner' of exercise of such powers, privileges or immunities.[50] It is clear that the CFA is reluctant to intervene in the legislative process or to determine the validity of an enacted law on the basis of procedural regularity unless relevant provisions in the Basic Law have clearly addressed such questions. A former senior legislator Dr Margaret Ng comments that the CFA's decision has established important constitutional principles that had a profound impact on the development of constitutional democracy.[51]

---

42 *Cheng Kar Shun and Leung Chi Kin v the Honourable Li Fung Ying and Others* [2009] HKEC 1587.

43 Ibid., para 99.

44 Ibid., para 220.

45 Ibid.

46 Ibid.

47 *Leung Kwok Hung v The President of the Legislative Council of the Hong Kong Special Administrative Region* [2014] HKEC 1604, paras 27–28.

48 Ibid., para 28.

49 Ibid., para 33.

50 Ibid., para 43.

51 Margaret Ng, '議會自主: 法庭不覆核議會內進行的程序 (Legislative Autonomy: The CFA Decided not to Intervene in Legco's Internal Processes)', *Ming Pao Daily News*, 8 October 2014.

Any Legco member who was dissatisfied with the procedures or decisions made by the President or committee chairpersons will find it difficult to seek relief by means of judicial intervention.[52] As far as Legco's external autonomy is concerned, the CFA decision narrows, if not eliminates, the space for Legco members to invite judicial intervention.

### Representation of Social Stratification

Up until 2007, Legco's membership of the HKSAR is stipulated by Annex II of the Basic Law. In the first term of Legco (1998–2000), 20 directly elected members were returned by GCs—which was also the case for Legco of 1995–97—and that number increased to 24 in 2000 and 30 in 2004 (see Table 2.1) through gradually reducing the number of seats returned by EC. The seats returned by FCs remained at 30 from 1998 to 2012. The fourth term Legco (2008–12) had the same composition as the third Legco (2004–08) because of the failure of the 2005 constitutional reform proposals. From 1998 to 2012, then, Legco had 60 members.

With regard to electoral arrangements after 2007, the Basic Law states that

> ...if there is a need to amend the provisions of this Annex, such amendments must be made with the endorsement of a two-thirds majority of all the members of the Council and the consent of the Chief Executive, and they shall be reported to the Standing Committee of the National People's Congress for the record.

On 24 and 25 June 2010, Legco passed two motions for constitutional reform, which provided that five more seats would be added to GCs and another five to the District Council sector of FCs, to be elected by means of 'quasi-universal suffrage',[53] and that the members of the Election Committee for the election of the fourth-term CE in 2012 would increase from 800 to 1200. The passage of these motions was regarded as 'a major breakthrough in Hong Kong's constitutional reform',[54] amending the Basic Law for the first time. Legco has had 70 members since its fifth term, with half returned by popular election.

### Functional Constituencies

FCs currently comprise 28 constituencies, having undergone a slight change in 2000 with the demise of the Urban Council and Regional Council sectors. The

---

52 Ibid.

53 Albert H.Y. Chen, 'An Unexpected Breakthrough in Hong Kong's Constitutional Reform', *Hong Kong Law Journal*, 40 (2010) 265.

54 Ibid.

TABLE 2.1 *Political orientation of Legco members, 1998–2016*

| Political orientation | 1998–2000 | | | | 2000–2004 | | | | 2004–2008* | | | 2008–2012 | | | 2012–2016 | |
|---|---|---|---|---|---|---|---|---|---|---|---|---|---|---|---|---|
| | FC | EC | GC | Total | FC | EC | GC | Total | FC | GC | Total | FC | GC | Total | FC | GC |
| Pro-Beijing | 18 | 10 | 5 | 32 | 19 | 6 | 7 | 32 | 18 | 12 | 30 | 21 | 11 | 32 | 25 | 17 |
| Pro-democracy | 5 | 0 | 14 | 19 | 6 | 0 | 16 | 22 | 7 | 18 | 25 | 4 | 19 | 23 | 9 | 18 |
| Independent | 7 | 0 | 1 | 9 | 5 | 0 | 1 | 6 | 5 | 0 | 5 | 5 | 0 | 5 | 1 | 0 |
| Total | 30 | 10 | 20 | 60 | 30 | 6 | 24 | 60 | 30 | 30 | 60 | 30 | 30 | 60 | 35 | 35 |

* There were 26 democrats in Legco after December 2007 when Mrs Anson Chan won a by-election.

Source: The author's calculation is based on the following sources: Ngok Ma, *Political Development in Hong Kong: State, Political Society, and Civil Society* (Hong Kong, London: Hong Kong University Press, 2007), 121–122; Yip Tin Sang (ed.), 香港選舉資料匯編: 1996–2000 (Electoral Facts in Hong Kong: 1996–2000) (Hong Kong: Hong Kong Institute of Asia-Pacific Studies, 2001); Yip Tin Sang (ed.), 香港選舉資料匯編: 2001–2004 (Electoral Facts in Hong Kong: 2001–2004) (Hong Kong: Hong Kong Institute of Asia-Pacific Studies, 2005); Legislative Council, *Members' Bibliographies*, <http://www.legco.gov.hk/general/english/members/yr08-12/biographies.htm>.

constituencies differ greatly in terms of the numbers and structure of the electorate. For instance, in the 2008 Legco election, the Education sector had 90,693 registered electors, mainly teachers and staff in educational institutions, whereas the Heung Yee Kuk sector had only 157 electors, including the Chairman and the Vice-Chairmen of the Heung Yee Kuk and the ex-officio, special and co-opted Councillors of the Full Council of the Kuk.[55] The number of pro-democracy Legco members returned by FCs has never exceeded seven before the 2012 Legco election.

FCs developed from the previous informal appointment system which ensured that 'specialist knowledge and valuable expertise had been provided to the Council'.[56] There are two assumptions that FCs are 'incorporating sectoral interests in policy making and tapping the idiosyncratic knowledge bases of different economic and professional sectors'.[57] Since the return of sovereignty to China, the future of the FC system has been the focus of debate. In 2007, Deputy Director of Hong Kong and Macau Affairs Office of the State Council Mr Zhang Xiaoming said that the FC system was not necessarily inconsistent with the concept of universal suffrage.[58] In 2010, Mr Qiao Xiaoyang, Deputy Secretary General of the NPCSC, defined universal suffrage as 'the equal right of election of all individuals' and further urged for 'an objective assessment of functional constituencies'.[59] These statements raised the concern about whether the CPG is determined to retain an FC system; moreover, pro-Beijing groups and individuals in Hong Kong have apparently begun to devise a scheme to adapt the existing FC system to the requirements of

55 The figures are available at '2008 Legislative Council Election', *Electoral Affairs Commission* [web page] (2008), <http://www.eac.gov.hk/en/legco/2008.htm>, accessed 1 June 2014. On the composition of both constituencies, see Legislative Council Ordinance, Cap 542, s 20(A) and 20(E). Heung Yee Kuk is a statutory advisory body with a constitution so framed as to ensure that it will as far as possible be truly representative of informed and responsible opinion in the New Territories, see Heung Yee Kuk Ordinance, Cap 1097.

56 Hong Kong Government, 'Green Paper: The 1987 Review of Developments in Representative Government' (1987) 22–23.

57 Rowena Y.F. Kwok and Chiu Tak Chow, 'The Dynamics of Social Policy Making in Hong Kong: The Role of Functional Representatives (1998–2004)', in Christine Loh and Civic Exchange (eds.), *Functional Constituencies: A Unique Feature of the Hong Kong Legislative Council* (Hong Kong: Hong Kong University Press, 2006), 262.

58 See Hong Kong and Macau Affairs Office deputy director, Mr Zhang Xiaoming's speech at a public forum on constitutional reform, Carrie Chan, 'Future of Functional Seats Disputed', *The Standard*, 31 December 2007, P04.

59 Editorial, 'Suffrage Statement Raises Fresh Concerns', *South China Morning Post*, 9 June 2010, EDT12.

universal suffrage, through technical optimisation of the franchise of FCs and competing for the power to 'correctly' interpret 'universal suffrage'.[60]

However, as Professor Norman Miners points out, FCs, intended to secure representation for minorities in other jurisdictions, have occupied the largest block of elected constituencies in Hong Kong to 'secure special representation for the richest and most privileged sectors of the community'.[61] Furthermore, the differing sizes of constituencies and the co-existence of corporate and individual voters are not conducive to the original objective of avoiding factional politics. The distance between the citizens and FC members generally makes people feel that although they are able to force political parties, whether pro-Beijing or not, to alter their position on some issues, it is difficult to exert any influence over those FC members without political affiliations. Hence, there is confusion about the role of FC members and which interests should be given priority by FC members: party interests, sectoral interests or the public interest? Such confusion is not conducive to shaping public expectations of Legco and eventually leads to diminishing popularity of Legco as a whole. Some scholars therefore argue that discussion on reforming FCs, rather than abolishing them, is incongruous in the prosperous and pluralistic community of Hong Kong.[62]

### Public Support

General support from the public is, in its simplest sense, connected with Legco's popularity. Surveys conducted by the Asian Barometer in 2001 and 2007 show that more than 50 per cent of Hong Kong people trust Legco, but fewer than 30 per cent trust political parties.[63] According to the public opinion programmes of the University of Hong Kong and the Chinese University of Hong Kong, the public's level of satisfaction with the performance of Legco since

60 See '梁爱詩:功能組別可符合普選定義 (Elsie Leung: Functional Constituencies could be Consistent with the Concept of Universal Suffrage)', *Hong Kong Economic Journal*, 9 June 2010, 16 (in Chinese); Eva Wu, 'Divisions Surface on Functional Constituencies', *South China Morning Post*, 31 December 2007, EDT3; and Fanny W.Y. Fung, 'NPC Local Deputy Proposes "One Man, Two Votes"', *South China Morning Post*, 3 January 2008, EDT3.

61 Miners and Tang, *The Government and Politics of Hong Kong*, 116.

62 Christine Loh and Civic Exchange, *Functional Constituencies: A Unique Feature of the Hong Kong Legislative Council* (Hong Kong: Hong Kong University Press, 2006), 1.

63 Ngok Ma and Kin-Man Chan, 'Asian Barometer—Hong Kong Report: The State of Democratic Governance in Hong Kong', *The Asian Barometer Conference on 'The State of Democratic Governance in Asia'* (Taipei, 20–21 June 2008), 24 <http://www.asianbarometer.org/newenglish/publications/conferencepapers/2008conference/sec.4.3.pdf>, accessed 10 September 2011.

1998 has barely exceeded 30 per cent, and the negative satisfaction rating is generally higher than the positive satisfaction rating.[64]

These results reveal the complicated public perception of Legco: trusting the institution but being dissatisfied with its performance. The trust of the public indicates that Legco has been recognised to be a legitimate representative body, but the reasons for dissatisfaction with its performance are relatively complicated. A survey in 2009 shows, in response to a question about executive–legislative relations, that 51.4 per cent of the respondents expected more checks on the executive by legislators whilst 37.9 per cent expected more cooperation between legislators and the executive.[65] The reasons for the dissatisfaction may be contradictory: those members of the public who want an active Legco may be dissatisfied with its lack of power to substitute and change public policy, whilst others may complain that lengthy debates in Legco and its occasional rejection of government proposals posed obstacles to the efficiency of the administration.

It is therefore doubtful whether a particular expectation of Legco is shared by the public. Expectations of the legislature, in Professor Mezey's words, are 'views about how a legislature should perform', that is, the 'appropriate legislative model'.[66] It is clear that legislators would gain less support from the public if they failed to conform to such a model.[67] However, there is not always public consensus or agreement on what constitutes an appropriate model. In Hong

64 For the survey result of HKU, see The University of Hong Kong Public Opinion Programme, '你對特區立法會成員既整體表現滿唔滿意? (Are You Satisfied with the Overall Performance of the Members of HKSAR Legislative Council?)', *HKU PoP Site* [web page] (2011) <http://hkupop.hku.hk/chinese/popexpress/sargperf/fourthlc/poll/datatables.html>, accessed 10 September 2011. And for the survey result of CUHK from April 1998 to October 2006, see Timothy Ka-Ying Wong and Shirley Po-San Wan, 'Citizen's Evaluations of Legitimacy in Post-Colonial Hong Kong: Results of a Longitudinal Study', in Joseph Yu-Shek Cheng (ed.), *The Hong Kong Special Administrative Region in Its First Decade* (Hong Kong: City University of Hong Kong Press, 2007), 90, table 2; for the result from April 2002 to April 2009, see The Chinese University of Hong Kong Institute of Asia-Pacific Studies, '表一:對特區政府各項施政的滿意度 (Table 1: Satisfaction with Various Policies of the HKSAR Government)', *CUHK* [web document] (20 April 2009), <http://www.cpr.cuhk.edu.hk/resources/press/pdf/4c43c7d775479.pdf>, accessed 10 September 2011.

65 See The Chinese University of Hong Kong Institute of Asia-Pacific Studies, '市民對立法會表現評價意見調查結果摘要 (Survey Results on Citizens' Opinions Towards the Legislative Council's Performance)', *CUHK* [web document] (29 July 2009), <http://www.cuhk.edu.hk/cpr/pressrelease/090729_survey.pdf>, accessed 10 September 2011.

66 Mezey (n 27), 32–33.

67 Ibid.

Kong society in the post-1997 year, a trend of social fragmentation and disintegration can be observed which is 'a combined result of an economic crisis of production and a political crisis of representation',[68] and Legco correspondingly appears to be divisive and to satisfy the public with difficulty.

Accordingly, given the overall low popularity of political parties and the importance of public support for an autonomous Legco, a crucial question is whether Legco can gradually rebuild the confidence of the public and shape clear expectations amongst citizens or not. Those components that do not favour building up clear public expectations and effective communication between Legco and the citizens need to be gradually dismantled. In this regard, the role of FCs is worth considering.

### Changing Political Environment

There are two perceptions regarding the evolving political environment in Hong Kong. One pertains to building a 'new political order' which 'complies with the original intentions of Beijing's policy towards Hong Kong', as summarized by Professor Lau Siu Kai.[69] The other is a 'mainlandization' policy which attempts 'to make Hong Kong politically and economically converge with the PRC' as analysed by Professor Sonny Lo.[70] Whilst the building of a 'new political order' focuses on how Beijing's OCTS policy is embedded in Hong Kong's political structure, discussion of 'mainlandization' stresses how 'Hong Kong's political and economic uniqueness' has been diluted through its convergence with the PRC.[71] Despite their distinct central points, both perceptions recognise the effect on political development of the transformation of Beijing's strategy towards Hong Kong since 2003, particularly the effect of Beijing's economic strategy on the political attitudes of Hong Kong people regarding the OCTS and democratic development, and eventually that on the political environment.[72] Beijing is regarded as having gradually abandoned the 'laissez faire policy' on Hong Kong during the first five years after reunification with the PRC, and as adopting a 'new policy' which 'emphasizes more central

68 Anthony B.L. Cheung, 'Restoring Governability in Hong Kong: Managing Plurality and Joining up Governance', in Julia Lai Po-Wah Tao, et al. (eds.), *Governance for Harmony in Asia and Beyond* (New York: Routledge, 2010), 173–175.

69 Lau, 'In Search of a New Political Order', 139.

70 Sonny Shiu-Hing Lo, 'The Mainlandization and Recolonization of Hong Kong: A Triumph of Convergence over Divergence with Mainland China', in Joseph Y.S. Cheng (ed.), *The Hong Kong Special Administrative Region in Its First Decade* (Hong Kong: City University of Hong Kong Press, 2007), 186.

71 Ibid., 184.

72 Ibid., 206; see also Lau (n 69), 152–153.

government engagement and involvement in Hong Kong's political development', as a mainland Chinese scholar points out.[73]

A new strategy has surfaced since 2004, when the interpretation of the Basic Law by the NPCSC, together with the 'patriotism propaganda' spread early in that year,[74] and weakened democrats' appeal for double universal suffrage.[75] Beijing was also alleged to have been involved in local elections, in particular the reported interference of the Central Liaison Office in the 2004 Legco election campaign.[76] The shift in Beijing's strategy towards Hong Kong has been influential in Hong Kong's political ecology. After the 2004 Legco election, the democracy movement is considered to have 'lost its direction or immediate goal' and experience a 'new impasse' in 2005 when Donald Tsang's constitutional reform proposals were vetoed by democrats.[77] The failure of the 2005 constitutional reform has 'intensified' the division between the pro-Beijing and the pro-democracy camps within Legco.[78]

Although Professor Lau Siu Kai argues that a loose governing coalition formed as one of main features of the 'new strategy' which was 'initially formulated during Tung's second term (2002–2005)' and 'inherited by Donald Tsang',[79] for quite some time the pro-Beijing political groups in Legco essentially lacked the incentive to provide absolute support for the executive. They do not share a common platform with the executive and, more importantly, cannot become the ruling party or a substantive part of the governing team. A winning candidate for the position of CE cannot be a member of any political party,[80] and the CE seldom appoints candidates with party affiliations as principal officials.[81] Instead, with the increased number of seats returned by GCs, political groups wanting more GC seats would have to assign more importance to the voice of their electorate. A division within the pro-Beijing camp between those who are pro-business and those who are pro-grassroots is also not conducive to a stable political coalition. The Liberal Party, until 2008 the

73 Jie Cheng, 'The Story of a New Policy', *Hong Kong Journal*, 15/July (2009) <http://web.archive.org/web/20120107011853/http://www.hkjournal.org/archive/2009_fall/1.htm>, accessed 2 January 2015.

74 Ma, 'Democratic Development in Hong Kong: A Decade of Lost Opportunities', 62.

75 Ibid., 65.

76 Lo (n 70), 206.

77 Ma (n 74), 65.

78 Chen (n 1), 34.

79 Lau (n 69), 152.

80 Chief Executive Election Ordinance, Cap 569, s 31.

81 On 28 June 2011, the CE appointed So Kam-leung as Secretary for Commerce and Economic Development. So is a member of and served as the Vice-chairman of the Democratic Alliance for the Betterment and Progress of Hong Kong (DAB).

sole political party representing the interests of local business sector, has revealed its decision to pursue more GCs seats and integrate various forces in Legco. Its leader, Mr James Tien, was the convener of the eight-party coalition which had put pressure on the executive during the 2001–02 session. In this sense the cross-party coalition is almost the opposite of the governing coalition, and would therefore be disallowed by the CPG and by the HKSAR government, which expects a strong executive. The shift of the Liberal Party's position on Article 23 of the Basic Law was a decisive event which led to its success in GCs election in 2004 but at the same time lost it the support and trust of the CPG and the Liaison Office (as discussed in the following chapter). In the 2008 Legco election the Liberal Party failed to secure its GC seat and subsequently split up, with four FC legislators breaking away to form Economic Energy, which was relatively more conservative. Accordingly, a governing coalition, if any, would be very unstable.

The 2012 CE election marked the commencement of a rather different era. Mr Leung Chun Ying defeated another pro-Beijing candidate, Mr Henry Tang, who had support from business tycoons and was a Principal Official in the government. Mr Leung is considered to have close ties with Beijing, given his experience serving as the Secretary General of the Consultative Committee for the Basic Law as early as 1988. In the later stages of the election, he apparently received strong support from the DAB and the Hong Kong Federation of Trade Unions (FTU), which are usually regarded as absolutely loyal to Beijing, in contrast to other pro-Beijing political forces. Mr Leung's assumption of office in 2012 caused a reshuffle of the political forces in Legco, particularly in FCs which seem to be easily controlled. After the 2012 Legco election, some long-term supporters of Mr Henry Tang in FCs were replaced by those having a stronger connection to Mr Leung Chun Ying, for instance, Mr David Li's replacement by Mr Ng Leung Sing in the Finance sector, Mr Lau Sau Sing's replacement by Mr Tony Tse in the Architectural, Surveying and Planning sector and Mr Ho Chung Tai's replacement by Lo Wai Kwok in the Engineering sector. Following a fierce election campaign, the objective of establishing a governing coalition in the early years of the HKSAR has been overwhelmed by the new government's desire for full control over Legco, and such control has been achieved on a narrower social base by excluding more potential allies than ever before.

### *Internal Characteristics: Rules, Committee Autonomy, Administrative Autonomy and Financial Autonomy*

Generally speaking, Legco enjoys administrative and financial autonomy through the Legislative Council Commission. The Commission usually has no more than 13 members, comprising the President as the Chairman, the Chairman and Deputy Chairman of the House Committee and other members elected from amongst the Legco membership.[82] The Legco Commission is independent of the executive and is responsible for administrative support and services to Legco through the secretariat. It provides funding for the work of Legco through a separate line of expenditure in the annual estimates of the government.[83] It is also responsible for employing staff and preparing the annual estimates of the Commission.[84] However, the allocation of additional resources depends on decisions made by the government.[85]

The secretariat contains a Legal Service Division and an Information Services Division. The Research Office of the Information Services Division is responsible for producing 'nonpartisan research services to the Council and its committees', including research reports, information notes, fact sheets, research briefs and reference notes.[86] There are currently nine research officers who provide stable, albeit disproportionate, research support for the seventy Legco members.

Leaders of the full Legco and its committees have the authority to make final decisions on its internal rules and procedures. The President is responsible for presiding over meetings, deciding on the agenda and other procedural matters concerning Legco meetings. However, government bills have priority in the agenda.[87] The effect of its leadership on Legco's internal operations can be revealed by examining the President's rulings on member's bills, motions and amendments and rulings of committee chairs on procedural affairs, as delineated in the following chapters. These chapters also show how Legco members communicate with the citizens and manage partisan control in committees. This section focuses on the evolution of the RoP and the allocation of committee leadership.

82 The Legislative Council Commission Ordinance, Cap 443, s 4.

83 The Legislative Council Commission, 'Report on the Activities of the Legislative Council Commission 2012–2013' (2013) <http://www.legco.gov.hk/general/english/sec/reports/c_1213.pdf>, accessed 1 June 2014, 15.

84 The Legislative Council Commission Ordinance, s 10.

85 The Legislative Council Commission (n 83).

86 See introduction to the Research Office of the Legco, available at: 'Research Office', *HKSAR Legislative Council* [web page] <http://www.legco.gov.hk/general/english/sec/corg_ser/research.htm>, accessed 1 June 2014.

87 Rules of Procedure of The Legislative Council of The Hong Kong Special Administrative Region (made by the Legislative Council on 3 July 1998, last amended 21 March 2014) (RoP hereinafter), Rule 18(1).

### Rules of Procedure

The RoP follows the main body of the Standing Orders of the colonial Legislative Council, with some modifications in accordance with the Basic Law. In addition to the SVM, a major modification concerns the method of voting. In colonial times, the passing of proposals put to Legco or its committees required 'a majority of the votes of the members present and voting' according to the Standing Orders.[88] However, Annex II of the Basic Law provides that 'the passage of bills introduced by the government shall require at least a simple majority vote of the members of the Legislative Council present' and that Legco members' initiatives require 'a simple majority vote of each of the two groups of members present', which have been incorporated into Rules 46 to 49. A 'majority vote of members present' means that the number of votes in favour exceeds the total number of 'those voting against, those abstaining from voting and those present but not voting'.[89] In practice, this makes it more difficult to get proposals passed than in colonial times. It gave rise to disagreement by the government when Legco was drafting the RoP. The government insisted that abstentions and the President (who never votes) should not be counted in determining the results of voting on government bills, on the ground that Annex II of the Chinese version of the Basic Law uses the Chinese character '票 [vote]'.[90] This character appears in the provision concerning the voting procedure for government bills but is absent in that for Legco members' initiatives.[91] A legal advisor to Legco disagreed with the government, pointing out that the only difference between the two voting procedures is the SVM,[92] and the difference alleged by the government was 'only a matter of style in writing'.[93] Hence, votes in the whole Council are always counted on the basis of the number of members 'present', regardless of whether voting is on government bills or members' bills or motions. However, it is noteworthy that the voting procedures in committees or panels have preserved the practice of counting 'a majority of members present and voting'.

---

88 Standing Orders of the Legislative Council of Hong Kong (ceased to apply on 1 July 1997). For full text, see Legislative Council Library, 'Legco Infopack 2011–2012', *HKSAR Legislative Council* [web document] (October 2011), <http://www.legco.gov.hk/general/english/library/infopacks/yr11-12/1112infopacks-lc-01-e.pdf>, accessed 1 June 2014.

89 Legislative Council Secretariat, 'Information Paper for the House Committee: Committee on Rules of Procedure Voting Procedures' (LC Paper No. CB(1) 72/98-99, 1998), para 2.

90 Ibid., paras 8–9.

91 Ibid., para 18.

92 Ibid., para 12.

93 Ibid., para 19.

Another significant dispute with the executive relates to the application of Article 74 to the RoP. The executive has asserted that the restrictions on private members' bills under Article 74 should also be applied to member's amendments to bills, and that the power to determine whether a member's bills or amendments are subject to Article 74 rests with the CE.[94] Legco has rejected these arguments and the President exercises the power to determine whether a member's bills or amendments fall within the scope of Article 74.

Following the enactment of the RoP, it has been amended several times since the return of sovereignty to China. These amendments aim to incorporate long-standing practice into the RoP, rectify discrepancies in the RoP or provide standing arrangements for exercising some activities, such as debates over subsidiary legislation.[95] The 2011 amendment is the most important and substantive after 1997 in terms of extending the power of the chairman of any committee. Pursuant to the amendment, the chairman of any committee has the power 'to order a member whose conduct is grossly disorderly to withdraw immediately from the Council or committees',[96] a power which was originally vested only in the President and the chairman of any standing or select committee. This amendment is usually deemed a constraint on activists within Legco who frequently take radical action at meetings; however, it imposes restrictions on members' behaviour overall, and whether this power can be used in a sound way depends on the experience and the impartiality of each chairman. Another amendment to authorise the chairman of any committee to discontinue the speech of a member who persists in irrelevance or tedious repetition, was vetoed without support from the Democratic Party and the Civic Party.

The latest development relating to the RoP and the practice of Legco is the publication of Legco's manual. In June 2014, Legco published the first part of its manual entitled 'A Companion to the history, rules and practices of the Legislative Council of the Hong Kong Special Administrative Region', which provides more detail about the practice and rules of Legco.

---

94 Committee on Rules of Procedure, 'Procedure in Dealing with the Introduction of Members' Bills as Provided in Article 74 of the Basic Law and the Interpretation of Article 48(10) of the Basic Law' (LC Paper No. CB(1) 45/98-99, 1998), paras 8, 11.

95 Hansard HK (2 December 2009), 2591.

96 Hansard HK (20 March 2013), 10220. Rule 45(1) of the RoP stipulates that: 'The President, the Chairman of a committee of the whole Council or the chairman of any standing or select committee, after having called the attention of the Council or the committee to the conduct of a Member who persists in irrelevance or tedious repetition of his own or other Members' arguments in the debate, may direct him to discontinue his speech'.

### Committee System and Leadership

An 'active and specialized' committee system is essential for an autonomous legislature to accumulate policy expertise.[97] Alongside gradual constitutional reform since the 1980s, Legco has developed a complete and institutionalised committee system, comprising permanent committees and panels, and ad hoc committees for specific purposes such as Bills Committee, investigation committee and select committee.[98] Similar to many other legislatures around the world, committees are where Legco exercises its functions and powers. Of the permanent committees, the House Committee and the Finance Committee have the same membership, that is, all members other than the President, but are responsible for different functions. The House Committee decides the manner of consideration of bills and subsidiary legislation, placing them with Bill Committees or subcommittees and considering the amount and priority of legislation; it may additionally consider any items concerning the business of Legco.[99] The Finance Committee, one of three standing committees of Legco together with the PAC and the Committee on Members' Interests, is responsible for deliberation over estimates and public expenditure. The PAC is another financial committee, possessing an audit function so that Legco can monitor the entire financial cycle, and usually has seven members. The number of panels which are parallel with the governmental departments are not fixed under the RoP, but has stood at 18 since the 2000–01 session, with the first term Legco (1998–2000) having 17. Within their respective jurisdictions, these panels consider policy matters referred to them by a member or the House Committee.[100] Only the standing committees have the power to summon witnesses and demand documents, whereas Legco uses a resolution to authorise a power of summons for other committees or panels.

Committee leadership, as an institutionalised position with higher status and authority in the legislature, is a suitable variable for measuring the performance of committees in legislatures.[101] The selection of chairmen for legislative committees varies between parliamentary systems and presidentialism. In

97 Carey, et al. (n 37), 573.

98 An investigation committee may be set up for the purpose of 'establishing the facts stated in the motion moved under Rule 49B(1A) (Disqualification of Member from Office), and giving its views on whether or not the facts as established constitute grounds for the censure'. A select committee may be appointed to consider certain issues or bills. See RoP, Rules 73A(1) and 78(1).

99 RoP, Rule 75.

100 RoP, Rule 77(3).

101 Robert L. Peabody, 'Leadership in Legislatures: Evolution, Selection, Functions', *Legislative Studies Quarterly*, 9/3 (1984) 445.

the US Congress, seniority is an important selection criterion for a committee chairman, whilst in the British parliament importance is attached to the neutrality of a committee chairman.[102] Parliamentary knowledge and experience, along with popularity, are also important for a strong candidacy.[103] In the British House of Commons, the majority does not necessarily gain a majority of the chairmanships of departmental committees.[104]

Legco has evident Westminster-style features, in the neutrality of its committee chairmen in past practice. The chairmen of committees or panels are often elected at the first meetings pursuant to the RoP. However, a true vote only takes place when political parties cannot reach a compromise on certain positions. Given the predominance of the pro-Beijing camp in Legco, the pro-democracy camp has always been allocated a minority of chairmanships. The awarding of some chairmanships is a matter of bargaining, but for others it is not. For instance, the House Committee has always been chaired by pro-Beijing members. Legislators with long professional experience, regardless of their political orientation, are more likely to obtain a chairmanship. Councillor Margaret Ng, a pro-democracy barrister, chaired the Panel on Administration of Justice and Legal Services until she decided not to stand for re-election. Neutrality and a good reputation assist pro-democracy members to defeat their pro-Beijing counterparts. For instance, Councillor Emily Lau, a leading democrat, was elected as the chairperson of the Finance Committee after defeating her pro-Beijing rivals in seven sessions.

However, the pro-Beijing camp has completely taken over the chairmanship of the Finance Committee since 2012 (during Mr Leung Chun Ying's term). A similar situation has occurred in allocating the chairmanships of the PAC and policy panels.

The authority of the PAC stems partly from its non-partisan and non-policy character. From 1998 to 2004, this committee was chaired by Councillor Eric Li, the representative of the Accountancy sector and also an independent. From 2004 to 2012, pro-Beijing legislator Philip Wong chaired the PAC whilst the representative of the Accountancy sector was appointed only as Deputy Chairman. In Legco's fifth term, the representative of the Accountancy sector, who is also a democrat, failed to gain even the position of deputy chairman.

---

102 David M. Olson, *Democratic Legislative Institutions: A Comparative View* (Armonk, N.Y.: M.E. Sharpe, 1994), 58.

103 Peabody (n 101), 455.

104 Robert Blackburn and Andrew Kennon (eds.), *Griffith & Ryle on Parliament: Functions, Practice and Procedures* (2nd edn., London: Sweet & Maxwell, 2001), 582.

The allocation of chairmanships of policy panels demonstrates changes in the political environment. As Figure 2.1 shows, after a relatively stable distribution of panel chairs between the pro-Beijing and the pro-democracy camps, a change appears at the beginning of the fifth term Legco, marking a vital shift of the pro-Beijing camp to full control over panel leaderships. In the 2012–13 session, the pro-democracy camp only obtained chairmanships in four panels (about 22.22 per cent), a clear contrast to vote of nearly 60 per cent that they obtained in the GC election.

In addition, the level of the parliamentary experience of panel leaders is dropping, with increasing numbers of new members assuming panel leaderships. In Legco's fifth term, more than 30 per cent of the panel chairs are awarded to new members who have little parliamentary experience; this was only 5.89 per cent in 1998 (Table 2.2). Lacking the necessary knowledge and reputation, such leaders often find it difficult to make appropriate and prompt decisions on disputes about questions of order during committee meetings.

It appears that this widening gap in the allocation of committee chairmanships between the pro-Beijing and the pro-democracy camps is linked to a more urgent policy agenda or a deeper political cleavage following Mr Leung Chun Ying's assumption of office in 2012. The pro-democracy camp, despite having nearly 60 per cent of the public's support, will feel more powerless. These changes, along with the decline in the parliamentary experience of

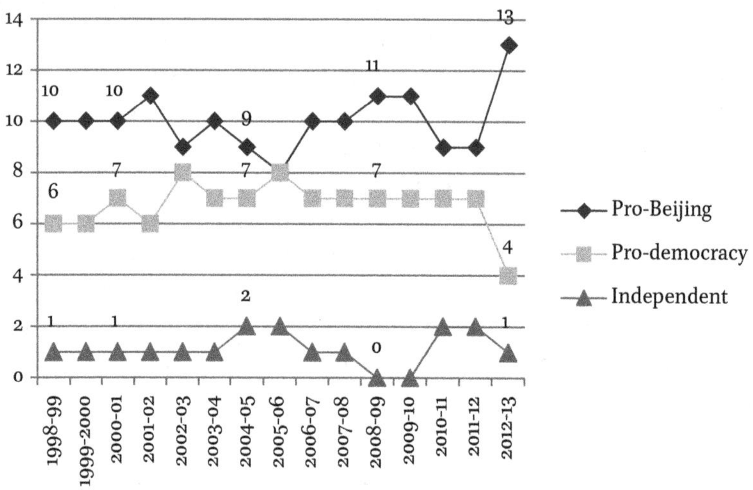


FIGURE 2.1 *Chairmanship of Legco panels (excluding Deputy Chairmanship), 1998–2013*
SOURCE: THE AUTHOR'S CALCULATION IS BASED ON THE MEMBERSHIP OF THE POLICY PANELS ON THE LEGCO WEBSITE.

TABLE 2.2 *Proportion of panel chairs without legislative experience in the first session of Legco terms*

| | 1st Legco 1998 | 2nd Legco 2000 | 3rd Legco 2004 | 4th Legco 2008 | 5th Legco 2012 |
|---|---|---|---|---|---|
| New member (%) | 5.89 | 13.89 | 25 | 22.22 | 30.55 |

SOURCE: THE AUTHOR'S CALCULATION BASED ON THE MEMBERSHIP OF THE POLICY PANELS ON THE LEGCO WEBSITE.

committee chairmen, predict the shift in the role of committee chairman from a neutral presiding officer to a participant having clear policy aims, which intensifies tension and conflict within committees. It is therefore doubtful that extending the power of the committee chairman would be helpful in restoring committee meetings to order. The interplay between various political groups and party control within committees may be revealed by close observation of the operation of committees, as discussed in the subsequent chapters.

## Conclusion

The Legislative Council of the HKSAR is a continuation of the colonial legislature in terms of its organisational structure and the rules and norms governing its internal work. With its checks and balances role embedded in the Basic Law, Legco possesses a genuine power to veto government bills and financial proposals. Furthermore, it has a specialised committee system and the necessary administrative and financial autonomy. During the course of drafting the RoP, Legco secured the power of its President to determine whether members' bills or amendments are subject to Article 74 and rejected the wishes of the executive regarding the voting procedure.

However, Legco has been facing serious challenges to its autonomy from both the external environment and the internal operations. Externally, Legco lacks effective means to hold the government accountable. Furthermore, with increasing conflict between the pro-Beijing and pro-democracy camps within Legco, the courts have been invited to intervene in the internal operations of Legco and have indeed established jurisdiction over the disputes concerning powers and practice of Legco. Owing to the deficiency in its representation system, namely the existence of the FC system, Legco has not shaped clear public expectations nor established effective communication with citizens. Internally, in recent years Legco has approved or has been considering some self-imposed restrictions in the RoP on members' activities. It seems doubtful whether or not these restrictions would be imposed in a sound way in view of the overall decline in the parliamentary experience of committee chairmen and their disputed impartiality.

From the preceding analysis, two preliminary observations deserve more attention: the first is that the objective of creating a governing coalition on a wider social base in the early years of the HKSAR has been overwhelmed by the government's desire for full control over Legco; the second is the shift in the role of the chairmen of important committees from that of a neutral presiding officer to a participant with clear policy aims. Both observations predict more future tension and conflict within or outside Legco.

This chapter provides a preliminary assessment of Legco's autonomy and the dynamics of the political system. The following chapters examines the way in which Legco performs its functions with such autonomy.

CHAPTER 3

# Scrutiny of Legislation

Since the return of sovereignty to China, Legco members' initiation power has received much more extensive restrictions under the Basic Law than under any colonial instruments. Further, the passage of member's bill and amendment is subject to a Separate Voting Mechanism (SVM) under Annex II of the Basic Law. The high success rate of government bills in Legco in the past may also impress people with a silent and weak legislature. However, Legco's actual impact on legislation depends on not only the constitutional power, but also various institutional factors, including the effectiveness of the committee work and interaction amongst political groups within Legco. To assess the legislative influence on public policy, many scholars develop the traditional notion of the law-making function of legislatures and provide broader perspectives for such assessment, including devising indicators for legislative 'viscosity',[1] conducting an issue-oriented examination of legislative activities,[2] and dividing distinct policy-making stages.[3] Using these measurement tools, this chapter examines the major aspects of Legco's law-making power, including private member's bills, Bills Committees' deliberation, members' Committee Stage Amendments (CSA) to government bills and subsidiary legislation, and illustrates ways in which legislators push the government into improving its drafts and changing public policy.

## Private Member's Bill under Article 74 of Basic Law

Hong Kong has followed the practice of introducing private member's bills as the former British colony. In the British Parliament, private member's bills refer to public bills introduced by members other than members of the government.[4]

1 The concept of 'viscosity' was suggested by Blondel to qualify legislative influence. Ma Ngok devised five 'viscosity indicators' for Hong Kong Legco: 1. the number of bill committees formed; 2. time spent on bill deliberation; 3. the number of government amendments; 4. the number of member' amendments; and 5. the number of members' amendments passed. See Ma, *Political Development in Hong Kong: State, Political Society, and Civil Society*, 122–123.

2 Ibid.

3 Mezey, *Comparative Legislatures*, 8.

4 Thomas Erskine May, W.R. Mckay, and Frank Cranmer, *Erskine May's Treatise on the Law, Privileges, Proceedings, and Usage of Parliament* (23rd edn., London: LexisNexis UK, 2004), 543.

 | DOI 10.1163/9789004276284_004

Legco members in the colonial period were not allowed to introduce a bill having 'an effect which would charge or dispose of the revenue of the Hong Kong government', without the express permission of the Governor.[5] After 1997, legislators can no longer propose bills relating to political structure, public expenditure or operation of the government. Moreover, member's bills relating to government policies shall require the written consent of the CE, according to Article 74 of the Basic Law. These restrictions were incorporated into Legco's Rules of Procedure (RoP) through Rules 51(3) and (4).[6] The President of Legco shall determine whether a member's bill falls within the scope of Article 74:

> Rule 51(3): Members may not either individually or jointly introduce a bill which, in the opinion of the President, relates to public expenditure or political structure or the operation of the Government.
>
> Rule 51(4): In the case of a bill which, in the opinion of the President, relates to Government policies, the notice shall be accompanied by the written consent of the Chief Executive in respect of the bill.

Any bill proposed by members is subject to restrictions of Rules 51(3) and (4) before its first reading. The President of Legco shall disallow the introduction of such a bill if it falls into the scope of Rule 51(3) or require the CE's written consent in the case that a bill relates to 'government policy' under Rule 51(4).

### *Decline of Private Member's Bills*

As Table 3.1 shows, Legco members introduced 25 public bills and 19 private bills from 1998 to 2013.[7] All private bills were passed whilst only seven private member's bills were enacted. Of 25 private member's bills, six were disallowed by the President in accordance with Rule 51(3) and ten relating to government policy were not tabled without the written consent of the CE. Of the remaining nine bills, two lapsed owing to the end of the Legco session. Therefore, only seven private member's bills were tabled before and eventually passed by Legco, including five bills concerning the composition of University Councils and two concerning the regulation of professional accountants. These successful bills do not have an effect on the public at large.

5 Max Wai-Lun Wong, 'The Meaning of "Charge": Private Member's Bills in the Legislative Council', *Hong Kong Law Journal*, 28 (1998) 231.

6 See Ruling by the President of the Legislative Council on the Employment (Amendment) Bill 1999 proposed by Hon. Andrew CHENG Kar-foo (16 July 1999), 14 <http://www.legco.gov.hk/yr98-99/english/pre_rul/990716.pdf>, accessed 21 September 2008.

7 The author's calculation based on Legco's official website: <http://www.legco.gov.hk>.

TABLE 3.1 *Result of bills introduced by members, 1998–2013*

| Type of bill | Negatived by President | Without CE's written consent | Lapsed | Passed | Total |
|---|---|---|---|---|---|
| Private bill | 0 | 0 | 0 | 19 | 19 |
| Public bill | 6 | 10 | 2 | 7 | 25 |
| Total | 6 | 10 | 2 | 26 | 44 |

SOURCE: THE AUTHOR'S CALCULATION BASED ON THE OFFICIAL RECORD OF PROCEEDINGS OF THE LEGISLATIVE COUNCIL (HANSARD HK HEREINAFTER), 1998–2013.

The aforementioned situation indicates that the CE's consent becomes a major determinant of the introduction of private member's bills. Bills without the CE's written consent in the past cover issues concerning employment, mandatory Provident Fund schemes, immigration, and import and export.[8] It appears that the government is reluctant to allow members to table public bills that have real policy impact and would rather issue written permission to private bills that usually handle the interests and benefit of individuals or private organisations such as banks and charity organisations.

The number of proposed private member's bills has decreased since 1997. Nearly a half of them were introduced during Legco's first and second terms. It is clear that Legislators are discouraged by low success rate of private member's bills and hope to use private member's bills as a negotiation weapon to push policy changes. However, such a weapon is not necessarily effective as both legislators and the government know the obstacles. Generally, private member's bills, as a means by which legislators are able to formulate public policy, have declined since 1997.

### *President's Rulings on Private Member's Bills*

In practice, most legislation more or less relates to public expenditure, government operation, political structure or government policies.[9] Hence, the President's interpretations of meanings of 'relate to' and the four categories in

8 The ten bills are Employment (Amendment) Bill 1999, Holiday (1999) Bill, Employment (Amendment) (No. 2) Bill 2000, Mandatory Provident Fund Schemes (Amendment) Bill 2001, Employment (Amendment) (No. 3) Bill 2000, The Smoking (Public Health) (Amendment) Bill 2009, The Mandatory Provident Fund Schemes (Amendment) Bill 2009, The Medical Registration (Amendment) Bill 2010, The Immigration (Amendment) (No. 2) Bill 2012, and Import and Export (Import and Export (General) Regulations) (Amendment) Bill 2013.

9 Ma (n 1), 117.

Article 74 are crucial to members' bills. At the time of making the RoP, the government criticised that the RoP is inconsistent with Article 74 of the Basic Law and insisted that the power to make such determinations rests with the CE.[10] However, the President of Legco never accepts the government's views.

From 1998 to 2013, the then Legco President Mrs Rita Fan and the present President Mr Jasper Tsang made rulings on 24 private member's bills, as shown in Table 3.2.[11] In her rulings, President Fan establishes a series of principles in interpreting 'public expenditure', 'political structure', 'operation of government', 'government policies' and the extent of 'relate to'. These principles are followed by her successor, President Jasper Tsang.

To propose public bills, members first 'seek the President's opinion in writing on whether the bill relates to any of the matters mentioned in Rule 51(3) and (4)'.[12] The administration is invited to submit views on whether the proposed bills satisfy the requirements in Article 74. Members have the opportunity to reply to the government's submissions. The President makes rulings on bills after hearing both parties. On her ruling-making process, President Rita Fan says that the President of Legco 'is not at liberty to consider views of other parties, apart from the Administration and the Member of Legco concerned, in reaching the Ruling'.[13] Also, President Fan's long-term service as the Legco President ensures the consistency in the President's rulings.

In her landmark ruling on Labour Relations (Right to Representation, Consultation and Collective Bargaining) Bill (Labour Relations Bill hereafter) proposed by Councillor Lee Cheuk Yan, the President pointed out that Article 74 is 'an enabling article which enables Members of the Legislative Council to introduce bills', imposing 'conditions and restrictions on such introduction'.[14] From time to time, the President's ruling on a private member's bill concerned more than one category under Article 74. As Table 3.2 shows, although almost

---

10 See Albert H.Y. Chen, 'Hong Kong's Legal System in the New Constitutional Order: The Experience of 1997–2000', in Jianfu Chen, Yuwen Li, and Jan Michiel Otto (eds.), *Implementation of Law in the People's Republic of China* (The Hague: Kluwer Law International, 2002), 239–240.

11 Of the 25 private member's bills, the University of Hong Kong (Amendment) Bill 2010 was not given a ruling by the President.

12 Legislative Council Secretariat, 'Legislative Council Procedures on Members' Bills' [web document] (3 January 2008) <http://www.legco.gov.hk/general/english/bills/mem-bill.pdf>, accessed 21 September 2008, para 4(c).

13 Interview with President Rita Fan on 1 December 2010.

14 Ruling by the President of the Legislative Council on the Labour Relations (Right to Representation, Consultation and Collective Bargaining) Bill (19 July 1999), para 12, <http://www.legco.gov.hk/yr98-99/english/pre_rul/990719b.pdf>, accessed 21 September 2008.

TABLE 3.2 *President's rulings on public bills introduced by members, 1998–2013*

| Type of test | Negatived | Passed | Approved by CE |
|---|---|---|---|
| Test of government policy | 24 | 0 | 8 |
| Test of operation of government | 1 | 6 | N/A |
| Test of public expenditure | 5 | 2 | N/A |
| Test of political structure | 0 | 0 | N/A |

SOURCE: THE AUTHOR'S CALCULATION BASED ON HANSARD HK, 1998–2013.

all private member's bills failed in the test of government policy, the President ruled that six of them did not relate to the operation of government and two did not relate to public expenditure. Even though these decisions in favour of members cannot change the final results of bills that failed in the test of government policy, they manifest the independence of the President.

(1) The test of Government Policies (GP). The test of GP is a two-step one: (a) whether there is a GP that is caught by Rule 51(4); (b) whether the proposed bill will have substantive effect on this policy.[15] The President defined government policies in ruling on Employment (Amendment) Bill 1999 as follows:[16]

(a) Policies that have been decided by the Chief Executive or Chief Executive in Council under Articles 48(4) and 56 of the Basic Law.
(b) Policies decided by former Governors or Governors in Council prior to the implementation of the Basic Law and which are still in force.
(c) Policies reflected in legislation are Government Policy for the purpose of Rule 51(4).
(d) Policies decided by authorised public officers.
(e) Policies promulgated by designated public officers in Legco or its Committee.

15 See Ruling by the President of the Legislative Council on the Holiday (1999) Bill Proposed by the Hon LEUNG Yiu-chung (15 September 1999), <http://www.legco.gov.hk/yr99-00/english/pre_rul/990915.pdf>; and President's Ruling on Mandatory Provident Fund Schemes (Amendment) Bill 2001 Proposed by Hon Andrew CHENG Kar-foo (26 February 2001) <http://www.legco.gov.hk/yr00-01/english/pre_rul/r010226e.pdf>, accessed 21 September 2008.

16 See Ruling on the Employment (Amendment) Bill 1999 (n 6), 20 .

Although all bills failed in the test of GP, the President excluded several types of policies from the scope of GP under Rule 51(4). In her ruling on Employment (Amendment) Bill 1999, the President clearly rejected the Administration's view that 'policies being formulated' were government policies for the purpose of Rule 51(4). In her ruling on the Mandatory Provident Fund Schemes (Amendment) Bill 2001, the President ruled that 'policy aims' or 'objectives' would not be considered government policies under Rule 51(4) unless 'concrete policy decisions have been made to achieve them'.[17] These principles have been applied to subsequent rulings concerning GP.

Since Mr Jasper Tsang's assumption of the presidency in 2008, he has applied Councillor Fan's principles to various rulings. In his ruling on the Medical Registration (Amendment) Bill 2010 proposed by Councillor Leung Ka Lau, President Tsang ruled that Councillor Leung's bill had a substantive effect on the government policy on the regulation of Managed Care Organisations which was contained in the administration's paper to the Panel on Health Services.[18] In his second reply letter, Councillor Leung insisted that the statements in the paper were only policy objects rather than policies.[19] The President rejected Councillor Leung's view on the ground that government policies 'include policies promulgated in the Legislative Council or its committees by public officers designated by the CE'.[20]

In addition to the definition of GP, the President has decided what constituted 'relate to'. In its view on the Labour Relations Bill, the administration asserted that 'relate to' meant having 'a direct, indirect, consequential or incidental bearing on the matter'. However, President Fan rejected the administration's view of 'having substantive effect'. In several rulings concerning GP, she defined 'relate to' as follows:

(a) The test of GP is '*neither* as high as requiring that the bill must have an important effect *nor* so low that it need merely have some tenuous link with a GP articulated by the Administration'.[21]

---

17 Interview with President Rita Fan on 1 December 2010.

18 President's Ruling on the Medical Registration (Amendment) Bill 2010 Proposed by Councillor Leung Ka Lau (25 June 2010), para 31, <http://www.legco.gov.hk/yr09-10/english/pre_rul/pre0625-ref-e.pdf>, accessed 20 October 2011.

19 President's reply letter to Councillor Leung Ka Lau (26 August 2010), <http://www.legco.gov.hk/yr09-10/english/pre_rul/pre0826-ref-e.pdf>, accessed 20 October 2011.

20 Ibid.

21 See the advice of the Counsel to Legco, in President's Ruling on Professional Accountants (Amendment) Bill 2004 Proposed by Dr Hon Eric LI Ka-cheung (4 March 2004), <http://www.legco.gov.hk/yr03-04/english/pre_rul/pre0304cb3-ref-e.pdf>, accessed 21 September 2008.

(b) 'A bill does not relate to GP simply because it seeks to amend an ordinance in order to address an issue which is merely *incidental* to a GP'.[22]

(c) 'A bill containing legislative proposals which are similar to or even exactly the same as what is being carried out as administrative measures for implementing a certain policy must, in principle, be considered as one that relates to GP'.[23] (Emphasis added)

Accordingly, there should be a measure of connection between the proposed bills and government policies. Incidental or tenuous connections would not be deemed 'relate to' for the purpose of Rule 51(4).

(2) The test of Public Expenditure (PE). In the colonial era, a major restriction on members' initiatives was the 'charging effect' that means 'the disposal of or charging any part of the revenue or other public moneys of Hong Kong' stipulated by the Royal Instructions. Councillor Andrew Wong, the President of the colonial legislature since 1995, adopted a systematic approach to determine the meaning of the 'charging effect',[24] with a view to establishing 'a framework on practice and procedure which could be applicable in future, even after the transfer of sovereignty'. He deemed the spirit of 'public expenditure' in the Basic Law similar to that of the 'charging effect' in the Royal Instructions.[25] After 1997, the restriction of the charging effect is applied to members' amendments to bills and motions through Rules 31 and 57(6) of the RoP.

However, the President of post-1997 Legco distinguished the two terms in her ruling on the Labour Relations Bill:[26]

(a) 'Charging effect' in Rules 31 and 57(6) has no relation to B[asic] L[aw] 74 and has no relevance to any ruling I make in respect of Public Expenditure under Rule 51(3).

(b) The term 'public expenditure' in Rule 51(3) is *wider* in scope than 'the disposal of or charging any part of the revenue or other public moneys of Hong Kong'. (Emphasis added)

22 The Counsel to Legco expressed such a view in President's Ruling on Forests and Countryside (Amendment) Bill 2006 proposed by Hon CHOY So-yuk (18 January 2007), <http://www.legco.gov.hk/yr06-07/english/pre_rul/pre0118-ref-e.pdf>, accessed 21 September 2008.

23 Ibid.

24 Wong (n 5), 246.

25 Ibid., 246–247.

26 Ruling on the Labour Relations Bill (n 14), 20.

This decision seems to adopt a more stringent criterion for members' bills than that for members' amendments and motions. For the purpose of Rule 51(3), the President ruled that a bill would relate to PE if it had the substantial effect of increasing or reducing PE that the President must not ignore,[27] '...unless the expenditure in question is one which only represents a minimal continuing demand on PE'.[28]

(3) The test of Operation of the Government (OG). The test of OG passed in six cases and was negated only once. In her ruling on the Employment (Amendment) (No. 2) Bill 1998, President Fan ruled that the 'government' only means the executive authorities defined under Article 59 of the Basic Law for the purpose of Rule 51(3), and thus rejected the administration's view of the 'government' including the judiciary for the purpose of Rule 51(3).[29]

In addition to narrowing the definition of the 'government', President Fan also laid down the requirement of an obvious, long-term and not temporary effect on the structure or procedure of executive authorities. In her ruling on the Labour Relations Bill, President Fan rejected regarding the Labour Tribunal as part of the government.[30] In her ruling on the Legal Aid (Amendment) Bill 2000, President Fan applied the requirement of 'not temporary effect'.[31] The 'effect' was also explained in rulings on Employment (Amendment) (No. 2) Bill 2001 and Forests and Countryside (Amendment) Bill 2006 and the crux is whether the proposed bill will result in changes to the structure or procedure of the executive authorities.[32] The passage of the OG test seems to be not of important significance for bills because the proposed bills are usually negatived on the ground of other tests. Even so, by establishing its own test principles, rulings

27 Ibid.

28 The Counsel to the Legco claimed this item and got confirmed by the President in her Ruling on the Fair Competition Bill Proposed by Hon Fred LI and Hon SIN Chung-kai (12 February 2001), <http://www.legco.gov.hk/yr00-01/english/pre_rul/e010212.pdf>, accessed 21 September 2008.

29 Ruling by the President of the Legislative Council on the Employment (Amendment) (No. 2) Bill 1998 Proposed by the Hon. LEE Cheuk-yan (19 July 1999), <http://www.legco.gov.hk/yr98-99/english/pre_rul/990719a.pdf>, accessed 21 September 2008.

30 Ruling on the Labour Relations Bill (n 14).

31 President's Ruling on Hon CHAN Kwok-keung's Proposed Legal Aid (Amendment) Bill 2000 (29 June 2000), <http://www.legco.gov.hk/yr99-00/english/pre_rul/000629.pdf>, accessed 21 September 2008.

32 President's Ruling on Employment (Amendment) (No. 2) Bill 2001 Proposed by Hon CHAN Kwok-keung, Hon LI Fung-ying, JP and Hon LEUNG Fu-wah, MH, JP (14 March 2002), <http://www.legco.gov.hk/yr01-02/english/pre_rul/pre0314cb3-ref-e.pdf>, accessed 21 September 2008; and the Ruling on Forests and Countryside (Amendment) Bill 2006 (n 22).

of the President on the meaning of 'operation of the government' indicate that Legco operates in accordance with its own rules and conventions, which ensure Legco's independence of the executive branch.

(4) The test of Political Structure (PS). The test of PS was only applied in rul ing on Legislative Council (Amendment) Bill 1997 in the Provisional Legco. President Fan ruled:

> to be caught by the provision of relate to political structure in the Rules of Procedure, it is not necessary that the proposed bill be in conflict with Article 68 and Annex II of the Basic Law and/or the decision of the Preparatory Committee; it is sufficient that the bill relates to them and thus relates to the political structure.[33]

In that case, as the functions and formation of Legco are stipulated in Chapter IV entitled 'political structure' and Annex II of the Basic Law, the proposed bill inevitably fell within the scope of PS. As the test of PS was never used in the SAR Legco, it remains to be seen whether the President adopts a broader or stricter interpretation for cases concerning PS.

The aforementioned findings indicate that the test of GP has become the primary barrier to private member's bills. The CE's consent power ensures that legislators are unable to change government policies by means of proposing bills.

### *Summaries*

The President's exclusive power to make decisions on private member's bills has manifested Legco's autonomy. Although Legco members or members of the public are 'free to make public their criticism or sort judicial review' against the President's rulings,[34] the President has always made rulings according to the RoP, free from any external interference. All principles established in the President's rulings have become precedents that the President of Legco must adhere to.[35]

Private member's bills still have particular implications, regardless of their low success rate. First, they provide alternatives to people and spark public debates over issues concerned. Councillor James To, a DP member said that a private member's bill constitutes an opportunity for the public to compare it to

---

33 President's Ruling on Legislative Council (Amendment) Bill 1997 (14 November 1997), <http://www.legco.gov.hk/yr97-98/english/pre_rul/971114.pdf>, accessed 21 September 2008.

34 Interview with President Rita Fan on 1 December 2010.

35 Ibid.

that introduced by the government.[36] The government may feel embarrassed or 'ashamed' if people accept proposals initiated by legislators who have fewer resources than those at the disposal of the government.[37] Second, by proposing bills, members expose legal vacuums and push the government into adding such issues into its legislative programme or incorporating particular provisions of a private member's bill into its draft. Hence, the utilisation of private member's bill has exceeded the traditional function of the law-making power. Whether legislators push policy change by providing alternatives and exposing flaws in government proposals is dependent on the extent to which members mould public opinion and seek popular support.

Overall, individual members' power to propose bills merely has indirect impact on public policy. However, the government needs to value private member's bills simply because its legislative programme does not necessarily come up to public expectation. If members' bills do gain support from the public and are of better quality, the government should value these proposals notwithstanding its reluctance to let members' bills go ahead, as the government has a responsibility to listen to people and provide better drafts for the legislative process.[38]

### Scrutiny of Bills: Bills Committees

When a bill is put forward at the Legco meeting, a Bills Committee (BC) may be set up under the House Committee (HC) for the purpose of considering the general merits, principles, detailed provisions of and any amendments to bills.[39] Legco members, other than the President, may join a BC. As members only examine the details of a bill at the later stage of the whole Council once debate on the second reading is resumed, a BC becomes an important arena for a comprehensive examination of the bill. Legislators, ordinary citizens and organisations can submit recommendations and views on the principles and provisions of the proposed bill to the BC. Once the BC has completed its work, a report is submitted to and discussed by the HC for the purposes of 'informing the members in preparation for the resumption of the second reading debate

36 Interview with Councillor James To on 14 October 2008.

37 Ibid.

38 For the government's constitutional responsibility to present the best possible bill to the legislature, see Albert Chen, 'Don't Ignore the Case for a White Bill', *South China Morning Post*, 28 December 2002.

39 RoP, Rule 76(7).

on the bill in Council'.[40] Normally, the HC does not make any substantial change to the BC report because it does not examine the bill in depth.

The BC's deliberation is deemed an indicator of 'legislative viscosity' that legislators spend much time in deliberating bills in BCs and frequently force the government to move amendments.[41] Under Rule 76 of the RoP, the BC Chairperson determines the time and the place for meetings, and decides on the time allotted for discussion of each item on the agenda of a meeting,[42] which means that deliberation over a particular bill may last for a long time if the BC members are discontented with the bill.[43] A prolonged process in the BC puts considerable pressure on the government if the bill bogged down is on the government's priority list.[44] Hence, on many occasions the government has to accept suggestions of legislators so that the second reading of the Bill is assumed as scheduled.

Members' amendments passed in the BC are usually moved in the name of the Chairperson at the Committee of the whole Council. However, any decisions of the BC 'shall not be binding on any member that is in Council, in the Committee of the whole Council or in the House Committee'.[45] This means that members can still vote as they wish or move their own amendments at the later stage of the Committee of the whole Council.

### *Bills Scrutinised by Bills Committees*

The BC is put on the waiting list if the total number of BCs in action has exceeded 16.[46] Also, they may not be activated finally at the end of a Legco term. Even though a BC is activated, it may be dissolved if the bill finally lapses. Apparently, only activated BCs have an opportunity to make a difference in bills.

As Table 3.3 shows, of the 337 BCs that were established from 1998 and 2012,[47] 316 completed their work. The past years have seen a steady increase in the percentage of BCs that completed their work, with all BCs completing their

40 RoP, Rule 76(10).

41 Ma (n 1), 122–123.

42 RoP, Rule 76(5); House Rules, Rule 24(m).

43 Members can go on with their questions and press government officials until they are satisfied with the response, according to Councillor Albert Ho Chun Yan. Interview with Councillor Ho on 17 February 2009. Councillor Ho is a directly elected Legislative Councillor and was the Chairman of the Democratic Party.

44 Interview with Councillor Albert Ho, ibid.

45 Ibid.

46 House Rules, Rule 21(a).

47 The statistics in this section do not include data in the 2012–13 session because BCs' work may continue during four years of a Legco term.

TABLE 3.3 *Proportion of bills committees that completed their work, 1998–2012*

| Legco session | BC formed (A) | BC completed work (B) | Perc. of BC completed work (C = B/A) |
|---|---|---|---|
| 1998–2000 | 86 | 73 | 84.88 |
| 2000–2004 | 106 | 98 | 92.45 |
| 2004–2008 | 72 | 72 | 100 |
| 2008–2012 | 73 | 73 | 100 |
| Total (perc.) | 337 | 316 | 93.77 |

SOURCE: THE AUTHOR'S CALCULATION BASED ON LEGCO'S ANNUAL REPORTS (1998–2012) AND INFORMATION UNDER THE CATEGORY OF 'BILLS COMMITTEES' ON THE LEGCO WEBSITE, <WWW.LEGCO.GOV.HK>.

TABLE 3.4 *Proportion of bills scrutinised by bills committees, 1998–2012*

| Legco session | BC formed (A) | BC not activated (B) | Effective BC (C = A – B) | No. of bill tabled (D) | Perc. of bill scrutinised by BC (C/D) |
|---|---|---|---|---|---|
| 1998–2000 | 86 | 12 | 74 | 174 | 42.53 |
| 2000–2004 | 106 | 6 | 100 | 148 | 67.57 |
| 2004–2008 | 72 | 0 | 72 | 102 | 70.59 |
| 2008–2012 | 73 | 0 | 73 | 92 | 79.35 |
| Total (perc.) | – | – | 319 | 516 | 61.82 |

SOURCE: THE AUTHOR'S CALCULATION BASED ON LEGCO'S ANNUAL REPORTS (1998–2012) AND INFORMATION UNDER THE CATEGORY OF 'BILLS COMMITTEES' ON THE LEGCO WEBSITE, <WWW.LEGCO.GOV.HK>.

work in Legco's third and fourth terms. It can be seen from Table 3.4 that from 1998 to 2012, there was a gradual increase in the percentage of bills scrutinised by BCs. In Legco's first term (1998–2000), only 42.53 per cent of bills introduced to Legco were scrutinised by BCs. In stark contrast, 70.59 per cent and 79.35 per cent of those were deliberated by BCs in Legco's third term (2004–2008) and Legco's fourth term (2008–2012) respectively.

Legco's first term was somewhat different from the others because 53 Adaptation of Law Bills out of 174 bills were tabled during the transition of the legal system. Many of them sought to make bills suitable for the new constitutional order after the return of sovereignty to China with technical or literal modifications. Even then, Legco in its first and second terms worked on bills with a full load, with 15 BCs always in action (the maximum number is 16) and 12 and 6 BCs on the waiting list at the end of the first and second terms respectively.[48]

The situation has been improved since Legco's third term, the 2005–06 session in particular, owing to a sharp decrease in both the number of bills tabled by the government and correspondingly the number of BCs newly formed in each session. In the 2005–06 session, only 16 bills were introduced and nine BCs were formed.[49] The decrease may be related to the then CE Mr Donald Tsang's assumption of the office in June 2005. A think tank, the SynergyNet's research reveals that the government under the rule of Donald Tsang 'shelved and postponed a large number of legislative initiatives that were originally included in its annual Legislative Programmes'.[50] And the administration seemed to 'steer away from controversy and is prepared to postpone difficult decisions when differences and criticisms were on the horizon'.[51] As Table 3.4 shows, the number of bills proposed has decreased year by year under the rule of Tsang, which demonstrates an obvious shift of the government to a stricter agenda control. However, an unexpected outcome appears that a decrease in the number of introduced bills eased Legco members' workload and led to more bills under BCs' deliberation. Accordingly, bills have been subject to more careful scrutiny by Legco over the years.

### *Legislators' Participation in BCs*

To examine members' participation in BCs, we can categorise BCs into four groups according to their membership: (1) BCs comprising 3–9 members; (2) BCs comprising 10–19 members; (3) BCs comprising 20–29 members and; (4) BCs comprising 30–59 members. As Figure 3.1 shows, with the exception of Legco's third term, more than 90 per cent of BCs comprise less than 20 members, with most BCs comprising 10–19 members since 2000. Owing to the large number of BCs in action and limited time and energy of members, each member is unable to join too many BCs concurrently. Even then, some BCs attracted more than half Legco members, those examining bills concerning constitutional and political issues in particular. In the 2000–01 session, 30 members joined the BC on the Chief Executive Election Bill.[52] In the 2004–05 session, 58 members joined the BC on the Chief Executive Election (Amendment)

48 The author's calculation is based on Legco's Annual Reports (1998–2012) and Hansard HK.

49 Ibid.

50 The Synergynet is a think tank based in Hong Kong. Synergynet, 'Review of the Governance Performance of the HKSAR Government 2010' (2010) <http://www.synergynet.org.hk/pdf/201012122320_en.pdf>, accessed 20 October 2011, 7.

51 Ibid.

52 The author's calculation is based on Legco's Annual Reports (1998–2012) and Hansard HK.

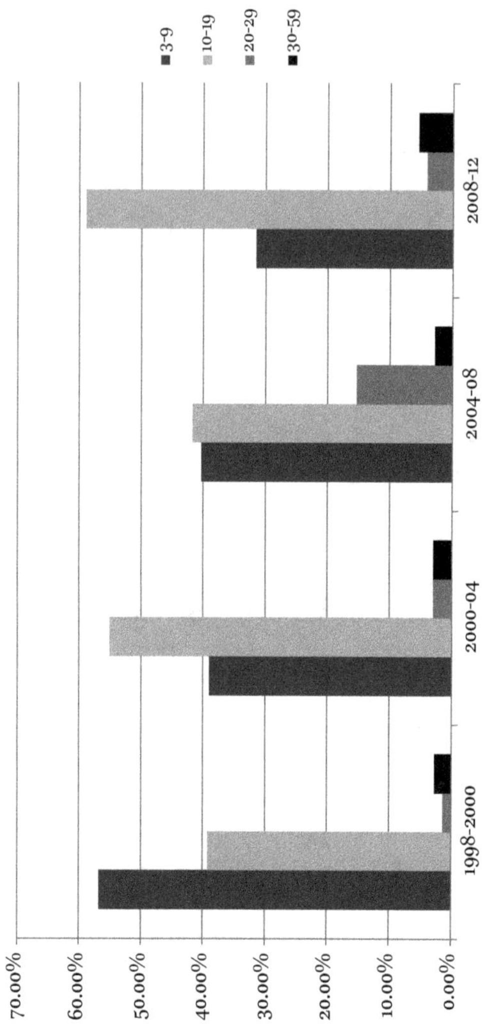


FIGURE 3.1 *Membership of Bills Committees, 1998–2012*

SOURCE: THE AUTHOR'S CALCULATION BASED ON LEGCO'S ANNUAL REPORTS (1998–2012) AND INFORMATION UNDER THE CATEGORY OF 'BILLS COMMITTEES' ON THE LEGCO WEBSITE, <WWW.LEGCO.GOV.HK>.

(Term of Office of the Chief Executive) Bill. Members were also willing to join BCs deliberating bills concerning civil liberties and people's livelihood. For instance, 34 and 50 members joined the BC on the Interception of Communications and Surveillance Bill in the 2005–06 session and BC on the National Security (Legislative Provisions) Bill (Legislation on Article 23) in the 2002–03 session respectively. In the 2008–09 session, 36 members joined the BC on Minimum Wage Bill.

These findings reveals that members were eager to participate in BCs which deliberate very important or controversial bills such as bills relating to constitutional and political affairs, and civil liberties, and the composition of these BCs often resembles the whole Council. BCs dealing with bills concerning livelihood issues, particularly those concerning labour and housing, were also attractive to legislators.

### *Deliberation in BCs*

Once a BC is formed, a bill cannot resume its second reading until the BC finishes deliberation. Hence, lengthy deliberation becomes an available strategy for legislators and a real threat to the government. In view of the decisive role of the BC Chairperson in presiding meetings, the government tries to lobby its allies to compete for the chairmanship and, if necessary, seek to hold back the prolongation of the deliberation period.[53] For instance, in the fifty-member BC on the National Security (Legislative Provisions) Bill in 2003, Councillor Ip Kwok Him, a DAB member, defeated a pro-democracy legislator Margaret Ng and was elected as Chairman by 30 votes to 14.[54] Councillor Ambrose Lau, a member of the Hong Kong Progressive Alliance (HKPA),[55] was elected as the Deputy Chairman by 27 votes to 13.[56] On 14 June 2003, the BC Chairman decided to put a motion to a vote 'stating that clause-by-clause scrutiny of the Bill was over and could not be reopened'.[57] This motion was carried unanimously in the absence of all pro-democracy members most of whom were attending a

53 Interview with Councillor Albert Ho on 17 February 2009.

54 See Bills Committee on National Security (Legislative Provisions) Bill, 'Minutes of Meeting Held on 6 March 2003' (LC Paper No. CB(2) 1612/02-03, 2003), paras 5–6.

55 The Hong Kong Progressive Alliance merged with the DAB in 2005.

56 See Bills Committee on National Security (Legislative Provisions) Bill (n 54), paras 5–6.

57 See Bills Committee on National Security (Legislative Provisions) Bill, 'Minutes of Meeting Held on 14 June 2003' (LC Paper No. CB(2) 2848/02-03, 2003); and Carole J. Petersen, 'Hong Kong's Spring of Discontent: The Rise and Fall of the National Security Bill in 2003', in Fu Hualing, Carole J. Petersen, and Simon N.M. Young (eds.), *National Security and Fundamental Freedoms Hong Kong's Article 23 under Scrutiny* (Hong Kong: Hong Kong University Press, 2005), 47.

conference on the very Bill.[58] Although the motion could not prevent further discussions in the community, the government obviously succeeded in rushing deliberation with a majority support in the BC. Hence, the opposition's strategy of lengthy deliberation was not effective. On many occasions, to seek a majority support, the government had to offer amendments and concessions to legislators, particularly handling bills on the government's priority list.

As most Committee Stage Amendments (CSA) to bills, if any, were formulated at the stage of the BC, the number of government CSA became a useful index for BCs' impact. Table 3.5 shows that from 1998 to 2012, 313 bills were passed with BCs' deliberation whilst 149 were passed without BCs formed. Of 313 bills which were examined by BCs, 275 (amounting to 87.86 per cent of them) were passed with government CSAs, whilst amongst 149 bills which were not deliberated in BCs, only 51 (amounting to 34.23 per cent of them) were passed with government CSAs. It is a stark contrast that strongly suggests the positive correlation between the establishment of BCs and the introduction of government CSAs. In other words, deliberation in BCs is conducive to 'wringing amendments out of government officials'.[59]

The preceding findings portray the general picture of BCs. A case study is helpful in exploring ways in which legislators pressed for government CSAs to bills.

TABLE 3.5 *Bills committees and government amendments, 1998–2012*

| | Bills passed with government amendment | | Bills passed without government amendment | | Total | |
|---|---|---|---|---|---|---|
| | Freq. | Perc. | Freq. | Perc. | Freq. | Perc. |
| BC formed | 275 | 87.86 | 38 | 12.14 | 313 | 100 |
| Without BC | 51 | 34.23 | 98 | 65.77 | 149 | 100 |
| Total | 326 | 70.56 | 136 | 29.44 | 462 | 100 |

SOURCE: THE AUTHOR'S CALCULATION BASED ON LEGCO'S ANNUAL REPORTS (1998–2012) AND INFORMATION UNDER THE CATEGORY OF 'BILLS COMMITTEES' ON THE LEGCO WEBSITE, <WWW.LEGCO.GOV.HK>.

58 Petersen, ibid.

59 See Ma's research, 'Comparison of viscosity indicators, 1991–2004', in Ma (n 1), 123, Tables 5.14 and 5.15.

***Case Study: Bills Committee on the Interception of Communications and Surveillance Bill***

The Interception of Communications and Surveillance Bill was first introduced as a private member's bill entitled 'the Interception of Communication Ordinance' (Cap 532) (IOCO) by Councillor James To on behalf of the DP on 28 June 1997, at the last moment of the colonial rule. However, neither the Governor prior to the handover nor the CE of the SAR government scheduled the commencement date of To's Bill. Hence, up till 2006, interception of communications had been regulated under s 13 of the Post Office Ordinance (Cap 98) and s 33 of the Telecommunications Ordinance (Cap 532).[60] In July 2005, the CE made an executive order to 'regulate covert surveillance activities undertaken by law enforcement agencies',[61] namely, the Law Enforcement (Covert Surveillance Procedures) Order. The making of the Order was criticised by some Legco members for replacing legislation and bypassing Legco.[62] Furthermore, it became urgent for the government to introduce new legislation regulating both the interception of communications and covert surveillance owing to its defeat in a judicial review case.[63] In *Leung Kwok Hung & Anor v Chief Executive of the HKSAR*, the applicants sought a declaration that the Chief Executive has 'acted unlawfully in breach of his statutory duty'[64] for failing to 'appoint a day to bring [the Interception of Communication Ordinance] into effect in its present form'.[65] On 9 February 2006, the Court of First Instance (CFI) dismissed the application. However, the court held that 's 33 [of the Telecommunications Ordinance], in so far as it authorises or allows access to, or the disclosure of, the contents of telecommunication messages is inconsistent with arts 30 and 39 of the Basic Law and, through Article 39, with Article 14 of the Bill of Rights'[66] and 'the Executive Order, as an administrative order, does not comply with art 30'.[67] Owing to the 'legal vacuum' brought about by these declarations, the CFI made a temporary validity order that s 33 and the Executive Order are 'valid and of

60 Legislative Council Secretariat, 'Report of the Bills Committee on Interception of Communications and Surveillance Bill' (LC Paper No. CB(2)2837/05-06, 2006).

61 See Legislative Council Secretariat, 'Background Brief (for Regulation of Surveillance and the Interception of Communications)' (LC Paper No. CB(2)1423/05-06(05), 2006), para 25.

62 Ibid., para 27.

63 In fact, two district court rulings found that 'there was no legislative framework in Hong Kong to regulate covert surveillance, and thus the minimum degree of legal protection to which Hong Kong citizens are entitled under article 30 of the Basic Law was lacking'. Ibid., 7.

64 *Leung Kwok Hung & Anor v Chief Executive of the HKSAR* [2006] HKEC 239, para 37(i).

65 Ibid., para 179.

66 Ibid., para 181.

67 Ibid., para 184.

legal effect for a period of six months from the date hereof'.[68] The case was subsequently appealed. In March 2006, the government proposed a bill to regulate the conduct of interception of communications and covert surveillance by law enforcement agencies.[69] Panel on Security of Legco held five meetings with the government in February and March 2006, at which a Bills Committee was recommended to set up.[70] On 12 July 2006, the Court of Final Appeal (CFA) made an order to set aside the CFI's temporary validity order and substituted a suspension of those declarations of unconstitutionality.[71] Such postponement would be for six months from the date of the CFI judgment of 9 February 2006.[72] However, 'the government is not shielded from legal liability for functioning pursuant to what has been declared unconstitutional'.[73]

### How Legislators Make a Difference

The courts' decisions compelled the government to introduce the Interception of Communication and Surveillance Bill (the Bill) to fill the legal vacuum. The Bill, concerning citizens' fundamental rights notwithstanding, was not given a public consultation and its provisions also aroused considerable controversy. Academics and legal professionals expressed their concern about the protection of legal professional privilege.[74] Other major controversial issues included the definition of public security, conditions for issue, renewal or continuance of prescribed authorization, powers of the Commissioner on Interception of Communications and Surveillance, and the creation of criminal offences.[75]

---

68 Ibid., paras 46 and 186.

69 Security Bureau, 'Proposed Legislative Framework on Interception of Communications and Covert Surveillance' (LC Paper No. CB(2)997/05-06(01), 2006), paras 7–8.

70 Legislative Council Secretariat, 'Legal Service Division Report on Interception of Communications and Surveillance Bill' (LC Paper No. LS44/05-06, 2006), 2.

71 *Koo Sze Yiu & Anor v Chief Executive of the HKSAR* [2006] 3 HKLRD 455. The Court of Final Appeal (CFA) held that 'the Government can, during the period of suspension, function pursuant to what has been declared unconstitutional, doing so without acting contrary to any declaration in operation. But, despite such suspension, the Government is not shielded from legal liability for functioning pursuant to what has been declared unconstitutional', see para 50.

72 Ibid., para 49.

73 Ibid., para 50.

74 See 'Submission from Professor Michael Jackson and J. Brabyn', LC Paper No. CB(2)2856/05-06(01), 6; 'Submission from Hong Kong Bar Association on 6 April 2006', LC Paper No. CB(2) 1685/05-06(01); and 'Submissions from Hong Kong Law Society on 16 July 2006', LC Paper No. CB(2) 2809/05-06(01).

75 Ibid.

With regard to the issues concerning covert surveillance, members questioned a proposed test of 'a reasonable expectation of privacy within the definition of covert surveillance' in a public place and queried whether a phone talking in a public place might be subject to surveillance without requirement of authorisation.[76] In addition, the Bill only covered 'covert surveillance using devices' and thus undercover operations did not require statutory authorization.[77] The focus of controversy was also on a sunset clause that the government needs to review the Bill, 'otherwise it will cease to have effect'.[78]

A BC was formed in March 2006, comprising 34 members 12 of which were pro-democracy members. Councillor Miriam Lau Kin Yee, a member of the Liberal Party (LP), was elected as the chairperson and a DAB member Councillor Lau Kwong Wah was elected as the Deputy Chairman. Within less than five months, the Committee had held about 50 meetings to request the government to explain policy intent and consider specific clauses.[79] However, eight members were absent from more than half the meetings.[80] Members who practiced as barristers and solicitors were active in deliberation and proposed a tremendous number of CSAs, particularly to provisions concerning controversial legal issues. The BC Report shows that the government did move many amendments at members' request during the BC meetings.[81] However, such amendments, in some pro-democracy members' opinion, were irrelevant and did not cover the most important matters in the Bill.[82]

It was meticulous deliberation as almost all clauses received amendments ranging from wording improvement to substantive modifications to the Bill. Recommendations accepted by the majority of the BC were included in amendments moved by the chairman on behalf of the Committee. On those unacceptable in the BC, members, mainly democrats, moved their own amendments to take a chance.[83] On 2 August 2006, the Bill comprising 69 clauses was

76 See Report of the Bills Committee on Interception of Communications and Surveillance Bill (n 60), paras 13–16.

77 Ibid., para 17.

78 Ibid., para 242.

79 The author's calculation is based on the minutes of the Bills Committee on IOCO.

80 Ibid.

81 See Report of the Bills Committee on Interception of Communications and Surveillance Bill (n 60).

82 See the speeches of Councillor James To and Councillor Margaret Ng, Hansard HK (2–5 August 2006). Observations are also based on the author's interview with Councillor James To on 14 October 2008.

83 For example, according to Councillor To, members occasionally won if some pro-government or independent members were persuaded into supporting the proposals opposed by the government, or if some members avoid voting by leaving the Chamber.

pushed to the second reading with 189 government amendments and more than 200 members' amendments.[84] All members' CSAs were moved by pro-democracy members and none of them passed at the Committee Stage of the whole Council. A serious question is thus raised about whether legislators made a difference in the Bill without any member's amendment being passed.

First, we must look at the origins and quality of government CSAs that passed at the Committee Stage of the whole Council.

With regard to the origins of government CSAs, a major CSA sponsor Councillor James To pointed that at least half the government amendments had incorporated members' proposals.[85] Furthermore, it can be seen from the BC Report that almost each government CSA was moved at the request of members who also represented organisations and the community. For instance, CSAs concerning the replacement of 'judicial authorization' with 'judge's authorization' originated in Hong Kong Bar Association's submission.[86] The government also moved some CSAs regardless of their same nature as that of members' CSAs, which attracted discontents amongst pro-democracy members.[87] On the government's handling of members' CSAs that it did not object, President Jasper Tsang points out that the government has insisted that members' CSAs be subject to the restrictions of public expenditure, the operation of government, political structure and government policy in accordance with Article 74 of the Basic Law, and it thus disallowed the introduction and passage of such members' CSAs and substituted with its own CSAs.[88]

With regard to the quality of the government's CSAs, a close examination of major issues addressed by those CSAs is helpful.

1. With respect to the definition of public security, some members concerned that it would include national security and was used for 'suppressing the right to freedom of expression or the right of peaceful assembly'.[89] The government thus introduced CSAs to 'define public security as the public security of Hong Kong' and 'expressly provide that advocacy, protest or dissent, unless likely to

84 Hansard HK (2–5 August 2006).

85 Ibid.

86 'Submission from Hong Kong Bar Association' (n 74).

87 Councillor James To and Councillor Margaret Ng's speeches (n 82) and the author's interview with Councillor James To.

88 Interview with President Jasper Tsang on 22 July 2011.

89 See Report of the Bills Committee on Interception of Communications and Surveillance Bill (n 60), para 36.

be carried on by violent means, is not of itself regarded as a threat to public security'.[90]

2. The government introduced CSAs to add the tests of reasonable suspicion and necessity, and that the authorising authority would consider 'other matters that are relevant in the circumstances',[91] in response to members' recommendations concerning the conditions for the issue or renewal or continuance of a prescribed authorisation.
3. The government introduced a CSA to provide express provisions for the scope of information which was required in the application for judge's authorisation.[92]
4. The government proposed CSAs to suggest the establishment of a mechanism for notification in limited circumstances by the Commissioner and the Commissioner may order the payment of compensation.[93]
5. Any regulations or amendments to Schedules 1, 2, 3 and 4 by the CE in Council would be subject to Legco's approval, namely, the positive vetting procedure.[94]

These examples do not constitute an exhaustive list of the government's CSAs having substantive consequences. Though the Bill's final version is far from being a satisfactory law, the government's CSAs have clearly improved the Bill owing to members' pressure.

Second, at least 32 members' suggestions were incorporated into the Code of Practice issued by the Secretary for Security, such as the guidance on the difference between type 1 and type 2 surveillance, the procedures for applications for the issue of emergency authorisation, and matters that law enforcement officers should take into account, including relevant provisions of the Basic Law, a public interest test and the importance of press freedom.[95] The Code of Practice comprises a series of executive orders regulating the implementation of the Bill by the law enforcement agencies. Although

90 Ibid., para 39.
91 Ibid., paras 50–51.
92 Ibid., para 96.
93 Ibid., paras 229 and 231.
94 Ibid., para 236.
95 See Legislative Council Secretariat, 'Issues Undertaken by the Administration to Be Incorporated in the Code of Practice to Be Issued by the Secretary for Security under the Bill' (LC Paper No. CB(2)2829/05-06(01), 2006).

most orders are related to practical procedures, there are such issues of great importance as the consideration of fundamental human rights included in the Code of Practice.

In addition, officials gave assurances in their speeches on the resumption of the second reading of the Bill in response to members' suggestions that they did not object in principle but were reluctant to include in the Bill or the Code of Practice. Such assurances can be deemed a concession to some extent and were conducive to elucidating principles and legislative intentions. For instance, the government assured members that 'any information subject to LPP [Legal Professional Privilege] that has been obtained during a covert operation will continue to be privileged'.[96]

### Anatomy of Bill: For Further Review

At the stage of the Committee of the whole Council, plenary meetings lasted five days and more than 200 amendments proposed by pro-democracy members were defeated.[97] The Bill was ultimately passed after the democrats' walkout which was sparked by the defeat of the 'sunset' clause proposed by Councillor Margaret Ng. However, deliberation over this Bill had 'broken many records in terms of the number of days and hours spent as well as the number of amendments'.[98] Why did pro-democracy members, Councillor James To and Margaret Ng in particular, spend lots of time in drafting and moving so many CSAs even if they were fully aware of there being little chance to win? Councillor Margaret Ng, a member of the Civic Party as well as a barrister, voiced the reason that 'what we were trying to do in that exercise was [to] expose every major fault in the law they are about to pass'.[99] What legislators have done is the anatomy of the Bill. In fact, the considerable number of amendments proposed to the Bill implied that the Bill might be problematic. In 2009, the Commissioner on Interception of Communications and Surveillance issued an annual report which exposed that the ICAC had conducted interception of communications relating to legal professional privileges without authorisation in four cases and destroyed recording materials and abstract files, regardless of

96 See Report of the Bills Committee on Interception of Communications and Surveillance Bill (n 60), 150.

97 The number of members' amendments was too big to be examined with other cases. This case will inevitably change the statistics of members' CSAs and lead to deviation.

98 Joseph Li, 'Legislators Good, Could be Better', *China Daily Hong Kong Edition*, 9 August 2006, P2.

99 Ambrose Leung, 'Spying Bill Passed after Stormy Debate', *South China Morning Post*, 6 August 2006, EDT1.

the Commissioner's request.[100] On 11 March 2009, Councillor Cyd Ho moved a motion to require the government to review the Interception of Communications and Surveillance Ordinance.[101] Although the motion was negatived, it exposed the flaw and loopholes of the Ordinance again. It is clear that the serious misconduct exposed by the Commissioner were exactly related to the most controversial issues during deliberation over the Bill, including the protection of legal professional privileges, the Commissioner's powers and the penalty provisions for non-compliance with the Ordinance. Therefore, members' diligent work is not in vain with its outcome recorded in the BC's minutes and reports, which proves significant for further review over the legislation.

### *Summaries*

The BC's scrutiny of bills has become the most important stage of the legislative process in terms of intensive meetings, the anatomy of a bill and the formulation of amendments. Data concerning BCs' scrutiny between 1998 and 2012 reveal at least three facts. First, legislators are active in joining 'important' BCs in order to exert their impacts on bills, particularly those concerning constitutional and political affairs, and issues regarding civil liberties, labour and housing. Second, scrutiny in BCs is conducive to squeezing government amendments. Third, most amendments or concessions from the government were formulated at this stage, rather than the later Committee Stage of the whole Council.

Despite the government's stricter control over agenda setting since the rule of Mr Donald Tsang, Legco has found its way to strengthen scrutiny of the bills with the growth in the proportion of bills scrutinised by BCs. Furthermore, the substantial impact of BCs has been manifested by the positive correlation between the establishment of BCs and the introduction of government amendments to bills, and has been vividly illustrated by case study on the BC on the Interception of Communications and Surveillance Bill.

However, members' strategy of squeezing government amendments or concessions such as lengthy deliberation is not necessarily effective if the government has obtained enough support in the BCs. Corresponding to the

100 The Commissioner on Interception of Communications and Surveillance complained that the ICAC destroyed the recording regardless of the express requirements of the Commissioner, see The Commissioner on Interception of Communications and Surveillance, 'Annual Report 2008 to the Chief Executive' (2008) <http://www.info.gov.hk/info/sciocs/eng/pdf/Annual_Report_2008.pdf>, accessed 20 October 2011, 60.

101 '檢討截聽條例動議遭否決 (Legco Vetoed Motion to Review the Interception Ordinance)', *Hong Kong Economic Journal*, 12 March 2009, P07.

composition of Legco, the BCs represent the major political groups of Legco, which makes it possible for the government to calculate the votes at this stage and decide what to do next: offering concessions, conducting relevant lobbying campaigns or adopting a firm stance. Usually, on issues unresolved in the BCs, members have less chance of winning over the government at the next stage—the Committee stage of the whole Council at which the government usually firmly insists on its attitude towards members' amendments unless it faces a danger of defeat or is under considerable pressure of public opinion.

Accordingly, involving the public more in the legislative process is not only a necessity for a more open democratic legislative procedure, but also a powerful means of pressing for more government concessions. In this sense, members' efforts in exposing loopholes and flaws of bills are still useful in sparking public debates over legislation.

## Scrutiny of Bills: Members' Committee Stage Amendments to Government Bills

Once a motion on the second reading of a bill is passed, Legco immediately sits as the Committee of the whole Council in which members go through the clauses and all amendments to the bill. At this stage, government amendments are easily passed because they often respond to members' views. Most members' CSAs, in contrast, find it difficult to get passed as they often concern the issues on which no consensus has been reached between legislators and the government at the stage of the BC's scrutiny. Furthermore, members' CSAs, like any other initiatives proposed by members, are subject to the Separate Voting Mechanism (SVM). Hence, it is unsurprising that few members' CSAs to government bills were passed. This section analyses restrictions on the introduction of members' CSAs and considers the determinants of the voting results of members' CSAs.

### *Restrictions on the Introduction of Members' CSAs*

The President of Legco has the power to rule members' CSAs out of order under the RoP, Rules 57 and 69(3) in particular.[102] In practice, the most frequently quoted rules are Rules 57(4)(a) and 57(6), as shown in Table 3.6.

102 Rule 57(4) of the RoP provides that

(4) The following provisions shall apply to amendments relating to bills:

(a) An amendment must be relevant to the subject matter of the bill and to the subject matter of the clause to which it relates.

TABLE 3.6 *President Rita Fan's rulings on members' CSAs, 1998–2008*[103]

| Main rule | Negatived | Passed | No ruling | Total | Per cent |
|---|---|---|---|---|---|
| Rule 57(6) | 16 | 25 | 0 | 41 | 11.48 |
| Rule 57(4)(a) | 38 | 24 | 0 | 62 | 17.37 |
| Rule 57(4)(c) | 0 | 2 | 0 | 2 | 0.56 |
| Rule 57(4)(d) | 0 | 3 | 0 | 3 | 0.84 |
| No ruling | 0 | 0 | 249 | 249 | 69.75 |
| Total (Freq. and Perc.) | 54 (15.08) | 54 (15.08) | 249 (69.84) | 357 (100) | 100 |

SOURCE: THE AUTHOR'S CALCULATION BASED ON INFORMATION IN THE CATEGORY OF 'PRESIDENT'S RULING' ON LEGCO'S OFFICIAL WEBSITE, ANNUAL REPORTS OF THE LEGISLATIVE COUNCIL (1998–2008) AND HANSARD HK.

Rule 57(4)(a): An amendment must be relevant to the subject matter of the bill and to the subject matter of the clause to which it relates.

Rule 57(6): An amendment, the object or effect of which may, in the opinion of the President or Chairman, be to dispose of or charge any part of the revenue or other public moneys of Hong Kong shall be proposed only by –

(a) the Chief Executive; or
(b) a designated public officer; or
(c) a Member, if the Chief Executive consents in writing to the proposal.

---

(b) An amendment must not be inconsistent with any clause already agreed to or with any previous decision of the committee upon the bill.
(c) An amendment must not be such as to make the clause which it proposes to amend unintelligible or ungrammatical.
(d) An amendment which is in the opinion of the Chairman frivolous or meaningless may not be moved.
(e) Where an amendment is proposed to be moved to a bill presented in both official languages the amendment shall be made to the text in each language unless it is an amendment that clearly affects the text in one language only. But an amendment which creates a conflict or discrepancy between the text in one language and the text in the other may not be moved.

Rule 69(3) provides that 'an amendment to any head of expenditure to reduce the sum allotted thereto in respect of any item therein may be moved by any Member, and shall take the form of a motion "that head…be reduced by $…in respect of (or by leaving out) subhead…item…"'.

103 The President may apply several rules to one ruing and the author selected the main clause in a specific ruling.

The procedure for the President's ruling on members' CSAs is a quasi-judicial one. After a member gives notice of a CSA to Legco, the administration may raise objection to such CSA. The President makes a ruling after hearing both parties. As Table 3.6 shows, President Rita Fan made rulings on about 30 per cent of CSAs moved by members and ruled 15.08 per cent of proposed CSAs out of order. After 2008, President Jasper Tsang made rulings on nearly 20 per cent of members' CSAs and ruled 7.03 per cent of proposed CSAs out of order. Rules 57(6) and 57(4)(a) are the most commonly cited rules by the government in its submissions to the President, as shown in Table 3.7.

### Dispute Concerning the Application of Article 74 to Members' CSAs

In accordance with the RoP, members' CSAs are not subject to the restrictions imposed by Article 74 of the Basic Law. In practice, the tests of GP, OG, PE and PS was never applied to members' CSAs. However, the government insists its objection to this matter.

The Department of Justice argued at the time of drafting the RoP in 1998 that both members' bills and CSAs should be covered by Article 74 on the ground that 'a generous and purposive interpretation should be given to Article 74',[104] and whether members' bills or CSAs were subject to Article 74 should be determined by the CE.[105] However, the Committee on Rules of

TABLE 3.7 *President Jasper Tsang's rulings on members' CSAs, 2008–2012*

| Main rule | Negatived | Passed | No ruling | Total | Per cent |
|---|---|---|---|---|---|
| Rule 57(6) | 4 | 10 | 0 | 14 | 10.93 |
| Rule 57(4)(a) | 5 | 3 | 0 | 8 | 6.25 |
| Rule 57(4)(c) | 0 | 0 | 0 | 0 | 0 |
| Rule 57(4)(d) | 0 | 0 | 0 | 0 | 0 |
| Others | 0 | 4 | 0 | 4 | 3.12 |
| No ruling | 0 | 0 | 102 | 102 | 79.69 |
| Total (Freq. and Perc.) | 9 (7.03) | 17 (13.28) | 102 (79.69) | 128 (100) | 100 |

SOURCE: THE AUTHOR'S CALCULATION BASED ON INFORMATION IN THE CATEGORY OF 'PRESIDENT'S RULING' ON LEGCO'S OFFICIAL WEBSITE, ANNUAL REPORTS OF THE LEGISLATIVE COUNCIL (2008–2012) AND HANSARD HK.

104 Committee on Rules of Procedure, 'Procedure in Dealing with the Introduction of Members' Bills as Provided in Article 74 of the Basic Law and the Interpretation of Article 48(10) of the Basic Law', para 8.

105 Ibid., para 11.

Procedure of Legco (the RoPC) rejected such arguments. The RoPC argued that Article 74 did not state the intent to cover members' amendments. If the scope of 'bills' was extended to cover 'amendments to bills', Legco would be deprived of the opportunity to discuss and agree to alternative proposals.[106] The exiting arrangement ensured checks and balances between the executive branch and Legco as well as the executive-led system.[107] With respect to the President's power to make a decision on member's initiative, the RoPC pointed out that this mechanism was similar to provisions of Legco's Standing Order in the colonial era and was widely adopted in other common law jurisdictions such as the UK, Canada and Australia.[108] Furthermore, the Committee deemed Rule 57(6) a self-imposed restriction concerning charging effect and not relevant to Article 74.[109] The government ultimately decided to take the stance of 'agree to disagree' with Legco.[110]

Councillor Albert Ho, a Democratic Party member, pointed out that President Rita Fan had played a crucial role in rejecting the application of Article 74 to members' CSAs.[111] In the President's ruling on Councillor Leung Yiu Chung's amendment to the Holidays (Amendment) Bill 1998, the government raised an objection to Councillor Leung's CSA on the grounds of charging effect under Rule 57(6) and government policy test.[112] President Fan pointed out that 'there [was] no restriction in the Rules of Procedure that CSA proposed by Members cannot relate to Government policy'.[113] In her subsequent rulings, the President also refused to make rulings on whether members' CSAs related to the operation of government and public expenditure. These precedents have been followed by her successor, President Jasper Tsang who has never made a decision on members' CSAs within the meaning of Article 74.

### Charging Effect

In her ruling on members' CSAs to the District Councils Bill, President Rita Fan ruled that an applicable test is 'whether the proposed statutory function required to be undertaken is one which is not provided for under existing

106 Ibid., para 14.

107 Ibid.

108 Ibid.

109 Ibid.

110 Interview with Councillor Rita Fan on 1 December 2010.

111 Interview with Albert Ho on 17 February 2009.

112 See Ruling by the President on the Charging Effect of Hon LEUNG Yiu-chung's Amendment to the Holidays (Amendment) Bill 1998 (23 July 1998), 1, <http://www.legco.gov.hk/yr98-99/english/pre_rul/980723.pdf>, accessed 21 September 2008.

113 Ibid., 4.

law'.[114] President Jasper Tsang followed President Fan's principle in his ruling on the Buildings (Amendment) Bill 2010 as follows.

> A clear principle has been established in past rulings that a CSA will have charging effect within the meaning of Rule 57(6) of the Rules of Procedure only if it imposes a new and distinct function on the Administration, i.e. a statutory function which is not provided in the existing law, and the President is satisfied that the performance of the new and distinct function will require the spending of an number of public money that is not nominal or negligible.[115]

### Subject Matter

From 1998 to 2012, a total of 43 members' CSAs were blocked by the test of 'subject matter' under Rule 57(4)(a) that any CSAs 'must be relevant to the subject matter of the bill and to the subject matter of the clause to which it relates'. During her presidency of the Provisional Legislative Council, President Rita Fan disallowed the introduction of some members' CSAs to several election bills on the ground of subject matter.[116] In 1999 and 2001, President Fan negatived CSAs that aimed to fundamentally change the formation method of Legco and the election of the CE on the ground that they went outside the scope of the Bill and were not relevant to the Bill's subject matter.[117] In 2006, Councillor Yeung Sum and Councillor James Tien's CSAs were disallowed on

114 President's Ruling on Hon Cyd HO's Proposed Amendment to Clause 59 (concerning the Functions of District Councils) in the District Councils Bill (8 March 1999), 2, <http://www.legco.gov.hk/yr98-99/english/pre_rul/990308b.pdf>, accessed 21 September 2008.

115 President's Ruling on Committee Stage Amendments to the Buildings (Amendment) Bill 2010 Proposed by Hon Kam Nai-wai (27 June 2011), 6, <http://www.legco.gov.hk/yr10-11/english/pre_rul/pre0627-ref-e.pdf>, accessed 20 October 2011.

116 See Ruling of the President of the Provisional Legislative Council on the Amendments Proposed to the Legislative Council Bill by the Hon Andrew Wong (24 September 1997), <http://www.legco.gov.hk/yr97-98/english/pre_rul/970924.pdf>; and Ruling of the President of the Provisional Legislative Council on the Amendments Proposed to the Legislative Council Bill by the Hon K.K. Fung (25 September 1997), <http://www.legco.gov.hk/yr97-98/english/pre_rul/970925a.pdf>, accessed 21 September 2008.

117 See President's Rulings on the Committee Stage Amendments proposed by Members to Legislative Council (Amendment) Bill 1999 (12 July 1999), <http://www.legco.gov.hk/yr98-99/english/pre_rul/990712.pdf>; and President's Ruling on the Committee Stage Amendments to Chief Executive Election Bill proposed by Hon Martin Lee Chu Ming (5 July 2001), <http://www.legco.gov.hk/yr00-01/english/pre_rul/r010705e.pdf>, accessed 21 September 2008.

the ground that what they sought to amend was not the subject of the Bill.[118] Similarly, Councillor Sin Chung Kai's amendment to expand the Information Technology Functional Constituency was disallowed as it did not aim to amend any provision of the proposed government bill which sought to update some information.[119] From 2008 to 2012, President Jasper Tsang made eight rulings on members' CSAs within the meaning of Rule 57(4)(a) and disallowed five CSAs of them amending the Telecommunications (Amendment) Bill 2009 and Legislative Council (Amendment) Bill 2010 respectively.

As the government intentionally blocked members' amendments by narrowing bills' long title,[120] the test of 'subject matter' has become an effective means of strengthening its control over members' initiatives.

### *Introduction of Members' CSAs*

This section considers the connection between the amount of members' CSAs and the sponsors' constituencies and political affiliation.

It is clear that GC members were more active in moving CSAs than FC members, as shown in Table 3.8. From 1998 to 2012, nearly 70 per cent of members'

TABLE 3.8 *Members' CSAs by sponsors' constituencies, 1998–2012*

| Year | FC | | GC | | EC | | Total | |
|---|---|---|---|---|---|---|---|---|
| | Freq. | Perc. | Freq. | Perc. | Freq. | Perc. | Freq. | Perc. |
| 1998–2000 | 39 | 29.77 | 89 | 67.94 | 3 | 2.29 | 131 | 100 |
| 2000–2004 | 34 | 39.53 | 49 | 56.98 | 3 | 3.49 | 86 | 100 |
| 2004–2008 | 36 | 25.71 | 104 | 74.28 | – | – | 140 | 100 |
| 2008–2012 | 33 | 25.78 | 95 | 74.22 | – | – | 128 | 100 |
| Total | 142 | 29.28 | 337 | 69.48 | 6 | 1.24 | 485 | 100 |

SOURCE: THE AUTHOR'S CALCULATION BASED ON HANSARD HK (1998–2012).

118 See President's Ruling on the Committee Stage Amendments to Chief Executive Election and Legislative Council Election (Miscellaneous Amendments) Bill 2006 proposed by Dr Hon Yeung Sum and Hon James Tien Pei Chun (4 May 2006), <http://www.legco.gov.hk/yr05-06/english/pre_rul/pre0504cb3-ref-e.pdf>, accessed 21 September 2008.

119 See President's Ruling on Committee Stage Amendment to Legislative Council (Amendment) Bill 2007 Proposed by Hon Sin Chung Kai (17 April 2008), <http://www.legco.gov.hk/yr07-08/english/pre_rul/pre0417-ref-e.pdf>, accessed 21 September 2008.

120 This argument was confirmed by Councilor Albert Ho in the author's interview with him on 17 February 2009.

CSAs were moved by GC members. Furthermore, the percentage of CSAs moved by GC members has exceeded 74 per cent since 2004.

Nearly 30 per cent of CSAs were moved by FC members. However, most of those were introduced by the democrats in FCs. As Figure 3.2 shows, whilst the percentage of FC democrats has never exceeded 30 per cent of FC members, they introduced nearly 80 and 90 per cent of FC members' CSAs in Legco's second and third terms, respectively. During Legco's fourth term (2008–2012), 63.63 per cent of FC members' CSAs were introduced by democrats who occupied merely 13.33 per cent of FC seats. This finding strongly suggests that the sponsors' political orientation is a more reliable indicator for members' performance in moving CSAs than their constituencies.

Table 3.9 indicates a more distinct division when considering members' political orientation. About 81 per cent of CSAs were introduced by pro-democracy members whilst only 13 per cent were moved by pro-Beijing members. This result proves that pro-democracy members in Legco are more active in amending government bills than pro-Beijing members regardless of their constituencies. In Legco's third term, more than 90 per cent of CSAs were introduced by democrats.

Pro-democracy members have displayed greater willingness to amend government bills than pro-Beijing members. However, this finding demonstrates that pro-Beijing members are likely to achieve their goals by other means. As the majority of Legco, the pro-Beijing camp has the advantage of negotiation with

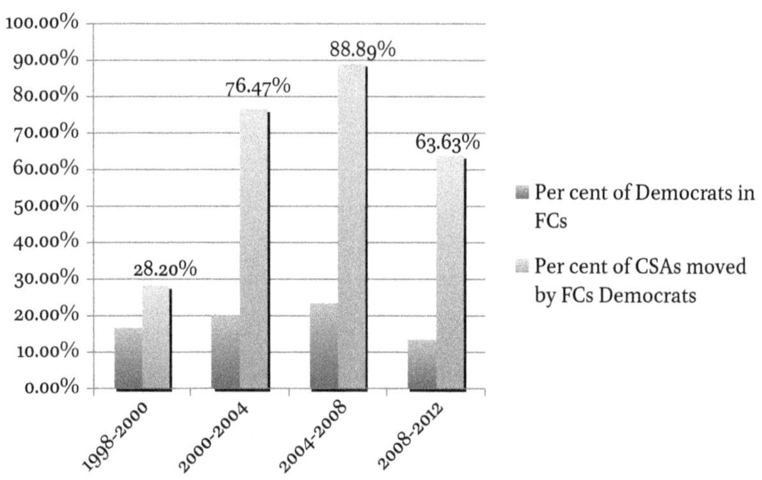


FIGURE 3.2 *Proportion of Democrats in FCs and Proportion of the CSAs Moved by Them, 1998–2012*

SOURCE: THE AUTHOR'S CALCULATION BASED ON HANSARD HK (1998–2012).

TABLE 3.9 *Members' CSAs by sponsors' political orientation, 1998–2012*

| Year | Pro-Beijing | | Pro-democracy | | Independent | | Total | |
|---|---|---|---|---|---|---|---|---|
| | Freq. | Perc. | Freq. | Perc. | Freq. | Perc. | Freq. | Perc. |
| 1998–2000 | 25 | 19.08 | 83 | 63.36 | 23 | 17.56 | 131 | 100 |
| 2000–2004 | 9 | 10.46 | 75 | 87.21 | 2 | 1.16 | 86 | 100 |
| 2004–2008 | 10 | 7.14 | 130 | 92.86 | 0 | 0 | 140 | 100 |
| 2008–2012 | 20 | 15.62 | 107 | 83.59 | 1 | 0.78 | 128 | 100 |
| Total | 64 | 13.19 | 395 | 81.44 | 26 | 5.36 | 485 | 100 |

SOURCE: THE AUTHOR'S CALCULATION BASED ON HANSARD HK (1998–2012).

the government over the pro-democracy camp. Since Legco's second term, particularly the rule of Mr Donald Tsang, the government has adopted the strategy of 'friend-or-foe dichotomy' and appointed the leaders of the major political parties as the Executive Councillors (as discussed in Chapter 2). If most substantive negotiations have been conducted before the Committee Stage, members of the major political parties do not need to use the weapon of moving CSAs. The fact that pro-Beijing members lack an incentive to introduce CSAs may suggest that the importance of deliberation at the Committee Stage is declining.

### *Determinants of Members' CSAs*

Although pro-democracy members are diligent in introducing amendments to government bills, they only achieved quite a low pass rate from 1998 to 2012, as shown in Table 3.10.[121] Of the 485 members' CSAs, only 19 (amounting to less than 4 per cent of those) were carried. 15 out of 19 successful CSAs were carried before 2004. Most successful CSAs received unanimous support in Legco and the government rarely raised objections to them. These CSAs chiefly dealt with rather technical and literal than substantive issues. For instance, Councillor Emily Lau's CSA to the Telecommunications (Amendment) Bill 2009 sought to add a statement of giving regard to the opinion of the public which did not bring about substantive changes in principal clauses.[122]

121 To some extent, the number and voting results of CSAs are difficult to calculate accurately, because some of them were voted on without divisions and on many occasions several relevant CSAs were determined by one round of voting. Hence, the following Tables provide an approximately comprehensive picture of members' CSAs.

122 Hansard HK (20 January 2010), 4452.

TABLE 3.10 *Result of members' CSAs to government bills, 1998–2012*[123]

| Result | 1998–2000 | | 2000–2004 | | 2004–2008 | | 2008–2012 | | Total | |
|---|---|---|---|---|---|---|---|---|---|---|
| | Freq. | Perc. | Freq. | Perc. | Freq. | Perc. | Freq. | Perc. | Freq. | Perc. |
| Negatived | 114 | 87.82 | 77 | 89.54 | 140 | 100 | 119 | 92.97 | 450 | 92.78 |
| Withdrawn | 3 | 2.29 | 6 | 6.98 | 0 | 0 | 3 | 2.34 | 12 | 2.47 |
| Not proceeding[124] | 2 | 1.53 | 0 | 0 | 0 | 0 | 2 | 1.56 | 4 | 0.82 |
| Passed | 12 | 9.16 | 3 | 3.48 | 0 | 0 | 4 | 3.13 | 19 | 3.92 |
| Total | 131 | 100 | 86 | 100 | 140 | 100 | 128 | 100 | 485 | 100 |

SOURCE: THE AUTHOR'S CALCULATION BASED ON HANSARD HK (1998–2012).

If we select all negatived CSAs and analyse the potential determinants of their results, we find out that in the first place, the Presidents disallowed about 13 per cent of members CSAs in accordance with the RoP, as shown in Table 3.11. Second, even though members' CSAs were put before the Committee of the Whole Council, nearly 12 per cent of those did not proceed under Rule 57(4)(b) which provides that '[a]n amendment must not be inconsistent with any clause already agreed to or with any previous decision of the committee upon the bill'. This rule has been applied to blocking a lot of members' CSAs because government CSAs, often the opposite of members' CSAs, were dealt with first. Finally, in addition to those withdrawn and not proceeding, the Committee of the whole Council voted down the remaining 334 (amounting to 71.67 per cent) of members' CSAs. The next section analyses the determinants of those negatived CSAs in detail.

### Separate Voting Mechanism (SVM)

The mechanism of voting by separate groups is usually criticised for blocking members' initiatives which could be carried by a simple majority. This section

123 The statistics of 2004–2012 Legco do not include the Interception of Communication and Surveillance Ordinance because amendments to this Bill were so numerous that they might cause a deviation from the whole statistics. The Interception of Communication and Surveillance Ordinance has been examined as a special case in the foregoing part.

124 In the cases where a member's CSA is the same as a government CSA which has been carried, the Committee of the Whole Council would not proceed to this member's CSA because the Committee has made a decision on the issue.

TABLE 3.11 *Determinants of unsuccessful CSAs, 1998–2012*

| Determinants/factors | Frequency | Per cent |
|---|---|---|
| President's ruling | 61 | 13.09 |
| Rule 57(4)(b) | 55 | 11.80 |
| Withdrawn | 12 | 2.58 |
| Not proceeding | 4 | 0.86 |
| Voted down by the committee of the whole council | 334 | 71.67 |
| Total | 466 | 100 |

SOURCE: THE AUTHOR'S CALCULATION BASED ON HANSARD HK (1998–2012).

TABLE 3.12 *Proportion of CSAs negatived by separate voting mechanism, 1998–2012*

| Year | CSAs negatived by SVM (A) | Negatived CSAs (B) | Perc. (A/B) |
|---|---|---|---|
| 1998–2000 | 14 | 89 | 15.73 |
| 2000–2004 | 2 | 49 | 4.08 |
| 2004–2008 | 4 | 99 | 4.04 |
| 2008–2012 | 3 | 97 | 3.09 |
| Total | 23 | 334 | 6.88 |

SOURCE: THE AUTHOR'S CALCULATION BASED ON HANSARD HK (1998–2012).

examines how many members' CSAs were negatived because of the SVM and analyse the correlation between the sponsors' political orientation and the voting behaviour of constituencies.

As Table 3.12 shows, of the 334 CSAs voted down by the Committee of the whole Council, 23 (amounting to 6.88 per cent) were negatived because of the SVM. This amount is less than that negatived by president's rulings (61) and Rule 57(4)(b) (55), respectively. Most cases occurred in Legco's first term. After that, no more than four CSAs were negatived because of the SVM in each term.

Of the 23 CSAs negatived by the SVM, six were voted down by GC members whilst 17 were vetoed by FC members, as shown in Table 3.13. All CSAs vetoed by GC members were proposed by pro-Beijing members or independents, whilst of the 17 CSAs vetoed by FC members, six were introduced by pro-Beijing members and 11 by democrats. Given the dominance of the pro-Beijing camp in FCs, it seems unusual that FC members vetoed six CSAs moved by pro-Beijing member. However, four of the six CSAs were related to livelihood issues

TABLE 3.13 *Members' CSAs negatived by different constituencies under the SVM controlling for sponsors' political orientation, 1998–2012*

| Sponsors' political affiliation | Negatived by GC | Negatived by FC | Total |
|---|---|---|---|
| Pro-Beijing | 4 | 6 | 10 |
| Pro-democracy | 0 | 11 | 11 |
| Independent | 2 | 0 | 2 |
| Total (Freq. and Perc.) | 6 (26.08) | 17 (73.91) | 23 (100) |

SOURCE: THE AUTHOR'S CALCULATION BASED ON HANSARD HK (1998–2012).

such as housing and labour.[125] Hence, this result exactly corresponds to the existence of a distinction between the pro-grassroots camp and pro-business camp which also exists within the pro-Beijing camp.

Table 3.14 shows the nature of the issues that CSAs concerned. Of the six CSAs vetoed by GC members, five were related to constitutional and political affairs. Ten of the 16 CSAs vetoed by FC members concerned livelihood issues, housing issues in particular. In addition, four CSAs concerning human rights were blocked by FC members.

The following conclusions can be drawn from these findings.

1. The SVM was employed more frequently in Legco's first term.
2. To date, FC members have employed the mechanism more frequently than GC members.
3. FC members primarily employ the mechanism to block members' CSAs concerning livelihood and human rights issues, housing and labour issues in particular, whilst their GC counterparts use it to block issues relating to constitutional and political affairs moved by pro-Beijing members.

In view of the proportion of CSAs vetoed by the SVM, it is a rather simplistic assessment to impute the overall low pass rate of members' CSAs to the mechanism. It is noted that although the SVM is indeed an unfair voting mechanism and an obstacle to amending government bills, most members' CSAs did not receive the majority support from Legco members, namely, pro-Beijing members from the political aspect and pro-business members from the aspect of social welfare, respectively.

125 The author's calculation based on Hansard HK.

TABLE 3.14 *Members' CSAs negatived by different constituencies under the SVM controlling for the nature of the issues, 1998–2012*

| | CSAs negatived by FCs | | CSAs negatived by GCs | | Total |
|---|---|---|---|---|---|
| | Issue | Freq. | Issue | Freq. | |
| People's livelihood | Housing | 6 | Constitutional and political affair | 5 | |
| | Labour | 3 | Economic Development Strategy and Policy | 1 | |
| | Welfare and social protection | 1 | | | |
| | Tax, fees and budget | 1 | | | |
| Human rights | | 4 | | | |
| Home affair | | 1 | | | |
| Environmental and conservation affair | | 1 | | | |
| Total | | 17 | | 6 | 23 |

SOURCE: THE AUTHOR'S CALCULATION BASED ON HANSARD HK (1998–2012).

### Political Orientation, the Nature of the Issues and Voting Behaviour of Constituencies

From 1998 to 2012, Legco voted on a total of 353 members' CSAs at the stage of the Committee of the whole Council, including 334 negatived and 19 successful CSAs. This section analyses the voting behaviour of different constituencies by considering the sponsors' political orientation and the nature of the issues.

Table 3.15 shows that FCs passed 10 of the 14 CSAs concerning constitutional and political affairs moved by pro-Beijing members, whilst only six of the 58 CSAs concerning constitutional and political affairs moved by pro-democracy members were passed in FCs. In addition, FCs passed only three CSAs of the 99 CSAs concerning livelihood issues and two of the 82 CSAs concerning human rights issues. Of the 15 concerning livelihood issues proposed by pro-Beijing members, only one were passed in FCs. These findings clearly prove the divisions into pro-Beijing and pro-democracy camps and pro-business and pro-grassroots camps, particularly the later within the pro-Beijing camp. In addition, FCs remain conservative in human rights issues overall.

TABLE 3.15 *Voting result in FCs by the nature of the issues controlling for sponsors' political orientation, 1998–2012*

| Nature of the issues | Moved by Pro-Beijing members | | Moved by Pro-democracy members | | Moved by independent | | Total |
|---|---|---|---|---|---|---|---|
| | Passed | Negatived | Passed | Negatived | Passed | Negatived | |
| Constitutional and political affair | 10 | 4 | 6 | 58 | 4 | 10 | 92 |
| Financial policy | 0 | 7 | 0 | 0 | 0 | 0 | 7 |
| Human rights | 1 | 2 | 1 | 82 | 0 | 0 | 86 |
| Tax, fees and budget | 0 | 5 | 1 | 14 | 1 | 0 | 21 |
| Environmental and conservation | 0 | 2 | 0 | 4 | 0 | 0 | 6 |
| Justice, legal service and legislation | 1 | 0 | 1 | 5 | 0 | 0 | 7 |
| Economy and development | 3 | 2 | 1 | 8 | 0 | 1 | 15 |
| People's livelihood | 1 | 14 | 2 | 81 | 0 | 1 | 99 |
| Public service | 0 | 1 | 0 | 7 | 0 | 0 | 8 |
| Home affair | 0 | 1 | 0 | 7 | 0 | 0 | 8 |
| Broadcasting | 0 | 1 | 1 | 2 | 0 | 0 | 4 |
| Total | 16 | 39 | 13 | 268 | 5 | 12 | 353 |

SOURCE: THE AUTHOR'S CALCULATION BASED ON HANSARD HK (1998–2012).

Table 3.16 shows the voting behaviour of GCs by considering the nature of the issues and the sponsors' political orientation. With respect to CSAs concerning constitutional and political affairs, GCs passed one of the 14 CSAs moved by pro-Beijing members and 30 of 64 CSAs moved by democrats. Of the 34 negatived CSAs concerning constitutional and political affairs moved by democrats, 27 were moved during Legco's first and second terms, particularly from 1998 to 2000.[126] This result seems reasonable because the pro-democracy camp had not dominated GCs until the 2000 election. The other seven were proposed and negatived in Legco's fourth term. Six of the seven were proposed by Councillor Margaret Ng to amend the Chief Executive Election (Amendment) Bill 2010 and the Legislative Council (Amendment) Bill 2010. On rare occasions, GCs

126 The author's calculation based on Hansard HK.

TABLE 3.16 *Voting result in GCs by the nature of the issues controlling for sponsors' political orientation, 1998–2012*

| Nature of the issues | Moved by Pro-Beijing members | | Moved by Pro-democracy members | | Moved by independent | | Total |
|---|---|---|---|---|---|---|---|
| | Passed | Negatived | Passed | Negatived | Passed | Negatived | |
| Constitutional and political affair | 1 | 13 | 30 | 34 | 2 | 12 | 92 |
| Financial policy | 0 | 0 | 7 | 0 | 0 | 0 | 7 |
| Human rights | 3 | 0 | 47 | 36 | 0 | 0 | 86 |
| Tax, fees and budget | 2 | 3 | 10 | 5 | 0 | 1 | 21 |
| Environmental and conservation | 1 | 1 | 2 | 2 | 0 | 0 | 6 |
| Justice, legal service and legislation | 1 | 0 | 6 | 0 | 0 | 0 | 7 |
| Economy and development | 2 | 3 | 6 | 3 | 0 | 1 | 15 |
| People's livelihood | 8 | 7 | 56 | 27 | 1 | 0 | 99 |
| Public service | 0 | 1 | 3 | 4 | 0 | 0 | 8 |
| Home affair | 1 | 0 | 4 | 3 | 0 | 0 | 8 |
| Broadcasting | 0 | 1 | 3 | 0 | 0 | 0 | 4 |
| Total | 19 | 29 | 174 | 114 | 3 | 14 | 353 |

SOURCE: THE AUTHOR'S CALCULATION BASED ON HANSARD HK (1998–2012).

unanimously vetoed CSAs moved by democrats. For instance, during deliberation over the Legislative Council (Amendment) Bill 1999, Councillor Sin Chung Kai, a DP member, moved a CSA to expand the corporate voters of the Information Technology Sector. This CSA was rejected unanimously by GC members in attendance but was supported by the LP members who intended to expand specific Functional Sectors.[127]

With respect to CSAs concerning livelihood issues, it can be seen from Table 3.16 that GCs vetoed seven moved by pro-Beijing members and 27 moved by pro-democracy member. These findings demonstrate that the pro-democracy camp does not necessarily take a unanimous stance on livelihood issues.

127 Hansard HK (15 July 1999), 10552–10553.

The following conclusions can thus be draw from these findings.

1. Livelihood issues and constitutional and political affairs are the focus of both the pro-government and pro-democracy camps.
2. FCs have blocked nearly all CSAs concerning livelihood issues, tax cuts and fee-reduction issues, regardless of the sponsors' political orientation.
3. As the usual majority of GCs, from time to time the pro-democracy camp split even over issues concerning constitutional and political affairs, and livelihood issues.

### Voting Behaviour of Major Political Groups

This section selects three sessions to compare the voting behaviour of various political groups, as shown in Table 3.17. This study on selected sessions is not complete statistics and specific controversial bills, such as the Minimum Wage Bill, may affect the conclusion. Hence, data are primarily used to study the division in the pro-Beijing and pro-democracy camps. The first seven political groups in Table 3.17 belong to the so called pro-Beijing camp and the other eight are often deemed the pro-democracy political groups.

It can be seen from Table 3.17 that the pro-Beijing camp as a whole had the inclination towards voting against members' CSAs. The pro-Beijing Hong Kong Federation of Trade Unions (FTU) and the Federation of Hong Kong and Kowloon Labour Unions (FLU) became the 'rebels' who voted for members' CSAs more frequently. CSAs that the FTU voted for or cast an abstention for were often related to labour, fee-cut or transport issues.[128] The FLU supported not only some CSAs concerning labour or fee-cut issues like the FTU, but also several concerning public service, and it also cast abstention votes on CSAs regarding human rights.[129] Amongst the pro-Beijing political groups, the Breakfast Group (the Alliance since 2004 and the Professional Forum since 2008) maintained the weakest party discipline over individual members' voting behaviour. The New People's Party (NPP) led by Councillor Regina Ip in early 2011 cast some votes deviating from major pro-Beijing political groups and attempted to burnish its alleged 'independent' public image.

It is evident that the pro-democracy camp is more willing to support members' CSAs than the pro-Beijing camp. However, fragmented voting on members' CSAs also existed within the pro-democracy camp. Casting the most negative votes on members' CSAs, the Hong Kong Association for Democracy and People's Livelihood (ADPL) became the 'dissent' on many occasions within the pro-democracy camp. Its voting behaviour on members' CSAs in the 2001–02

128 The author's calculation based on Hansard HK.

129 Ibid.

TABLE 3.17 *Voting behaviour of the major political groups on members' CSAs in selected years*

| | Political groups | 2001–2002 | | | | 2005–2006 | | | | 2009–2010 | | | |
|---|---|---|---|---|---|---|---|---|---|---|---|---|---|
| | | P | N | A | As | P | N | A | As | P | N | A | As |
| 1 | DAB | 0 | 14 | 0 | 0 | 0 | 14 | 0 | 0 | 2 | 26 | 2 | 0 |
| 2 | LP | 1 | 13 | 0 | 0 | 0 | 14 | 0 | 0 | 1 | 29 | 0 | 0 |
| 3 | BG* | 0 | 14 | 0 | 0 | 0 | 14 | 0 | 0 | 2 | 24 | 4 | 0 |
| 4 | FTU | 0 | 14 | 2 | 0 | 5 | 6 | 0 | 3 | 14 | 10 | 6 | 0 |
| 5 | FLU | 3 | 5 | 3 | 3 | 0 | 7 | 1 | 6 | 16 | 9 | 5 | 0 |
| 6 | ES | N/A | N/A | N/A | N/A | N/A | N/A | N/A | N/A | 0 | 30 | 0 | 0 |
| 7 | SPI/NPP | N/A | N/A | N/A | N/A | N/A | N/A | N/A | N/A | 5 | 19 | 0 | 6 |
| 8 | DP | 14 | 0 | 0 | 0 | 14 | 0 | 0 | 0 | 23 | 6 | 1 | 0 |
| 9 | CTU | 13 | 1 | 0 | 0 | 9 | 0 | 0 | 5 | 26 | 3 | 0 | 1 |
| 10 | ADPL | 3 | 9 | 0 | 2 | 8 | 5 | 0 | 1 | 22 | 6 | 0 | 2 |
| 11 | NWSC | 7 | 0 | 0 | 7 | 13 | 0 | 0 | 1 | 26 | 4 | 0 | 0 |
| 12 | Frontier | 13 | 1 | 0 | 0 | 10 | 0 | 0 | 4 | N/A | N/A | N/A | N/A |
| 13 | CP | N/A | N/A | N/A | N/A | 14 | 0 | 0 | 0 | 26 | 3 | 1 | 0 |
| 14 | LSD | N/A | N/A | N/A | N/A | N/A | N/A | N/A | N/A | 15 | 1 | 2 | 12 |
| 15 | CA | N/A | N/A | N/A | N/A | N/A | N/A | N/A | N/A | 24 | 1 | 0 | 5 |

* BG refers to the Alliance after 2004 and Professional Forum after 2008.
Note 1: P, Pass; N, Negative; A, Abstention; As, Absent.
Note 2: BG, Breakfast Group; FTU, The Hong Kong Federation of Trade Unions; FLU, The Federation of Hong Kong and Kowloon Labour Unions; ES, Economic Synergy; SPI/NPP, Savants Policy Institute/New People's Party; CTU, Hong Kong Confederation of Trade Unions; ADPL, Hong Kong Association for Democracy and People's Livelihood; NWSC, Neighbourhood and Worker's Service Centre; CA, Civic Act-up
SOURCE: THE AUTHOR'S CALCULATION BASED ON HANSARD HK (1998–2012).

session seemed to be more similar to the FLU and other pro-Beijing political groups, rather than other pro-democracy political groups.

The 2009–10 session saw the growing fragmentation in both the camps. There have been more political groups in Legco since the 2008 Legco election owing to the split of political parties and the emergence of new political parties in both camps. It became more difficulty to maintain unanimity amongst each camp. With the exception of the Economic Synergy, the pro-Beijing political groups cast at least one positive vote on members' CSAs. In addition, the frequency of abstentions increased. The pro-democracy political groups cast more negative votes and abstentions on members' CSAs than in previous sessions.

TABLE 3.18 *Division over members' CSAs in various camps by the nature of the issues in selected years*

| Nature of issue | Division in Pro-Beijing camp | Division in Pro-democracy camp |
|---|---|---|
| Labour | 20 | 3 |
| Tax cuts, fees and budget | 6 | 4 |
| Public service | 3 | 2 |
| Human rights | 2 | 7 |
| Transport | 2 | 0 |
| Constitutional and political affair | 1 | 0 |
| Housing | 0 | 1 |

SOURCE: THE AUTHOR'S CALCULATION BASED ON HANSARD HK (1998–2012).

Table 3.18 further shows types of the issues each camp split over. The pro-Beijing camp often split over members' CSAs concerning labour and fee-reduction issues. Other such issues included human rights, public services and transport. The major division amongst the pro-democracy political groups often appeared whilst voting on issues regarding human rights, labour, tax cuts and fee-reduction. Furthermore, CSAs concerning public services and housing also caused disagreement within the pro-democracy camp.

These findings demonstrate the growing fragmentation in Legco over recent years and thus the government finds it more difficult to target its potential allies and secure enough votes in Legco.

### *Filibuster: An Unusual Procedural Weapon*

Findings in the preceding sections suggest that members' CSAs rarely imposed crucial impact on bills. In these circumstances, some legislators, radical democrats in particular, have gradually developed unusual procedural means to achieve their goals.

In May 2012, a filibuster ('lai bo' in Cantonese) action was taken by several pro-democracy members to block the passage of the Legislative Council (Amendment) Bill 2012 (the Bill) which sought to inhibit a Legco member who has resigned from being a candidate in any by-elections in the same Legco held within six months of that resignation.[130] This Bill was regarded as the response

130 Constitutional and Mainland Affairs Bureau, 'Legislative Council Brief on the Legislative Council (Amendment) Bill 2012' (CMAB C1/30/5, 2012).

to the incident in 2010 in which five members of Legco resigned to trigger by-elections in all five GCs, namely 'five-constituency resignation', so as to put the government's 2010 constitutional reform plan to a de-facto referendum.[131]

A total of 1,306 CSAs were moved by Councillors Wong Yuk Man and Albert Chan Wai Yip of the People Power and were allowed to move by the President.[132] After the second reading of the Bill was resumed on 2 May 2012, deliberation over the Bill immediately entered into the Committee Stage of the whole Council at which all CSAs would be debated and voted. Councillors Wong and Chan, together with several other pro-democracy members began lengthy speeches, raised points of order and made enquiries on the presence of a quorum.[133] The abortion of the Legco meeting occurred on 3 May owing to the absence of a quorum.[134] On 9 May, Councillor Audrey Eu's motion to adjourn debates on the Bill was negatived and Legco continued its deliberation over the Bill. A joint debate on the Bill's clauses and proposed amendments began on 10 May and took place overnight on 16 May.[135] By 4:30 pm on 17 May, the joint debate has lasted more than 33 hours.[136] Three members, including Wong, Chan and Councillor Leung Kwok Hung from the League of Social Democrats (LSD), used 'irrelevance or tedious repetition' in their over 20 times of speeches, respectively.[137] On 17 May, the President made a decision to terminate the debate under Rule 92 of the RoP at the request of Councillor Philip Wong.[138] The Bill was passed on 1 June 2012 after 110-hour deliberation since the resumption of the second reading.[139]

The President's decision to 'cut the cloth' encountered challenge in the court. Councillor Leung Kwok Hung filed an application to the Court of First Instance for judicial review of the President's ruling. He sought a court order to quash the President's ruling and a declaration that the President acted *ultra*

131 P.Y. Lo, 'Lai Bo and Other "Procedural Kills": A Study of Discontent in the Legislative Council', *Hong Kong Law Journal*, 42 (2012) 287.

132 President's Ruling on Closing the Joint Debate at the Committee stage of the Legislative Council (Amendment) Bill 2012 (22 May 2012), <http://www.legco.gov.hk/yr11-12/english/pre_rul/pre0522-ref-e.pdf>, accessed 10 September 2012.

133 Lo (n 131), 288.

134 Ibid.

135 President's Ruling on Closing the Joint Debate (n 132).

136 Ibid.

137 Ibid.

138 Lo (n 131), 291. Rule 92 states: 'In any matter not provided for in these Rules of Procedure, the practice and procedure to be followed in the Council shall be such as may be decided by the President who may, if he thinks fit, be guided by the practice and procedure of other legislatures'.

139 Ibid.

*vires* in closing debate on the Bill.[140] The court held that there is no constitutional right of Legco members to filibuster.[141] The court made reference to *Cheng Kar Shun v Li Fung Ying* and held that the courts do have the jurisdiction to determine whether the practice of Legco is in accordance with the Basic Law, but there must be very 'exceptional circumstances' that are deemed appropriate by the court to intervene in the legislative process.[142] Following the principle of parliamentary privilege, the proper interpretation of the RoP concerned rests with Legco and the President under Article 72 of the Basic Law.[143] Thus, the court decided not to intervene in the present case.[144] The case was appealed to the Court of Appeal after the passage of the Bill and Councillor Leung's appeal converted to challenge to the validity of the Bill on the basis of the alleged invalidity of the President's ruling.[145] The appeal was dismissed by the Court of Appeal.

In December 2013, the Court of Final Appeal (CFA) granted permission for an appeal of the case on the basis that two questions of great public importance were raised in the appeal: first, under what circumstances a decision made by the Legco President during the legislative process can be judicially reviewed and, second, whether the President's decision to end a debate is amenable to judicial review.[146] The CFA agreed with the Court of Appeal that Article 73(1) of the Basic Law does not confer on a Legco member a constitutional right to participate in the legislative process.[147] Applying the common law doctrine of the separation of powers and the 'non-intervention principle',[148] the CFA recognised 'the exclusive authority of the legislature in managing its own internal processes in the conduct of its business, in particular its legislative processes',[149] and would not 'intervene to rule on the regularity or

140 *Leung Kwok Hung v The President of the Legislative Council of the Hong Kong Special Administrative Region* [2012] 3 HKLRD 470, 478.

141 Ibid., 488.

142 Ibid., 481.

143 Ibid.

144 Ibid., 489.

145 *Leung Kwok Hung v The President of the Legislative Council of the Hong Kong Special Administrative Region* [2014] HKEC 1604, para 13.

146 Ibid., para 2. See also Francis Moriarty, 'Legislator Granted Permission to Appeal', *RTHK*, 16 December 2013, <http://rthk.hk/rthk/news/englishnews/news.htm?all&20131216&56&970845>, accessed 1 June 2014; Eddie Luk, 'Long Hair Wins Right to Appeal Filibuster Ruling', *The Standard*, 17 December 2013.

147 Ibid., para 25.

148 Ibid., paras 27–28.

149 Ibid., para 28.

irregularity of the internal processes of the legislature but will leave it to determine exclusively for itself matters of this kind'.[150] In respect of the validity of the Bill based on the alleged invalidity of the President's ruling, the CFA pointed out that Article 73(1) does not 'address the question whether non-compliance with "legal procedures" [in Article 73(1)] will result in invalidity of a law',[151] and the court seemed to refuse to deem compliance with procedural regularity in the law-making processes of a legislature a condition of the validity of an enacted law.[152] Therefore, the CFA insisted the application of the non-intervention principle to the present case. The court has jurisdiction 'to determine the existence of a power, privilege or immunity of Legco' and its President but not 'to determine the occasion or the manner of exercise of any such powers, privileges or immunities either by LegCo or the President'.[153] With respect to the question whether Rule 92 authorises the President to close debate on the Bill, the CFA pointed out that 'the President has power to set limits to and terminate a debate' and such power 'is inherent in' Article 72(1) of the Basic Law setting out the President's powers.[154] The court thus refused to determine whether or not the power was properly exercised by the President.[155] The CFA ultimately dismissed the appeal.

In addition to the obstruction of Legco business on the agenda, a more far-reaching consequence of the filibuster was the postponement of the governmental plan to re-organise the Government Secretariat which was announced by then CE-elect Mr Leung Chun Ying. To push through the plan in Legco before the new CE's assumption of office on 1 July 2012, the government moved a motion on 20 June which sought to give priority to its proposed resolution on the reorganisation plan. The motion was surprisingly defeated and the Chief Secretary announced the postponement of the plan on 9 July.[156] It is believed to be a blow to Mr Leung Chun Ying.

Filibusters or similar activities are 'well-practised' tactics in legislatures around the world.[157] And it was not the first use of this obstruction tactic in Hong Kong's legislature. In 1999, during deliberation over the Provision of Municipal Services (Reorganisation) Bill which sought to abolish the

150 Ibid., para 28.
151 Ibid., para 36.
152 Ibid., para 33.
153 Ibid., para 43.
154 Ibid., para 46.
155 Ibid.
156 Lo (n 131), 295.
157 Ibid., 296.

Provisional Urban Council and Regional Council, given the absence of some supporters for the Bill at the Legco meeting held on 1 December 1999, pro-Beijing members made lengthy speeches to delay a vote.[158] The Bill was finally voted and passed the next day when the Council meeting resumed and pro-Beijing members came back to the meeting. A similar situation occurred in the Finance Committee when it was examining an appropriation with a cost of HK$66.9 billion for the construction of the Hong Kong section of the Guangzhou-Shenzhen-Hong Kong Express. To block the appropriation, pro-democracy members raised hundreds of questions and motions at the meetings of the Finance Committee held on 18 December 2009, 8 January and 15 January 2010. This impeded the vote on the appropriation that was not voted and approved until 16 January 2010.

A filibuster against the Legislative Council (Amendment) Bill 2012 is just the beginning of obstruction tactics employed frequently in subsequent sessions. The Appropriation Bill 2013 received more than 700 members' CSAs and deliberation lasted 16 days.[159] In 2014, members moved a total of 1,917 CSAs to the Appropriation Bill and 1507 of them were moved by Councillor Leung Kwok Hung.[160] In his ruling, the President paid special attention to 909 'sequential CSAs' which sought to 'reduce the appropriation to a Head of Expenditure for a specific purpose by sequentially varying amounts'.[161] Although the President allowed such type of members' CSAs in his previous rulings on the Appropriation Bill 2013, he noticed that those sequential CSAs in 2013 did not provide 'fair and genuine choices for members' and 'achieved no purpose other than taking up the Council's time in completing the necessary proceedings'.[162] With respect to 909 sequential CSAs to the Appropriation Bill 2014, the President ruled that they '[did] not serve any purpose reasonably connected with the function of the committee of the whole Council' and infringed Rule 57(4)(d) of the RoP 'for being frivolous or meaningless'.[163] Given the previous experience and foreseeable obstructions on Legco's 'proper exercise and discharge of its constitutional powers and functions' by those sequential CSAs,[164] the President

158 '1999 年建制派曾拉布 (Pro-establishment Camp Filibustered in 1999)', *Ming Pao Daily News*, 7 May 2012.

159 Hansard HK (29 May 2013), 12585–12586.

160 President's Ruling on Committee Stage Amendments Proposed by 14 Members to the Appropriation Bill 2014 (27 April 2014), <http://www.legco.gov.hk/yr13-14/english/pre_rul/pre0417-ref-e.pdf>, accessed 1 June 2014.

161 Ibid., para 7.

162 Ibid., para 11.

163 Ibid., para 13.

164 Ibid., para 18.

ruled them inadmissible. After nearly two-month debates and voting, the Bill was passed on 4 June 2014, with a total of 1,192 members' CSAs tabled and negatived.[165]

Rule 38 of the RoP excludes the application of the restriction on the times of members' speech on a question to members' speeches at the Committee stage, which constitutes the procedural 'loophole' that allows a filibuster. However, the CFA decision on *Leung Kwok Hung* case signifies that the President is able to exercise the power to close lengthy debates free from judicial intervention.

### *Summaries*

Members' power to amend government bills is of great significance, as their initiation power has been largely curbed by Article 74 of the Basic Law. The struggle for legislative power continues between the executive branch and legislature. During debate on the application of Article 74, Legco members, particularly the President of Legco, refused to impose the restriction stipulated by Article 74 on members' CSAs, which has proved crucial to maintaining Legco's autonomy. Furthermore, the Presidents' rulings on members' CSAs have become significant precedents. These features constitute the characteristics of an independent and autonomous legislature.

Given the extremely low success rate of members' CSAs, it is clear that the importance of deliberation at the Committee Stage has been declining. Most success members' CSAs just concerned technical and literal modifications. However, it is useful to discuss how various constituencies and political groups have interacted with each other.

It can be seen from the previous study on BCs that most concessions and agreements were reached between the government and legislators, pro-Beijing members in particular, during deliberation in BCs or panels. Pro-Beijing members, as the majority of Legco, do not need to achieve their goals by means of moving CSAs. Thus most CSAs were moved by the democrats and rarely passed for lack of majority support in Legco. It is also unsurprising that the SVM did not have overwhelming impact on the voting results of members' CSAs. However, data on FC members' voting behaviour demonstrate that this mechanism were primarily employed by and benefited FC members to block members' CSAs regarding housing, labour and human rights, despite the sponsors' political orientation. Data on the voting behaviour of the major political groups across the constituencies further shows the similar inclination of pro-Beijing political groups towards vetoing members'

165 Hansard HK (4 June 2014) (Chinese version only), 363.

CSAs, with the exception of FTU and FLU whilst voting on specific CSAs concerning labour issues.

The growing fragmentation within Legco and long-term powerlessness of democrats have fed on unusual procedural moves. Lengthy speeches at the Committee Stage in May 2012 effectively obstructed the passing of important government proposals, which was followed by the unusual procedural move by the President to terminate debate. In the foreseeable future, Legco will witness more clashes and tensions not only between members and the government, but also between members belonging to different camps.

## Study of Several Bills: Government's Defeats

Most government bills can pass and ultimately become laws. However, the government was defeated or forced to cease the legislative process on rare occasions for various reasons. For instance, the withdrawal of the National Security (Legislative Provisions) Bill was most likely caused by the strong objection from the public, whilst the government's defeat over clause 58 of the Race Discrimination Bill resulted primarily from the division within Legco.

### *National Security (Legislative Provisions) Bill*

The National Security (Legislative Provisions) Bill (the Bill) was proposed to implement Article 23 of the Basic Law.

> [The HKSAR] shall enact laws on its own to prohibit any act of treason, secession, sedition, subversion against the Central People's Government, or theft of state secrets, to prohibit foreign political organisations or bodies from conducting political activities in the Region, and to prohibit political organisations or bodies of the Region from establishing ties with foreign political organisations or bodies.

As the Bill was concerned with national security, human rights protection and civil liberties, it became the most contentious legislative proposal in the history of the HKSAR. On 24 September 2002, the government issued a consultation paper entitled 'Proposals to implement Article 23 of the Basic Law Consultation Document' (consultation document).[166] From September 2002

166 Security Bureau, 'Proposals to Implement Article 23 of the Basic Law Consultation Document' (2002) <http://www.info.gov.hk/archive/consult/2002/bl23-e.pdf>, accessed 21 September 2008.

to July 2003, notwithstanding the interruption by the SARS crisis, the Hong Kong community was engaged in the wide-ranging debates and discussions on the legislation on Article 23. The consultation document attracted a total of 97,097 submissions involving 340,513 signatures.[167] Organisations and individuals that expressed views came from almost all walks of life, including the business community, trade unions, professional associations, religious organisations and ethnic minority groups.[168] Legal professionals submitted detailed legal suggestions and scholars wrote articles in the newspapers to express their views on the principles or specific legislative suggestions in the consultation document.[169] It was a comprehensive and open discussion in terms of both quantity and quality.[170]

Some scholars argued that some technical amendments to the existing law would be enough to fulfil the constitutional duty imposed by Article 23 of the Basic Law as most issues that Article 23 concerned had been covered in the existing law.[171] It was also suggested that some outdated provisions in the existing law be amended to meet the modern principles of human rights protection.[172] More critics, legal professionals in particular, pointed out the ambiguity and uncertainty in consultation document, and the potential danger of the Bill to human rights protection and civil liberties.[173] In addition, whether a white bill should be published to lengthen the consultation period aroused considerable controversy.[174]

---

167 See 'Foreword (to the Conpendium of Submissions)' (2003) <http://www.basiclaw23.gov.hk/english/download/forward-e.pdf>, accessed 21 September 2008.

168 See 'List of Submissions' (2003) <http://www.basiclaw23.gov.hk/english/download/forward-e.pdf>, accessed 21 September 2008.

169 In addition to submitting their opinions and petitions, law professors, such as Professor Albert Chen, gave their comments on every aspect of consultation paper in the newspapers.

170 See Security Bureau, 'Legislative Council Brief: National Security (Legislative Provisions) Bill' (SBCR 2/1162/97, 2002), 6.

171 See Albert Chen, 'Existing Law May Be Good Enough', *South China Morning Post*, 23 September 2002. Tom Kellogg argues that there was no legal vacuum in Hong Kong's national security law, see Tom Kellogg, 'Legislating Rights: Basic Law Article 23, National Security, and Human Rights in Hong Kong', *Columbia Journal of Asian Law*, 17/2 (2004) 312.

172 See Chen, ibid.

173 The Article 23 Concern Group, 'Article 23 Legislation' (2002). The leading members of the Article 23 Concern Group formed the Civic Party in 2006.

174 Not only did democratic advocators and legal professionals call for a white bill, the public at large continued to be concerned about the white bill as well. South China Morning Post published several editorials and commentaries from October to December in 2002, discussing the advantages of a white bill. See Editorial, 'No Need to Rush', *South China*

### Legco Panels' Work

After the issue of the consultation document, the Panel on Security and Panel on Administration of Justice and Legal Service of Legco held joint meetings to receive public submissions,[175] to invite public officers and the representatives of various deputations to present their views and to discuss the response from the government. At these meetings, members raised their concern about the timing of introducing the legislation, a necessity to publish a white bill, applications of principles of human rights protection, the issues concerning the proscription of local organisations and such issues of concepts as the definition of treason.[176]

Some members recognised the necessity to publish a white bill to set out the details of legislative proposals for consultation before the publication of a blue bill,[177] thereby urging the government to avoid taking a determined stand on the provisions in a blue bill.[178] Such concern did reflect the views from the public. In October 2002, some influential features and organisations expressed, one after another, their demands for a white bill.[179] As the main difference between having a white bill and not having one lay in the timing of the legislation,[180] the publication of a white bill would be deemed 'a sign that the government respects our history, tradition and constitutional convention of consulting the community

---

*Morning Post,* 2 October 2002; Chen (n 38); and Editorial, 'General Interest', *Ming Pao Daily News*, 17 January 2003.

175 Legislative Council Secretariat, 'Legal Service Division Report on National Security (Legislative Provisions) Bill' (LC Paper No. LS61/02-03, 2003).

176 Legislative Council Secretariat, 'Summary of Concerns and Queries Raised by Members at the Joint Meetings on 26 September 2002, 21 October 2002, 19 December 2002 and 7 January 2003' (LC Paper No. CB(2) 1082/02-03(01), 2003).

177 Ibid., 3.

178 Ibid., 4.

179 Those features included Anson Chan (former Chief Secretary for Administration), the Law Society, the Bar Association and Ms Margaret Ng (representative of Legco's Legal sector). Mrs Anson Chan's speech was given in Washington on 2 October 2002, and others submitted their joint letter on 7 October 2002. See Stella Lee, 'Lawyers urge White Bill for Article 23', *South China Morning Post,* 8 October 2002, EDT4. However, President of the Law Society, Simon Ip, subsequently gave up his insistence on a white bill, which gave rise to some doubts, See Ambrose Leung, 'Law Society Boss Backs Away from Demand for Article 23', *South China Morning Post,* 10 October 2002, EDT3. Others claimed for a white bill. For instance, academics signed a petition demanding a white bill on Article 23. See Ambrose Leung and May Sin-mi Hon, 'Artists, Teachers and Academics Fear Repression', *South China Morning Post,* 2 November 2002, EDT3. The democrats conducted a poll and declared that 70 per cent of the 589 people surveyed called for a white bill. See Ambrose Leung, '70pc Call for White Bill to Be Drafted', *South China Morning Post,* 18 October 2002, EDT4.

180 Chen (n 38).

through white bills on important legislative issues'.[181] However, the government rejected such suggestions on the grounds that, first, a blue bill and a white bill could equally serve the purpose of providing details,[182] and second, it was not usual practice to issue a white bill.[183] Such grounds sounded unconvincing in view of the complexity and importance of the legislation on Article 23.

Discussion on the proscription of local organisations also indicates a persuasive approach rather than a consultative approach taken by the government.[184] Members' queries mainly included that (1) whether it is appropriate for the Secretary for Security to proscribe a local organisation 'on the basis of a proscription by the Central Authorities of a Mainland organisation to which it was affiliated' whilst the decision of the Central Authorities was not based on common law principles;[185] (2) an accused may be unable to defend himself if the nature of evidence considered by an appeal tribunal was highly confidential whilst the court would only consider points of law.[186] The government argued that the proscription of a Mainland organisation by the Central Authorities would be a fact that 'the court must accept'.[187] Furthermore, there would be a mechanism for the proscription of local organisations that the Secretary for Security must be satisfied by such preconditions as the affiliation of the local organisation to the proscribed Mainland organisation, a threat to national security, and the necessity and proportionality to proscribe the local organisation.[188] The government also stressed that it was 'an established practice to establish tribunals to handle appeals on points of facts' and both the decisions of the Secretary for Security and the tribunal would be subject to judicial review.[189] However, the government's promise of good will to enforce the law was not enough to remove members' serious doubts about whether the Mainland's legal system would be introduced into Hong Kong.

The major political groups of Legco split over the legislation. For instance, with respect to issues concerning the proscription of local organisations, the DAB, as 'the most politically loyal force supportive of Article 23',[190] questioned

181 Ibid.
182 Legislative Council Secretariat (n 176), 3–4.
183 Ibid.
184 Petersen (n 57), 23.
185 Ibid., 8.
186 Ibid., 9.
187 Ibid., 8.
188 Ibid.
189 Ibid., 8–10.
190 Sonny Shiu-Hing Lo, *The Dynamics of Beijing-Hong Kong Relations: A Model for Taiwan?* (Hong Kong: Hong Kong University Press, 2008), 154.

that definition of local organisation in proposed document 'might be too narrow' as it only covered organisations registered under the Societies Ordinance.[191] By contrast, most critical queries were raised by pro-democracy members and members from the LP also expressed their concern about the power of the Secretary for Secretary to make a decision on the proscription.[192]

With the publication of the Compendium of Submissions on the Consultation Document (Compendium of Submissions) in January 2003, members shifted their focus to the Compendium of Submissions. At the Legislative Council meeting held on 26 February 2003, a DP member Councillor Sin Chung Kai moved a motion to condemn the government for compiling the Compendium of Submissions 'in a slipshod, incomplete and inequitable manner, distorting the views expressed by the public and organisations'.[193] Councillor Howard Young on behalf of the LP moved an amendment to Mr Sin's motion which substituted 'expresses disappointment with' for 'condemn', and described the government's manner as 'slipshod' and 'incomplete', and held it as 'categorizing wrongly' the submission.[194] Although neither the original motion nor Mr Young's amendment passed, it appeared that even the LP, one of its important allies, did not recognised the government's approach in dealing with submissions. In addition, a research team comprising scholars from several local universities also joined in the questioning about the impartiality of the Compendium of Submissions and the method of analysis used by the government.[195]

After the close of the consultation, the government made nine-point clarification to elucidate important definitions and to abolish the offence of misprision of treason and the offence of possession of seditious publications.[196] However, such clarification did not help to remove people's doubts. Furthermore, although the major pro-Beijing political groups such as the DAB, FTU and LP

---

191 See Panel on Security and Panel on Administration of Justice and Legal Services, 'Minutes of Joint Meeting Held on 15 February 2003' (LC Paper No. CB(2)2035/02-03, 2003), para 45.

192 Ibid., para 32.

193 For legislators' discontent, see motion debates on 'Compendium of Submissions on the Consultation Document on Proposals to Implement Article 23 of the Basic Law' moved by Councillor Sin Chung-kai, Hansard HK (14 February 2003), 4182–4257.

194 Ibid.

195 For the critics by research teams, see Chan Kin-Man and Robert Ting-Yiu Chung, 'Redress for the Public Voice', *HKU pop Site* (2003) <http://hkupop.hku.hk/english/columns/columns20.html>, accessed 21 September 2008.

196 HKSAR Government, 'Government Further Clarifies Legislative Proposals to Implement BL 23' (LC Paper No. CB(2)1069/02-03(02), 2003).

expressed their support for the legislation, Councillor Young's motion expressing disappointment with the government might foreshadow the subsequent division of the 'governing coalition' over the legislation of Article 23.

The pro-democracy camp mobilised the public to join in the discussions on the consultation document by constantly explaining the proposals to the public in detail and claiming that the proposals 'affect everyone'.[197] The mobilisation proved successful. Opinion polls conducted by the Hong Kong Transition Project indicated that the level of 'very worried' about personal freedoms of Hong Kong people in late November 2002 rose to double digits in contrast to that in August 2002, higher than any of those previously surveyed since 1997.[198] This sharp rise was deemed related to the consultation over legislation on Article 23.[199]

In this case, joint meetings of two panels have served as a forum for conveying the views of the public and consolidating public opinion. Furthermore, the government was afforded an opportunity to respond to questions and queries addressed by legislators and deputations in attendance.

### Bills Committee on National Security (Legislative Provisions) Bill

Despite heated controversy, the government published a blue bill in the Gazette on 14 February 2003 and introduced it to Legco on 26 February. The Bills Committee on National Security (Legislative Provisions) Bill (the Committee) was established on 28 February. Fifty members joined the BC. Councillor Ip Kwok Him of the DAB and Councillor Ambrose Lau of the HKPA were elected as the Chairman and Deputy Chairman, respectively.[200] The Committee held a total of 29 meetings between March and June 2003,[201] four of which were held for inviting individuals and representatives of the deputations to present their views on the Bill in Legco.[202]

It was a fierce battle over deliberation on the Bill between pro-Beijing members and pro-democracy members at the BC meetings. On 10 June 2003,

197 Martin Lee, 'Officials Must Reveal True Colour of Article 23', *South China Morning Post*, 1 October 2002.

198 The Hong Kong Transition Project, 'Accountability & Article 23: Freedoms, Fairness and Accountability in Hong Kong ' (2002) <http://hktp.hkbu.edu.hk/article23/article23.pdf>, accessed 21 September 2008, 8–9.

199 Ibid.

200 See Bills Committee on National Security (Legislative Provisions) Bill (n 54).

201 Legislative Council Secretariat, 'Report of the Bills Committee on National Security (Legislative Provisions) Bill' (LC Paper No. CB(2)2646/02-03, 2003), 2.

202 These meetings were held on 12 April 2003, 26 April 2003 and 3 May 2003.

Councillor Martin Lee moved a motion to defer the resumption of the second reading of the Bill and giving more deliberation time for the Bill.[203] It was negatived by 15 to 24.[204] The BC also vetoed another suggestion from Councillor Lee rescheduling the meeting originally scheduled to be held on 14 June because of the clash with a seminar on the Article 23 Legislation to be held on the same day.[205] Hence, at the meeting held on 14 June, with the absence of almost all democrats, the BC conducted clause-by-clause deliberation and passed a motion declaring the close of the clause-by-clause deliberation with the exception of follow-up issues.[206] The passage of this motion sharpened debates on the resumption of the second reading of the Bill at the meeting on 17 June. The pro-democracy members were attempting to rescind the motion carried on 14 June and moved a no confidence motion in the BC Chairman.[207] Both motions were defeated and the motion to resume the second reading on 9 July was passed.[208] At the meeting held on 26 June, the Chairman declared that the BC had completed its work regardless of objections from the democrats.[209] The deep cleavage in the BC demonstrated the widening division in the community to some extent.[210]

During deliberation by the BC, members and the government moved a lot of amendments. Most sponsors for members' CSAs were members from the Article 23 Concern Group, DP, Frontier and ADPL.[211] Four amendments were proposed by members from the LP and DAB.[212] CSAs moved by the democrats primarily sought to delete provisions concerning handling seditious publication, expanded investigation power and the proscription mechanism.[213] The democrats also introduced new provisions concerning the public interest

203 Bills Committee on National Security (Legislative Provisions) Bill, 'Minutes of Meeting Held on 10 June 2003' (LC Paper No. CB(2) 2838/02-03, 2003), 4–5.

204 Ibid.

205 Ibid., 5.

206 Bills Committee on National Security (Legislative Provisions) Bill, 'Minutes of Meeting Held on 14 June 2003' (LC Paper No. CB(2) 2847/02-03, 2003).

207 Bills Committee on National Security (Legislative Provisions) Bill, 'Minutes of Meeting Held on 17 June 2003' (LC Paper No. CB(2) 2962/02-03, 2003).

208 Ibid.

209 Bills Committee on National Security (Legislative Provisions) Bill, 'Minutes of Meeting Held on 26 June 2003' (LC Paper No. CB(2) 2893/02-03, 2003).

210 For the divide in the community, see Kuan Hsin-chi's Comments, in Chris Yeung, 'Conversation with the Post', *South China Morning Post*, 21 December 2002, P15.

211 Legislative Council Secretariat (n 201) Appendix IV, V, VI and VII.

212 Ibid.

213 Ibid.

defence and an interpretation principle that the provisions of the Bill should be interpreted, applied and enforced in a manner consistent with Chapter III of the Basic Law.[214]

The government's CSAs on 28 June partly responded to members' requirements. The government incorporated amendments proposed by members from the LP and DAB into the Bill.[215] Some requirements imposed by the democrats, for instance, the manner of interpretation, enforcement and application having to be consistent with Chapter III of the Basic Law, were satisfied.[216] However, most substantive CSAs were not accepted by the government until 5 July 2003 when the government proposed the fifth set of amendments, namely, 'three concessions'.[217] It was believed that these concessions were offered in response to the big march on 1 July 2003 with more than 500,000 protesters.[218] However, these concessions seemed too late to convince the public and to remedy the situation.[219] A further challenge that the government was facing was another march on 9 July 2003 organised by the democrats once Legco resumed the second reading of the Bill.[220]

The Bill was ultimately shelved after the resignation of Councillor James Tien from the Executive Council and the shift of the LP, which meant that the government might be defeated in Legco. It is clear that the government was reluctant to offer significant concessions until the unprecedented protest on 1 July 2003. The final withdrawal of the Bill was announced after 'calculating the inevitable defeat in Legco' owing to the 'rebellion' of LP members.[221] As far as the whole legislative process was concerned, the hasty legislative agenda, including the refusal of a white bill and the last minute concessions, fuelled people's doubts and fears, and fostered strong opposition to the legislation.

---

214 Ibid.

215 House Committee of the Legislative Council, 'Minutes of the 31st Meeting Held on 27 June 2003' (LC Paper No. CB(2) 2979/02-03, 2003), 10–11.

216 See Bills Committee on National Security (Legislative Provisions) Bill, 'Paper No. 111' (2003) <http://www.legco.gov.hk/yr02-03/english/bc/bc55/papers/bc55-111-e.pdf>, accessed 21 September 2008.

217 Petersen (n 57), 51. The three concessions included the deletion of the proscription mechanism and the expanded investigation powers, on the one hand, and the introduction of the public interest defence, on the other. See 'Chief Executive's Transcript on Basic Law Article 23' [webpage] (5 July 2003) <http://www.info.gov.hk/gia/general/200307/05/0705158.htm>, accessed 21 September 2008.

218 Petersen (n 57), 50–51.

219 Lo (n 190), 159.

220 Ibid.

221 Ibid., 156–157.

Committee Work, Public Opinion and Street Politics

Deliberation in panels, the BC and plenary meetings of Legco shows how legislators conveyed views of the public, provided alternative proposals, and squeezed concessions from the government. The lapse of the Bill resulted from the shift of the LP to a large extent, and might also have a connection with the downturn in the economy as a consequence of the SARS outbreak and then CE's poor political skills.[222] Even then, strong opposition from the public and social movement in the street were the ultimate causes for the failure of the Bill.

In this case, Legco could not fully represent the public and build effective communication with citizens. The peculiar nature of the legislation on Article 23, namely, national security, determined that the pro-Beijing camp, in particular the DAB, FTU and other representatives of conservative business sectors must take a rather tough stand on the legislation. They controlled the schedule of the legislative process by a majority in Legco plenary meetings as well as its panels and committees. The pro-democracy camp, obtaining the majority votes in direct elections notwithstanding, can only occupy the minority seats in Legco. In these circumstances, Legco and its committee could not play their role as an arena for effectively reflecting and bringing public opinion into the legislative process. The government ultimately had to bow to popular pressure in consideration of the unprecedented big march and another incoming protest.

### *Government's Defeat in Race Discrimination Bill*

Another case is the government's defeat in introducing a new clause to the Race Discrimination Bill (the Bill). The Bill was tabled in December 2006 to fill the legislative gap as 'Hong Kong has an international obligation to prohibit all forms of racial discrimination'.[223] The Bill was studied by the Bills Committee under the chairmanship of Councillor Margaret Ng who introduced five CSAs on behalf of the BC.[224] One of the most contentious issues was Clause 58 providing

---

222 Councillor Tam Yiu-chung, President of the DAB, regarded the SARS outbreak and the 'agitation' of the democrats as important reasons for the strong opposition of the public. He admitted that, at the later stage of the legislative process, the crux was not about how many concessions would be given because people did not try to understand the provisions of the legislation. Nonetheless, the government firmly insisted on proceeding with the legislative process. Interview with Councillor Tam on 11 February 2009. On poor political skills of the then CE, see Lo (n 190), 154–159.

223 Legislative Council Secretariat, 'Report of the Bills Committee on Race Discrimination Bill' (LC Paper No. CB(2)2478/07-08, 2008), 1.

224 Others were the application of the Bill to the Government (Clause 3), the scope of circumstances constituting indirect discrimination (Clause 4), and the exclusion of new arrivals

an exception of language for the provision of goods, services and facilities.[225] Committee members expressed their strong dissatisfaction with this clause and decided to move a CSA to exclude the provision of vocational training courses and medical treatment within the meaning of Section 2 of the Medical Clinics Ordinance (Cap 343) from the exception of language.[226] This CSA received the support from the pro-democracy camp and several pro-grassroots members from the pro-Beijing camp,[227] including Councillor Chan Yuen Han from the FTU and Councillor Li Fung Ying from the FLU.[228] The FTU and FLU are often characterized by pro-grassroots orientation, attaching importance to labour rights and social welfare. This factor increased the uncertainty of voting on Clause 58, notwithstanding the support from the DAB and LP.[229] Members' CSAs to narrow down the scope of exception of language were negatived because of the SVM. However, clause 58 proposed by the government was also voted down by 24 to 26. Thus the exception for language discrimination was not added to the Bill. Some commentaries attributed the government's defeat to objections from the FTU and Councillor David Li who was the representative of the Bank Sector, and the absence of two members from the Alliance, namely, Councillors Abraham Shek and Patrick Lau who were supposed to vote for the government.[230] It was unusual for 'legislators usually considered friendly to the Administration' to vote against the government.[231]

Notwithstanding some accidental factors such as the absence of some pro-Beijing members, the defeat exposed the loose cooperation between the government and its allies over non-political issues. Some FTU members were concurrently holding a DAB membership at the time, but the FTU and DAB do not necessarily toe the same party line and achieve consensus on livelihood issues.[232] In

from the Mainland from the scope of the Bill (Clause 8). See Margaret Ng's speech on behalf of the Bills Committee in the Legco meeting for the resumption of the Second Reading debate on the Race Discrimination Bill, Hansard HK (9 July 2008), 10551–10554.

225 Legislative Council Secretariat (n 223), 16.

226 Ibid., 17.

227 Ibid.

228 Ibid.

229 Ibid.

230 '關鍵六票令政府滑鐵盧 (The Critical Six Votes Defeated the Government)', *Ming Pao Daily News*, 11 July 2008, A06.

231 Editorial, 'Race Bill Imperfect But Still Welcome', *South China Morning Post*, 11 July 2008, EDT.

232 Interview with Legislative Councillor Tam Yiu Chung on 11 February 2009. Councillor Tam is a directly elected member and the President of DAB. He is also a former member of the FTU.

addition, to maintain its role as the 'critical minority' in Legco,[233] members from the Alliance in FCs stressed its independent and professional image, which further added to the uncertainty of a strong 'governing coalition'.

### Scrutiny of Subsidiary Legislation

Subsidiary legislation or subordinate legislation in the legal sources of Hong Kong refers to 'any proclamation, rule, regulation, order, resolution, notice, rule of court, bylaw or other instrument made under or by virtue of any Ordinance and having legislative effect'.[234] It is also called delegated legislation as it is usually made by a delegated law-making body or an official.[235] After the return of sovereignty to China, subsidiary legislation has remained one of the legal sources of Hong Kong Law, together with common law, rules of equity, ordinances and customary law under Article 8 of the Basic Law. It is considered significant as far as its quantity on the statute books and extensive interference with citizens' rights is concerned.[236]

The number of subsidiary legislation has always exceeded that of primary legislation or ordinances.[237] For instance, during the 2003–04 session, 37 ordinances were enacted whilst 192 pieces of subsidiary legislation were examined by Legco.[238] In addition to the quantity, the diversity in the names of subsidiary legislation indicates the wide-ranging nature of the issues it concerns. As Professor Wesley-Smith points out, 'Regulations' mostly concern changes to the substantive law, 'rules' usually relate to procedural matters and 'bylaws' are often municipal in nature or are restricted to a small geographical area.[239] The diversity and flexibility of subsidiary legislation seem to support two major functions stated by Professor Miners: first, preventing 'the overloading of the legislature with technical details' and second, being 'a flexible means for quickly incorporating minor changes without the need to go through the whole process of amending the original law'.[240]

---

233 'The Critical Six Votes Defeated the Government' (n 230).

234 Interpretation and General Clauses Ordinance, Cap 1, s 3.

235 Peter Wesley-Smith, *Constitutional and Administrative Law in Hong Kong* (Hong Kong: Longman Asia Ltd, 1994), 163; Miners and Tang, *The Government and Politics of Hong Kong*, 127.

236 Wesley-Smith, ibid.

237 Miners and Tang (n 235), 127.

238 Legislative Council, 'The Legislative Council Annual Report, 2003–04' (2004) <http://www.legco.gov.hk/general/english/sec/reports/a_0304.pdf>, accessed 21 September 2008, 3.

239 Wesley-Smith (n 235), 164.

240 Miners and Tang (n 235), 127. Peter Wesley-Smith expresses the similar views that the delegated legislation 'relieve the primary legislature of discussing technicalities and

### *Results of Subsidiary Legislation*

The enactment of subsidiary legislation is subject to the supervision of Legco and the courts. The courts may declare a piece of subsidiary legislation void if such legislation has gone beyond powers delegated by its parent or principal ordinance.[241] It is Sections 34 and 35 of the *Interpretation and General Clauses Ordinance* (Cap 1) (IGCO) that secure all subsidiary legislation subject to Legco's deliberation through commonly called procedures of 'positive vetting' and 'negative vetting':

1. Negative Vetting procedure in s 34 of the IGCO
   (1) All subsidiary legislation shall be laid on the table of the Legislative Council at the next sitting thereof after the publication in the Gazette of that subsidiary legislation.
   (2) Where subsidiary legislation has been laid on the table of the Legislative Council under subsection (1), the Legislative Council may, by resolution passed at a sitting of the Legislative Council held not later than 28 days after the sitting at which it was so laid, provide that such subsidiary legislation shall be amended in any manner whatsoever consistent with the power to make such subsidiary legislation, and if any such resolution is so passed the subsidiary legislation shall, without prejudice to anything done thereunder, be deemed to be amended as from the date of publication in the Gazette of such resolution.
2. Positive Vetting procedure in s 35 of the IGCO
   Where any Ordinance provides that subsidiary legislation shall be subject to the approval of the Legislative Council or of any other authority, or contains words to the like effect, then the subsidiary legislation shall be submitted for the approval of the Legislative Council or other authority; and the Legislative Council may by resolution or the other authority may by order amend the whole or any part of the subsidiary legislation.

Both are substantive and mandatory procedures as legislators have the final say on subsidiary legislation. Even then, there is a clear difference between the two vetting procedures. Subsidiary legislation proposed under the negative vetting procedure becomes effective as provided in the subsidiary legislation unless it is amended or repealed in the form of a resolution by Legco within

details; and to provide flexibility and speed of legislative change'. See Wesley-Smith (n 235), 164.

241 Miners and Tang (n 235), 128.

28 days which may be extended by resolution, whilst Legco's approval is required for the enactment of subsidiary legislation proposed under the positive vetting procedure. The positive vetting procedure rather resembles the legislative procedure for primary legislation and legislators can play a more important role in deliberating subsidiary legislation.

It is seen from Table 3.19 that Legco deliberated a total of 411 pieces of subsidiary legislation under the positive vetting procedure from 1998 to 2013. The government withdrew 63 (amounting to 15.33 per cent) most of which were resubmitted with revisions and eventually passed by Legco. Members proposed 20 amendments to nine pieces of subsidiary legislation and none was carried.[242] In the 2010–11 session, Legco vetoed a resolution under the Public Finance Ordinance which sought funds to enable the government to carry on its services before the Appropriation Bill 2011 came into operation.[243]

Table 3.20 shows that as many as 2,950 pieces of subsidiary legislation were laid before Legco under the negative vetting procedure from 1998 to 2013. Legco cannot deliberate them all in detail owing to a huge number of such legislation. From 1998 to 2013, 136 pieces of such legislation (amounting to 4.61 per cent of all legislation) passed with amendments and 19 were repealed by resolutions moved by members or the government. However, the percentage of

TABLE 3.19 *Result of subsidiary legislation under positive vetting procedure, 1998–2013*

| Term | Passed | | Withdrawn | | Negatived | | Total |
|---|---|---|---|---|---|---|---|
| | Freq. | Perc. | Freq. | Perc. | Freq. | Perc. | Freq. |
| 1998–2000 | 53 | 86.89 | 8 | 13.11 | 0 | 0 | 61 |
| 2000–2004 | 97 | 88.99 | 12 | 11.01 | 0 | 0 | 109 |
| 2004–2008 | 89 | 94.68 | 5 | 5.32 | 0 | 0 | 94 |
| 2008–2012 | 82 | 74.55 | 27 | 24.55 | 1 | 0.91 | 110 |
| 2012–2013 | 26 | 70.27 | 11 | 29.73 | 0 | 0 | 37 |
| Total | 347 | 84.43 | 63 | 15.33 | 1 | 0.24 | 411 |

Note: The number of subsidiary legislation under positive vetting procedure in this table is bigger than that in the Annual Report because the author separately calculated every piece of subsidiary legislation proposed in one resolution.

SOURCE: THE AUTHOR'S CALCULATION BASED ON HANSARD HK (1998–2013).

242 The author's calculation is based on Hansard HK (1998–2013).

243 Hansard HK (9 March 2011).

TABLE 3.20 *Result of subsidiary legislation under negative vetting procedure, 1998–2013*

| Year | Passed with amendments | | Repealed | | Passed without amendments | | Total | |
|---|---|---|---|---|---|---|---|---|
| | Freq. | Perc. | Freq. | Perc. | Freq. | Perc. | Freq. | Perc. |
| 1998–2000 | 6 | 1.02 | 5 | 0.85 | 579 | 98.13 | 590 | 100 |
| 2000–2004 | 58 | 6.95 | 12 | 1.44 | 765 | 91.61 | 835 | 100 |
| 2004–2008 | 37 | 4.62 | 1 | 0.13 | 763 | 95.25 | 801 | 100 |
| 2008–2012 | 28 | 4.65 | 1 | 0.17 | 573 | 95.18 | 602 | 100 |
| 2012–2013 | 7 | 5.74 | 0 | 0 | 115 | 94.26 | 122 | 100 |
| Total | 136 | 4.61 | 19 | 0.64 | 2759 | 93.53 | 2950 | 100 |

SOURCE: THE AUTHOR'S CALCULATION BASED ON HANSARD HK (1998–2013).

subsidiary legislation under the negative vetting procedure passed with amendments or repealed has decreased since 2004, as shown in Table 3.20.

Table 3.21 shows that of the 139 amendments moved by the government, 134 were carried. In addition, Legco also passed two resolution of repeal moved by the government. In a startling contrast, only five of the 42 members' amendments and 17 of the 70 members' resolution of repeal were carried. Legco seemingly reached the peak of its power over subsidiary legislation in its second term, namely, the 2000–04 sessions during which members and the government moved more resolutions to amend or repeal subsidiary legislation than in other terms. This period, particularly the 2001–02 session, overlapped with the active period of the eight-party coalition of Legco.

These findings on subsidiary legislation under both vetting procedures indicate that Legco members have found it difficult to amend or repeal subsidiary legislation by means of moving resolutions, in particular since 2004. A practicable means to make a difference in legislation for Legco members is to force the government to proactively amend or withdraw proposals. However, given the decreasing number of the government's amendments to subsidiary legislation moved under the negative vetting procedure since 2004, it is doubtful that such means is still as effective as in the earlier period of the HKSAR.

### *Negative Vetting or Positive Vetting*

It is clear that under the SVM, tabling subsidiary legislation under the negative vetting procedure is more likely to obtain results in favour of the government than under the positive vetting procedure. As Table 3.22 shows, assuming that

TABLE 3.21 *Result of amendments to subsidiary legislation under negative vetting procedure, 1998–2013*

| | 1998–2000 | 2000–2004 | 2004–2008 | 2008–2012 | 2012–2013 | Total |
|---|---|---|---|---|---|---|
| Passed amendments moved by government | 6 | 53 | 37 | 31 | 7 | 134 |
| No. of amendments moved by government | 6 | 54 | 40 | 32 | 7 | 139 |
| Passed repeal moved by government | 0 | 1 | 1 | 0 | 0 | 2 |
| No. of repeal moved by government | 0 | 1 | 1 | 0 | 0 | 2 |
| Passed amendments moved by members | 0 | 5 | 0 | 0 | 0 | 5 |
| No. of amendments moved by members | 2 | 17 | 6 | 17 | 0 | 42 |
| Passed repeal moved by members | 5 | 11 | 0 | 1 | 0 | 17 |
| No. of repeal moved by members | 7 | 50 | 4 | 9 | 0 | 70 |

SOURCE: THE AUTHOR'S CALCULATION BASED ON HANSARD HK (1998–2013).

TABLE 3.22 *Votes required to make subsidiary legislation effective under different vetting procedures, 1998–2012*

| Vetting procedure | Form of proposal | No. of votes required to make proposed subsidiary legislation effective |
|---|---|---|
| Positive vetting | Government's resolution | 31 |
| Negative vetting | Members' repeal resolution | 15 |

all the 60 members are present, the government has to secure at least 31 votes to make the subsidiary legislation effective under the positive vetting, whereas under the negative vetting, the government needs only 15 votes in FCs or GCs to defeat members' resolutions to amend or repeal subsidiary legislation.

In addition, Legco's positive vetting means more time spent and more members involved, resembling the legislative process of a parent bill. In fact, whilst examining some very important and controversial parent bills, an important requirement of legislators is that relevant subsidiary legislation would be made through the positive vetting so that Legco can play more influential role in deliberation over the issues concerned.[244]

An extreme example is what occurred during deliberation over the Urban Renewal Bill in 2000. Clause 1 of the Bill states that the commencement date of the Bill would be given in the form of a notice under the negative vetting procedure. The Bill aroused considerable controversy over such important issues as compensation, rehousing and the criteria for flexible rehousing.[245] Councillor James To moved a CSA to substitute the vetting procedure with the positive vetting, which meant that the commencement date of the Bill would be subject to Legco's prior approval.[246] Councillor Jasper Tsang of the DAB stated that, although Councillor To's CSA was 'unprecedented', they also needed to 'see the fulfilment of the undertakings and assurances made by the Government'.[247] Although the CSA received support from the DAB and FTU, it was defeated because of the SVM. It was not rare practice of putting the commencement date of parent bill under the positive vetting procedure. On some occasions, the government was willing to table issues including the commencement dates of primary legislation under the positive vetting procedure as required by legislators.[248]

The case of Land (Compulsory Sale for Redevelopment) (Specification of Lower Percentage) Notice (the Notice hereafter) further shed light on the difference between the two vetting procedures. The Notice was published in the gazette and tabled before Legco in January 2010 under the negative vetting procedure. It aimed to lower the application threshold for compulsory land sales from 90 percentage to 80 percentage of the undivided shares in a lot.[249] The Notice aroused considerable controversy within the community as it concerned the right of private ownership of property. Furthermore, any incautious handling of such issues by the government was likely to create a public

244 Councillor James To's Speech, Hansard HK (26 June 2000), 8693.

245 Ibid.

246 Ibid.

247 Councillor Jasper Tsang's speech, Hansard HK (26 June 2000), 8700.

248 To's speech,, Hansard HK (26 June 2000), 8708.

249 Development Bureau, 'Legislative Council Brief on Land (Compulsory Sale for Redevelopment) (Specification of Lower Percentage) Notice' (DEVB(PL-UR)70/41/85, 2010), para 1.

perception that the legislation 'allows developers to force citizens to sell them their properties at reservation prices'.[250]

On 1 March 2010, the Subcommittee on the Notice passed a motion to urge the authorities to withdraw the Notice on the ground that the Notice 'cannot provide effective protection for minority owners' interests nor resolve building safety issues, and that the authorities have failed to set up a mediation mechanism promptly'.[251] During two-day debates over the legislation, six members moved 14 amendments but all were negatived. The Notice was ultimately carried without any amendments being passed on 17 March 2010. Of the 14 amendments, one moved by Councillor James To to delay the commencement date of the Notice for a year obtained 29 yes-votes and 22 no-votes, but it was finally defeated because of the SVM, with 11 to 16 votes in FCs.[252]

People may ask why such an important issue was examined by means of a less stringent legislative procedure, namely, the negative vetting procedure. It was the principal Ordinance, the Land (Compulsory Sale for Redevelopment) Ordinance (Cap 545) passed by the Provisional Legislative Council (PLC) on 7 April 1998 that authorises the CE in the Council to specify a percentage lower than 90% of the undivided shares in a lot by notice in the Gazette (s 3(5)). The provisions of the principal Ordinance secure the powerful control over the issue by the government. However, this is a highly debatable decision made by the PLC to deal with an issue concerning such important right of citizens through a relatively weaker vetting procedure, namely, no Legco's approval required. The motion carried by the Subcommittee and the voting result of members' amendments to delay the effect of the Notice have shed light on that the majority of Legco members had considerable reservations regarding the proposed lower threshold.

The SVM has provided more protection for the government when dealing with subsidiary legislation under the negative vetting procedure, thereby encouraging the government in seeking quick voting, rather than consensus in Legco and in the community. Accordingly, it is unsurprising that the executive branch and the legislature continue their fight for the power to control subsidiary legislation. The following study provides such a case of competition between the executive and legislature.

---

250 Editorial, '未保障小業主權益 強拍門檻不應降低 (Compulsory Sale Law should Protect Small Owners and Threshold should not be Lowered)', *Ming Pao Daily News* (16 March 2010), A03.

251 Legislative Council Secretariat, 'Report of the Subcommittee on Land (Compulsory Sale for Redevelopment) (Specification of Lower Percentage) Notice' (LC Paper No. CB(1)1362/09-10, 2010), para 53.

252 'Council Meeting (Voting Result) 17 March 2010' [web page] (2010) <http://www.legco.gov.hk/yr09-10/english/counmtg/voting/v201003172.htm>, accessed 20 October 2011.

### *Case Study: Country Parks (Designation) (Consolidation) (Amendment) Order 2010*

The Country Parks (Designation) (Consolidation) (Amendment) Order 2010 (the Order hereafter) originated in the government's plan to extend the South East New Territories landfill.[253] S 14 of the Country Parks Ordinance (Cap 208) stipulates that 'where the Chief Executive in Council has approved a draft map under s 13 and it has been deposited in the Land Registry, the Chief Executive shall, by order in the Gazette, designate the area shown in the approved map to be a country park'. On 4 June 2010, the CE gazetted a revised map of the Country Park by means of the Order. The existing map would be replaced with the newly approved map designated in the Order which excised 5 hectares from the area of Clear Water Bay Country Park to expand the landfill.[254]

The proposed landfill extension aroused grave concern and objections from Tseung Kwan O residents who were living quite near the landfill.[255] Under the negative vetting procedure, the Order was about to come into operation on 1 November 2010 unless it was repealed or amended by means of a resolution. In June 2010, a Subcommittee was established for deliberation of the Order, comprising five pro-democracy members and four pro-Beijing members. Councillor Tanya Chan, a member of the CP, was elected as the Chairperson.[256] The Subcommittee held one meeting to receive the views of the public and another six to meet with officials.[257] Given the odour problem in Tseung Kwan O, the Subcommittee passed a motion to request the CE to repeal the Order at its meeting held on 27 September 2010,[258] and the Chairperson gave notice of a resolution to repeal the proposed Order.

In its submissions to the President, the executive contended that member's resolution to repeal the Order was 'unlawful' on the ground that the resolution would be inconsistent with the CE's power to make the Amendment Order

253 Environmental Protection Department and Agriculture, Fisheries and Conservation Department, 'Legislative Brief on Country Parks (Designation) (Consolidation) (Amendment) Order 2010' (EP CR 9/25/15, 2010).

254 Ibid.

255 '擴建將軍澳堆填區遭反對 (Objections to Extension of Tseung Kwan O Landfill)', *Wen Wei Po*, 28 September 2010, A15.

256 Legislative Council Secretariat, 'Report of the Subcommittee on Country Parks (Designation) (Consolidation) (Amendment) Order 2010' (LC Paper No. CB(1)3017/09-10, 2010), 4.

257 Ibid.

258 Subcommittee on Country Parks (Designation) (Consolidation) (Amendment) Order 2010, 'Minutes of the Fourth Meeting Held on 27 September 2010' (LC Paper No. CB(1)38/10-11, 2010).

under s 14 of Cap 208.[259] And the statutory intention and purpose of Cap 208 were not 'to empower the CE to repeal the Amendment Order and undo the elaborate statutory process for the designation which covers several stages'.[260] The Department of Justice cited the legal advice of Mr Michael Thomas that s 14 imposed a duty upon the CE to designate the area of the country Park, which meant that the CE had no power to decide not to designate the area that had been approved by the CE in Council under s 14, notwithstanding some discretion on the timing and the commencement date of the Order.[261] In this case, 'the act of the CE in designating the newly mapped area by order in the Gazette constitutes the subsidiary legislation within the definition given in s 3 of Cap 1'.[262] As Legco has the same power as the original maker under s 34(2) of the IGCO, Legco did not have such power to repeal the Order.[263]

The President quoted Mr Philip Dykes' views on the constitutional principle that 'Legco must have effective oversight of the exercise of all legislative power and relevant legislation governing the exercise of law-making powers, such as the IGCO (Cap 1) should be construed so as to give effect to this principle'.[264] The President further stated that:

> My view is that Legco has the constitutional duty to scrutinise subsidiary legislation and correspondingly has the power to amend or repeal when it is appropriate to do so. The statutory provisions in any ordinance which grant powers to make subsidiary legislation should not in the absence of clear words or manifest legislative intention be interpreted to mean that Legco has abdicated its control over the exercise of those powers.[265]

Hence, the President should consider whether Legco 'had agreed to abdicate its control over the power for CE to make orders under section 14' when Cap

259 President's Ruling on Proposed Resolution to Repeal the Country Parks (Designation) (Consolidation) (Amendment) Order 2010 Proposed by Hon Tanya CHAN (7 October 2010), para 6.

260 Ibid., para 7.

261 See Department of Justice, 'Summary of the Advice Given by Mr Michael Thomas, Q.C., S.C. On the Power of Legco to Repeal the Country Parks (Designation) (Consolidation) (Amendment) Order 2010' (CB(1)2988/09-10(01), 2010), paras 7–8.

262 Ibid., para 5.

263 See the Administration's response, Department of Justice, 'Legal Implications Concerning Repeal of the Country Parks (Designation) (Consolidation) (Amendment) Order 2010' (CB(1)2976/09-10(01), 2010).

264 Ibid, para 16.

265 Ibid, para 18.

208 was passed.[266] As the CE's power to designate the proposed map by means of the Order published in the Gazette is the 'final step' in the statutory process for the designation, the act of the CE in designation is 'not merely for the purpose of notification'.[267] The President thus concluded that interpretations adopted by the executive 'clearly render the negative vetting procedure ineffective and deprive Legco of its function of overseeing the exercise of powers in relation to subsidiary legislation'.[268] The President ultimately made a decision to allow Councillor Tanya Chan to move her resolution.

The resolution was carried by 27 to 1, with one abstention in FCs, and by 28 to 1 in GCs.[269] In fact, two members voting against the resolution were members of the Exco, thereby casting their votes in line with the executive. Legco members reached an overwhelming consensus on the objection to the proposed Order. Critics believe that the government seemed to be negligent in a variety of potential disputes and factors such as the opposition from the district, the subsequent District Councils elections and the preservation of country parks.[270] Their electoral interest became the incentive for the LP and FTU to actively object to the extension of landfill and the DAB refused to offer its hand to the government in consideration of the political wind.[271]

After the passage of the resolution to repeal the Order, the government was planning to apply for a judicial review to clarify the powers of Legco.[272] However, the CE shortly issued a statement announcing that 'the government would not do anything [to extend the landfill] without the approval of the Legco'.[273] On 5 January 2011, then Chief Secretary Mr Henry Tang revealed that the government would not seek judicial review, notwithstanding maintaining its stance that Legco had no power to repeal the CE's Order.[274] The government's decision not to seek judicial review helped to avoid a constitutional

266 Ibid, para 20.

267 Ibid, para 22.

268 Ibid, para 23.

269 Hansard HK (13 October 2010).

270 Brian Fong, '廢令風波折射行政立法矛盾 (Repeal Resolution Reflected Executive-Legislative Conflict)', *Ming Pao Daily News*, 16 October 2010, A26.

271 Ibid.

272 '港府擬覆核立會堆填區"廢令" (Government will Seek Judicial Review to Quash Repeal Resolution)', *Sing Tao Daily*, 30 November 2010, A02.

273 '立會大比數廢堆填指令 (Legco Vetoed Tseung Kwan O Landfill Notice by a Landslide)', *Ming Pao Daily News*, 14 October 2010, A13.

274 '立會廢特首指令　政府不提覆核 (Government Decided not to File the Judicial Review)', *Ming Pao Daily News*, 5 January 2011, A06.

crisis temporarily. However, legal dispute over Legco's power to examine subsidiary legislation remains unresolved.

### *Summaries*

The President in his ruling on the Country Park Order clearly stated that Legco had no inclination to 'abdicate' its power to scrutinise subsidiary legislation, notwithstanding the huge number of subsidiary legislation which the executive has been delegated the power to deal with for reason of efficiency. The findings on the results of subsidiary legislation from 1998 to 2013 indicate that the most effective means to make changes in subsidiary legislation is to squeeze amendments or withdrawal from the executive. However, the effectiveness of such means has been declining since the third Legco term.

The fight for legislative power and public mandate has continued. The clash between the executive and the legislature has been intensified over the extent of Legco's power to examine subsidiary legislation. Despite unresolved legal disputes and heated debates from time to time, a solution of 'agree to disagree' in the case of the Country Park Order could be a feasible way to deal with such disputes and enable the legislature and the executive to fulfil their respective constitutional roles properly.

## Conclusion

The legislative power of the post-1997 Legco is considered incomplete,[275] because of not only the curtailment of initiation power but also the restrictions on the scrutiny of bills. In addition, subsidiary legislation proposed under the negative vetting procedure does not require Legco's prior approval.[276] However, despite the government's objections, the Presidents of Legco have established their exclusive authority over procedural matters concerning the introduction of private member's bills and members' CSAs, which defines Legco of the HKSAR as an autonomous legislature in terms of internal characteristics.

Most government bills, those with BCs formed in particular, were enacted with amendments that often incorporated members' recommendations, rather than in their original versions. Therefore, a major means employed by legislators to make a difference in legislation, including principal legislation and subsidiary legislation, is to force the government to proactively propose

275 Interview with Albert Ho on 17 February 2009.

276 Interpretation and General Clauses Ordinance, Cap 1, s 34 and s 35.

amendments, withdraw bills or offer assurances on specific issues. This interplay pattern of anticipated reactions demonstrates that the legislature maintains its impact on legislation without or rarely using the power to veto or amend legislation.

The line of division between the pro-Beijing camp and the pro-democracy camp remains the most important angle for observers to analyse the political groups within Legco and the executive-legislative relationship. However, the nature of the issues and public reactions to the issues have become influential determinants for the legislative process. Legislation on Article 23 clearly exemplifies how public opinion was conditioned and expressed through the forum of Legco committees, and how a public outcry and street protests have led to the split amongst the pro-Beijing camp within Legco in turn and ultimately the collapse of the bill.

Accordingly, a legislature with limited legislative power does not necessarily have a minor role in the legislative process. These findings in this chapter suggest a necessity to conduct more detailed analysis of committee work and explore the way in which individual political groups have interacted with the public and the executive branch, rather than merely relying on the pass rate of bills and members' CSAs.

CHAPTER 4

# Scrutiny of Public Finance

The aim of financial, or fiscal accountability is to keep citizens informed of the mobilisation of financial resources and their use in meeting the needs of the community and, ultimately, to avoid institutional recidivism and improve financial management.[1] The impetus for enhancing financial accountability may come in large part from distrust of the government and/or its officials.[2] With the shift in responsibility to representatives of the people or indeed to the people themselves, legislatures have become one of the most important governmental institutions for achieving financial accountability and transparency.[3] Legislative scrutiny of public finance is thus an obligation for legislatures the world over, and is a fundamental requirement enshrined in many constitutions.[4] Legislative scrutiny of budget proposals and other financial measures is particularly important in jurisdictions in which electoral accountability is weakly developed because such scrutiny is conducive to improving budget transparency and establishing broad-based consensus.[5]

The budget process comprises four distinct stages: the draft, legislative, execution and audit stages.[6] There is also a clear distinction between the oversight of future performance and that of past performance, that is, between *ex ante* scrutiny and *ex post* scrutiny.[7] *Ex ante* scrutiny focuses on the content and

1 Arigapudi Premchand, 'Public Financial Accountability', in Salvatore Schiavo-Campo (ed.), *Governance, Corruption, and Public Financial Management* (Manila: Asian Development Bank, 1999), 178.

2 Ibid., 152.

3 Ibid., 172–173.

4 Joachim Wehner, 'Assessing the Power of the Purse: An Index of Legislative Budget Institutions', *Political Studies*, 54 (2006) 767.

5 Ibid.

6 Joachim Wehner and Winnie Byanyima, 'Parliament, the Budget and Gender' (Inter-Parliamentary Union, United Nations Development Programme, World Bank Institute, and United Nations Fund for Women, 2004) <www.ipu.org/PDF/publications/budget_en.pdf>, accessed 20 October 2011, 30.

7 Riccardo Pelizzo and Rick Stapenhurst, 'Tools for Legislative Oversight: An Empirical Investigation', in Rick Stapenhurst et al. (eds.), *Legislative Oversight and Budgeting: A World Perspective* (Wbi Development Studies; Washington DC: World Bank, 2008), 13; Joachim Wehner, *Back from the Sidelines? Redefining the Contribution of Legislatures to the Budget Cycle* (Series on Contemporary Issues in Parliamentary Development; Washington DC: World

 | DOI 10.1163/9789004276284_005

direction of budget policy, whilst *ex post* scrutiny focuses on the quality of that policy's implementation.[8] In practice, the legislative scrutiny approach adopted varies by country, and generally corresponds to the country's constitutional structure, party politics and other country-specific elements.[9]

Westminster-style legislatures usually stress audit examination.[10] In Britain, for example, the Public Accounts Committee, one of the most important financial committees of the House of Commons, exercises *ex post* scrutiny of public finance.[11] However, this kind of *ex post* approach is less widely accepted in other countries, most notably the United States, which focuses on *ex ante* scrutiny.[12] Both Houses of the US Congress have unfettered powers to amend the President's draft annual budget.[13] Further, enactment of the Congressional Budget and Impoundment Control Act of 1974 saw the founding of a non-partisan Congressional Budget Office to support budget-related analyses and compile other budget information.[14]

Hong Kong's legislature has inherited most of the structural arrangements of the British parliament, including a standing Public Accounts Committee (PAC) and a passive role in approving budget proposals. The Finance Committee is the only Legco organ that examines budget proposals. In addition, most of the financial proposals submitted by the government need to be approved by the Finance Committee which receives recommendations from its two subcommittees: the Establishment Subcommittee (ESC) and Public Works Subcommittee (PWSC).

This chapter first discusses the constitutional restrictions on and institutional framework for financial scrutiny by Legco. It then analyses Legco's role at the budget and audit stages using data on the results of financial proposals and public hearings held by the PAC to show how and to what extent Legco affects public expenditure and supervises public finance.

---

Bank Institute, 2004), 5–6. Some researchers use terms of 'post facto' check and 'a priori' control, Nevil Johnson, 'Financial Accountability to Parliament', in Bruce L.R. Smith and Douglas Chalmers Hague (eds.), *The Dilemma of Accountability in Modern Government: Independence versus Control* (London: Macmillan, 1971), 283–291.

8 Wehner (n 7), 6.

9 Ibid., 8.

10 Johnson (n 7); Premchand (n 1).

11 Johnson, ibid., 284.

12 Ibid., 283.

13 Ian Lienert, 'Who Controls the Budget: The Legislature or the Executive?' (IMP WP/05/115, International Monetary Fund, 2005) <www.imf.org/external/pubs/ft/wp/2005/wp05115.pdf>, accessed 1 June 2014.

14 Ibid.

## Institutional Framework for Financial Scrutiny by Legco

### *Legco's Power to Amend and Approve Public Expenditure*

The constitutional basis of Legco's financial control power is established by Article 73 of the Basic Law. Article 73(2) and (3) read as follows: '[Legco shall exercise the following powers and functions] to examine and approve budgets introduced by the government; to approve taxation and public expenditure'. Article 64 of the Basic Law corresponds to these two clauses and provides that 'the Government of HKSAR...must be accountable to Legco...it shall obtain approval from the Council for taxation and public expenditure'. In accordance with these constitutional provisions, legislative endorsement is required for all budget, taxation and public expenditure issues, which ultimately ensures government accountability to Legco. Part II of the Public Finance Ordinance (PFO) (Cap 2) further stipulates the examination by Legco of revenue, expenditure and appropriation estimates.[15]

An Appropriation Bill is usually introduced together with the annual Draft Estimates of Expenditure, which contain the government's estimated expenditure on all services for the current or succeeding financial year.[16] After debate on the second reading of the Appropriation Bill has been adjourned, the expenditure proposals 'may be referred by the President of Legco to the Finance Committee for detailed examination before consideration of the Appropriation Bill in committee of the whole Council'.[17] Once the estimates of expenditure have been approved by Legco, 'no change shall be made except with the approval of the Finance Committee upon a proposal of the Financial Secretary'.[18] However, the Finance Committee may delegate authority to the Financial Secretary (FS) to approve changes subject to certain conditions.[19] For example, the FS has been delegated the power to:[20]

(a) approve supplementary provisions and to increase and create capital account commitments in respect of expenditure under the General Revenue Account each with a limit of $10 million;

15 See Public Finance Ordinance, Cap 2, s 6, 7, 8 and 9.
16 RoP, Rule 67(1).
17 RoP, Rule 71 (11); Finance Committee, 'The Appropriation Bill and the Estimates and Implementation of the Budget Proposals' (LC Paper No. FC48/10-11(01), 2011), 4.
18 Public Finance Ordinance, Cap 2, s 8(1).
19 Ibid., s 8(3).
20 Finance Committee (n 17).

(b) create Category D items in the Capital Works Programme each up to $21 million;
(c) create financial commitments each up to $10 million for projects on major systems and equipment, and computerization under the Capital Works Reserve Fund;
(d) establish and delete non-directorate posts subject to the establishment ceiling not being exceeded; and
(e) create supernumerary directorate posts for not more than six months.

Any other expenditure proposals require the approval of the Finance Committee. The ESC and PWSC may be appointed to assist the Finance Committee if the proposals concern the establishment of the government or use of the Capital Works Reserve Fund,[21] although the Finance Committee is not obliged to accept their recommendations.[22] Generally, all items submitted to the Finance Committee have been discussed by subcommittees or policy panels, but it is the Finance Committee itself that determines whether financial proposals are accepted.

The revenue proposals in budgets are often consolidated in a Revenue Bill or subsidiary legislation, and other taxation proposals are introduced in the form of bills or subsidiary legislation. Legco may set up Bills Committees or Subcommittees to deliberate such bills or subsidiary legislation and move amendments.

The examination of government accounts is another important aspect of financial scrutiny by Legco. As one of Legco's three Standing Committees, the PAC conducts *ex post* scrutiny by examining audit reports, holding public hearings, and producing conclusions and recommendations.

However, not all financial proposals require the prior approval of the Finance Committee or Legco. The PFO stipulates that any fee or charge payable to the government or any public body or public officer may be reduced or varied by order of the Chief Executive (CE), 'provided that no variation shall cause such fee or charge to exceed the original figure'.[23] In addition, there are a number of grey areas that require clarification, for instance, whether use of the Fiscal Reserve Fund requires Legco's approval and what the exact scope of general revenue is (see discussion in the following section).

21 RoP, Rule 71(5).

22 See Finance Committee Procedure, para 3.

23 Public Finance Ordinance, Cap 2, s 39A.

TABLE 4.1 *Restriction on members' power to move financial initiatives or amendments to financial proposals*

| Type of motion | Restriction | Related rule | Related article of the Basic Law |
|---|---|---|---|
| Private member's bills | Public expenditure | Rule51(3) | Article 74 |
| Members' CSAs | Charging effect | Rule 57(6) | – |
| Members' motions and amendments | Charging effect | Rule 31 | – |
| Members' amendments to the budget | Not increasing the sum | Rule 69(1) | – |

SOURCE: THE AUTHOR'S COMPILATION BASED ON THE BASIC LAW AND THE ROP.

### *Restrictions of 'Public Expenditure' and 'Charging Effect'*

Article 74 of the Basic Law stipulates that members shall not introduce bills relating to public expenditure, a stipulation that has been incorporated into Rule 51(3) of the Legco Rules of Procedure of Legco (RoP). Furthermore, Rule 57(6) of the RoP stipulates that amendments to bills, 'the object or effect of which may, in the opinion of the President or Chairman, be to dispose of or charge any part of the revenue or other public moneys of Hong Kong shall be proposed only by: (a) the Chief Executive; or (b) a designated public officer; or (c) a Member, if the Chief Executive consents in writing to the proposal'. The restriction of this 'charging effect' is also applicable to members' motions and amendments, according to Rule 31. With regard to amendments to Appropriation Bills, 'any amendment which, in the opinion of the Chairman of the Whole Committee, would increase the sum, shall only be moved by a designated public officer'.[24] Table 4.1 lists the restrictions on members' power to propose or amend financial proposals.

The President of Legco has ruled that 'public expenditure' in Article 74 and Rule 51(3) has no relevance to the 'charging effect' in Rule 57(6).[25] Moreover, the scope of public expenditure has been deemed wider than 'the disposal of or charging any part of the revenue or other public moneys of Hong Kong', namely, the 'charging effect'.[26]

24 RoP, Rule 69(1).

25 For the disputes surrounding Article 74 and the Rules, see Chapter 3 of this book.

26 Ruling by the President of the Legislative Council on the Labour Relations (Right to Representation, Consultation and Collective Bargaining) Bill Proposed by the Hon. LEE Cheuk-yan (19 July 1999), 20.

In 2006, the constitutional validity of Rule 57(6) was challenged by Councillor Leung Kwok Hung who applied for judicial review to seek two declarations: (1) that a member's Committee Stage Amendment (CSA) that has an impact on public expenditure or has a charging effect is not a bill relating to public expenditure within the meaning of Article 74 and, (2) that Rule 57(6), which seeks to preclude a Legco member from proposing a CSA that has a charging effect on revenue, contravenes Articles 73(1) and 74 of the Basic Law.[27]

The Court of First Instance (CFI) dismissed the application. The court held that it has jurisdiction to determine 'whether rules of procedure enacted by Legco are consistent with the Basic Law',[28] but noted that 'it is a jurisdiction which, having regard to the sovereignty of Legco under the Basic Law, should only be exercised in a restrictive manner'.[29] The court declined to determine the first declaration on the ground that it was not necessary to give a 'broad and definitive interpretation of the nature and effect…of art. 74' in the present case.[30] However, it did deem it necessary to 'consider Article 74 as a stepping-stone to determining the core issue' in the second declaration.[31] The court further held that 'Article 74 circumscribes the right of members before anything has been brought within the purview of Legco while proposing amendments to bills takes place after bills have been brought within the purview of Legco'.[32] Therefore, Article 74 should not be read as engaging the enacting process, and members' power to propose amendments is a matter independent of the scope of Article 74.[33] Accordingly, Rule 57(6) 'is not rendered inconsistent with the Basic Law by the application of Article 74'.[34]

This judgment established the jurisdiction of Hong Kong courts over the constitutional validity of the RoP, but it left open the question of whether Article 74 should be applied to members' CSAs. In practice, whilst the government has always maintained its stance with regard to the scope of Article 74's application, Legco Presidents have never applied the public expenditure restriction to any member initiatives other than private members' bills.

27 *Leung Kwok Hung v The President of The Legislative Council of The Hong Kong Special Administrative Region and Another* [2007] 1 HKLRD 387.

28 Ibid., para 24.

29 Ibid., para 31.

30 Ibid., para 44.

31 Ibid., para 45.

32 Ibid., para 69.

33 Ibid., para 71.

34 Ibid., para 72.

## *Ex ante* Scrutiny: Control over Budget and Public Expenditure

A Finance Committee responsible for examining all financial matters proposed by the Governor of Hong Kong was established in 1872.[35] The Finance Committee had the final say on government expenditure, giving its members a voice on public policies.[36] Since the return of sovereignty to China, the Finance Committee has consisted of all Legco members other than the President.[37] The Committee's function is to scrutinise and approve the public expenditure proposals put forward by the government,[38] the annual Draft Estimates of Expenditure and Appropriation Bills in particular. There are two major differences between the voting procedures of the Finance Committee and those of plenary meetings of Legco. First, a Separate Voting Mechanism is not applied to the Finance Committee,[39] and, second, 'a majority' in the Finance Committee means 'a majority of members *present and voting*', whilst votes in the whole Council are counted on the basis of the number of members *present* (emphasis added).

### *Examination of Budget Proposals*

After the introduction to Legco of estimates of expenditure in conjunction with an Appropriation Bill, the Finance Committee is charged with examining those estimates. Members may submit written questions within two weeks of the Bill's introduction. As Figure 4.1 shows, it is common for more than one thousand questions to be submitted. The Finance Committee holds consecutive special meetings at which the Directors of Bureaus, Heads of Departments and other controlling officers are invited to give preliminary answers to members' written questions and to explain the estimates to members,[40] who have an opportunity to follow up their concerns and queries. Upon resumption of the debate on the second reading of the Appropriation Bill, each member can speak about the estimates for up to fifteen minutes. Appropriation Bill debates usually last for two consecutive days, with voting taking place at the

---

35 See G.B. Endacott, *Government and People in Hong Kong 1841–1962: A Constitutional History* (Hong Kong: Hong Kong University Press, 1964).

36 Miners and Tang, *The Government and Politics of Hong Kong*, 134.

37 See RoP, Rules 71(1).

38 See Public Finance Ordinance, Cap 2, Part II.

39 RoP, Rule 71(5B).

40 See Finance Committee, 'Report on the Examination of the Estimates of Expenditure' (1998–2010); and interview with Councillor Emily Lau on 24 April 2009. Councillor Lau is a member of the Democratic Party.

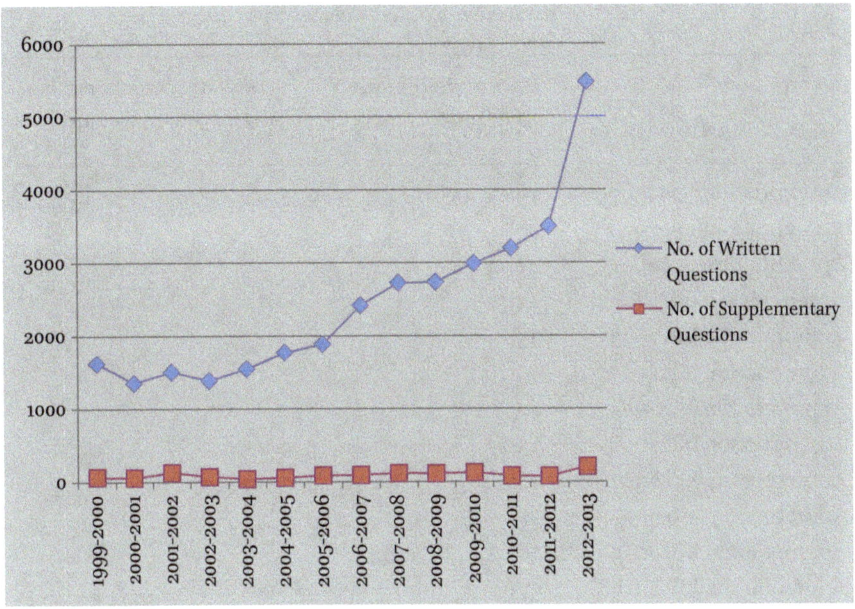


FIGURE 4.1 *Questions and Requests Raised by Members of the Finance Committee, 1998–2013*
SOURCE: THE AUTHOR'S COMPILATION BASED ON FINANCE COMMITTEE OF LEGCO, *REPORTS ON THE EXAMINATION OF THE ESTIMATES OF EXPENDITURE*, 1998–2013.

next plenary meeting. The presentations and explanations of government officials and statistics on members' questions are compiled and published in a *Report on the Examination of the Estimates of Expenditure* within several months of the Finance Committee finishing its work, usually in June.[41]

### Time Spent on Budget Proposals

Table 4.2 shows the amount of time spent by Legco on examination of the annual estimates of expenditure from 1998 to 2013. The number of days of deliberation indicates how many days Legco spent on an Appropriation Bill between its first and third readings. In its first term (1998–2000), Legco spent less than one month on Bill deliberation, whilst a marked increase was seen in its second term (2000–04), particularly in the days of deliberation over Appropriation Bill 2002. Since 2008, the deliberation process has usually taken nearly two months, with something of a record achieved in 2013 when Legco spent 83 days on the Appropriation Bill for that year because of a filibuster organised by members from People Power and the League of Social Democrats.

41 See Finance Committee, ibid.

TABLE 4.2 *Time spent on the examination of the estimates of expenditure, 1998–2013*

| Year of the bill | Days of deliberation* | Days of special meetings in the finance committee |
|---|---|---|
| Appropriation bill 1999 | 28 | 4 |
| Appropriation bill 2000 | 28 | 4 |
| Appropriation bill 2001 | 28 | 4 |
| Appropriation bill 2002 | 42 | 3 |
| Appropriation bill 2003 | 35 | 4 |
| Appropriation bill 2004 | 49 | 4 |
| Appropriation bill 2005 | 42 | 4 |
| Appropriation bill 2006 | 35 | 4 |
| Appropriation bill 2007 | 49 | 4 |
| Appropriation bill 2008 | 56 | 5 |
| Appropriation bill 2009 | 56 | 5 |
| Appropriation bill 2010 | 57 | 5 |
| Appropriation bill 2011 | 50 | 5 |
| Appropriation bill 2012 | 57 | 5 |
| Appropriation bill 2013 | 83 | 5 |

* Days are calculated between the Date of 1st Reading and the Date of Third Reading.
SOURCE: THE AUTHOR'S CALCULATION BASED ON HANSARD HK (1998–2013).

The Finance Committee generally meets over three to five consecutive days, inviting government officials and other relevant persons and organisations to provide information or explanations and/or to produce any records or documents the Committee requires in performing its duties.[42] Given the lengthier examinations of Appropriation Bills over time, special meetings, too, generally last longer, as shown in Table 4.2. The steady increase in the amount of time spent on budget proposals implies more intensive study by Legco members and more questions for government officials to answer, which may in turn be prompting government officials to exercise greater caution in expenditure planning.

### Members' Questions and Requests

There has indeed been a gradual increase in the number of written questions asked and requests made by Finance Committee members during their

42 RoP, Rule 71 (12).

examination of the estimates of expenditure. As Figure 4.1 shows, they rose from 1,616 in 1999 to 5,471 in 2013, and the number of supplementary questions has also increased accordingly. This growth in the number of questions/requests issued by members may have a connection with the gradual increase in the number of directly elected Legco seats between the 2000 and 2004 elections, with pro-democracy legislators now playing a more active role in monitoring the government. In addition, public awareness of the need for government transparency has also increased over the years, according to Councillor Emily Lau.[43] Legco members, particularly those who have been popularly elected, have a responsibility to enhance budgetary transparency by urging officials to explain the government's rationale for the allocation of resources. As all meetings of the Finance Committee are open to the public, the responses and explanations that officials provide are offered not only to legislators, but also to the general public directly.[44] More careful questions by members and honest and transparent responses from government officials are clearly helpful in enhancing public understanding of budget proposals.

### Members' Amendments to Appropriation Bills

After the Finance Committee completes its work on budget proposals, the Appropriation Bill undergoes a second reading in the Committee of the Whole Council. If members wish to amend the estimates of expenditure at this point, they need to move CSAs to the Bill. Between 1998 and 2012, sixty-two members' CSAs to Appropriation Bills were proposed.[45] All of them were moved by members of the pro-democracy camp, and all were negatived. The aim of some was to cut government posts by reducing executive expenditures. For example, Councillor Emily Lau proposed a CSA to cut the provisions of the Constitutional Affairs Bureau,[46] and Councillor Yeung Sum moved one stipulating a remuneration reduction for Deputy Directors of Bureaus and Political Assistants.[47] Councillor James To or one of his colleagues in the Democratic Party (DP) moves an amendment every year to scrap expenditure on the Complaints Against Police Office unit. None of these amendments was likely to pass, as the pro-Beijing camp would not allow such changes to the government structure. Therefore, the introduction of CSAs can more usefully be seen as political posturing to highlight the poor performance of certain government departments.

43 Ibid.

44 Ibid.

45 The author's calculation based on Hansard HK.

46 Hansard HK (9 April 2003) 5470.

47 Hansard HK (23 April 2008) 6330.

Members have the power to approve, reject or reduce the expenditures proposed in the Appropriation Bill.[48] However, many of them, particularly those sympathetic to grassroots issues, find it difficult to allocate resources to areas to which the government is unwilling to distribute funds through budget amendments. Furthermore, rejecting the full set of budget proposals poses a political risk because the government may be unable to function properly without its estimates of expenditure being passed. Consider the resolution on the annual provisional appropriation in 2011 as an example. After Legco vetoed it, the public's satisfaction with the overall performance of Legco members plunged sharply by ten percentage points.[49] An opinion poll credited the plunge to Legco's rejecting of the initial expenditure estimates.[50]

Therefore, the virtually all-or-nothing nature of the deliberation process on the estimates of expenditure considerably narrows the space for members to make a difference in the budget process. Accordingly, members and political groups regularly try to compel the FS to proactively offer giveaways and tax cuts and/or impose a freeze on fees and charges. To secure enough votes for the government's budget proposals, the FS often negotiates with the major political groups, particularly the pro-Beijing political forces. Concessions may also be made to minority members (usually democrats) if the FS hopes to earn greater support for budget proposals.[51] Further, the popularity rating for budget proposals amongst the public also tends to exert sometimes unexpected pressure on officials.

The controversy surrounding the 2011 Appropriation Bill is a case in point. The FS made a sudden swerve in the face of strong criticism of the budget proposals by the public, announcing that the government would hand out HK$6,000 to every Hong Kong Permanent Resident over the age of 18. The so called 'Scheme $6000' subsequently led to a budget deficit. Although the FS's move was criticised for deviating from the long-held principle of prudent financial management,[52] it constituted a substantive concession that exceeded public expectations. It is a clear case of the FS reacting to fierce public opposition that was reflected and conditioned by Legco members.

---

48 The situation is similar with that in the colonial era, Miners and Tang (n 36) 136.

49 The Public Opinion Programme of the University of Hong Kong, 'HKU POP Releases Figures of People's Satisfaction with Legco Members in general, the Hong Kong Police Force and the PLA Hong Kong Garrison', [Web Page] (12 April 2011), <http://hkupop.hku.hk/english/release/release823.html>, accessed 1 June 2014.

50 Ibid.

51 Interview with Councillor Lee Cheuk Yan on 11 February 2009.

52 Gary Cheung and Tanna Chong, 'Should John Tsang Resign, Government Survey Asks', *South China Morning Post*, 17 March 2011, EDT5.

### Negatived Government Revenue Proposals

Revenue Bills are proposed to give effect to the revenue proposals in the FS's budget speech. Any revenue proposals that would result in higher or lower levels of government revenue require Legco approval, with fee-hike proposals more likely to encounter opposition than fee-reduction proposals. The 1999–2001 period was a rather active one for blocking government fee hikes.

In 1999, the executive introduced an amendment to increase the maximum fees for the use of metered and pay-and-display parking spaces to HK$4.[53] This government amendment was negatived and resubmitted in the form of Revenue (No. 2) Bill 2001, which proposed increasing the maximum fees from HK$2 to HK$3, a smaller rise than that in Revenue Bill 1999. It was again blocked by members from the Democratic Alliance for the Betterment of Hong Kong (DAB), Hong Kong Federation of Trade Unions (FTU) and most pan-democrats. The revenue proposals in the proposed 2000–01 budget encountered the most defeats. In his budget speech, the FS proposed increases in tobacco duty, the duty on certain alcoholic beverages, driving licence and vehicle licence fees, and on-street parking meter charges,[54] of which only the tobacco and alcohol duty increases were approved. The proposed driving licence and vehicle licence fee hikes met strong cross-party opposition, with members from such major political parties as the Liberal Party (LP), DAB, DP and Hong Kong Confederation of Trade Unions (CTU) raising objections.

These defeats demonstrate that the coalition of Legco members between 1999 and 2001 extended beyond the usual divisions into pro-Beijing and pro-democracy camps and pro-business and pro-grassroots camps. In the face of such circumstances, the government was forced to formulate its proposals quite carefully and to attempt to secure every single vote through intensive lobbying. Hence, a cross-party coalition in Legco can pose a real threat to government proposals. The next section analyses the rise and fall of just such a coalition, which is commonly called the 'eight-party coalition'.

### Short-Lived Cross-Party Coalition

The precursor of the eight-party coalition was the 'seven parties and one group' established in 1998 to study 'the issue of people's livelihood and the ways to boost [the] economy'.[55] During the 2001–02 session, an eight-party coalition was proposed by Councillor Emily Lau and convened by LP leader Councillor

53 Hansard HK (8 July 1999), 9798.

54 The Financial Secretary's speech on 2001–02 budget, see Hansard HK (7 March 2001) 3874.

55 Hansard HK (8 July 1998).

James Tien. The coalition was a loose non-political coalition comprising seven political parties and the Breakfast Group, a loosely affiliated group primarily comprising Functional Constituency members. The first parties to join were the LP, CTU and The Frontier, and the second were DAB, the Hong Kong Political Alliance (HKPA), the Hong Kong Association for Democracy and People's Livelihood (ADPL) and the Breakfast Group.[56]

Councillor James Tien connected the powerful influence of the eight-party coalition with the ongoing economic downturn.[57] It was also noted that because neither 2001 nor 2002 was an election year, there was no fierce competition amongst the political parties.[58] Regardless of the reasons for its growing influence, the eight-party coalition provoked wide-ranging discussion in the community at large in the 2001–02 session, as shown in Table 4.3. The then Secretary for Constitutional Affairs recognised that ideas originating from the eight-party coalition were 'valuable in facilitating the government's governance'.[59] The coalition reached its zenith in the 2001–02 session, when it comprised 50 Legco members, although its influence has declined in the years since.

This instance of cross-party cooperation began with what became known as the Seven-point Consensus on 9 October 2001, which was directed primarily at the CE's Policy Address. Although the CE said that the government had adopted six of the seven-point consensus,[60] in fact, fewer proposals had actually been accepted by the government. As Table 4.4 shows, members' suggestions to reduce the rents for public housing and shops under Housing Authority management and defer the payment of salaries tax were both rejected. The coalition held several meetings and proposed more suggestions concerning the

56 '八黨: 民生合作政治免問 (Eight-Party Coalition: Yes for People's Livelihood, No for Politics)', *Wen Wei Po*, 17 August 2002, A09; '政府圖瓦解八黨聯盟 (Government Tended to Disintegrate the Eight-Party Coalition)', *Apple Daily*, 2 April 2002, A17.

57 Mr James Tien said that eight-party coalition appeared in 2001 for the bad economy. See Smile Cheung, '田北俊: 集體負責及保密制已過時 (James Tien: Principles of Collective Accountability and Confidentiality have been Outdated)', *Hong Kong Economic Journal*, 17 June 2002, P24.

58 '八黨聯席前景未定 (Uncertain Future of the Eight-Party Coalition)', *Ming Pao Daily News*, 22 August 2002, B12.

59 See Stephen Lam Sui-lung's speech at the RTHK programme commemorating the 10th anniversary of Party Line, 'Political parties key gauge of public opinion' [web page] (23 November 2002), <http://archive.news.gov.hk/isd/ebulletin/en/category/administration/021125/html/021125e01002.htm>, accessed 20 October 2011.

60 See the CE's answer to questions on Policy Address in Legco, Hansard HK (11 October 2001) 51.

TABLE 4.3 *Articles containing 'Eight-party Coalition/八黨聯盟' in Hong Kong newspapers, 1998–2010*

| Session | Number of relevant articles in newspaper |
|---|---|
| 1998–2001 | 0 |
| 2001–2002 | 328 |
| 2002–2003 | 48 |
| 2003–2004 | 39 |
| 2004–2005 | 22 |
| 2005–2006 | 14 |
| 2006–2007 | 12 |
| 2007–2008 | 6 |
| 2008–2009 | 2 |
| 2009–2010 | 4 |

SOURCE: THE AUTHOR'S CALCULATION BASED ON SEARCH RESULT OF THE HEADLINE OR CONTENT WITH KEY WORDS 'EIGHT-PARTY COALITION' OR '八黨聯盟' IN ARTICLES OF 38 HONG KONG NEWSPAPERS WHICH ARE AVAILABLE IN WISENEWS DATABASE.

budget proposals, including more specific fee-cut proposals such as waiving water and sewerage charges and reducing tuition fees, medical charges, business registration fees, and vehicle and driving licence fees. These suggestions, along with some of the government's seven-point response, were mentioned to varying degrees by the FS in his budget proposals.

It should be noted that there was a deficit budget at the time, and public finances were facing considerable pressure from the continuing economic downturn. In fact, at the outset of his policy address, the CE limited the maximum amount to be waived from public housing rents to HK$2,000[61] and firmly rejected suggestions to waive water and sewerage charges. He also announced that the government had appointed an Advisory Committee to study ways to increase government revenue through a broader-based tax system. However, several months later, the FS decided to waive water and sewerage charges, and announced that the level of rent waivers for public housing would increase to HK$5,000. In addition, no new tax levies were created. This very clear shift in policy can be traced by observing the budget proposal drafting process, which in turn reflects the influence of the eight-party coalition.

61 See CE's Policy Address in 2001, Hansard HK (10 October 2001) para 103.

TABLE 4.4 *Eight-party consensus on the 2001–02 budget proposals and government response*

| Date | Eight-party consensus | Related motion | Government response |
|---|---|---|---|
| Seven-point package on economic relief measures on 9 October 2001 | Waiving the government rates for all the four quarters | Motion on 2/6/2002 was approved unanimously. | Budget Speech: to reduce rates payments, by raising the level of waiver from $2,000 to $5,000. |
| | Creating 20 000 temporary posts in addition to posts created by infrastructural projects | | Policy Address speech: 30 000 Jobs opportunities will be created.[62] |
| | Expediting infrastructural projects to create more jobs | | Policy Address speech mentioned this point.[63] |
| | Reducing the rentals for shopping arcades and markets under the management of the Housing Authority | Motion on 1/16/2002 was approved unanimously. | rejected |
| | Reducing public housing rents | Motion on 1/16/2002 was approved unanimously. | rejected |
| | Deferring salaries tax payment | Motion on 10/24/2001 was amended and approved. | rejected |

62 Ambrose Leung, 'Budget Met Our Needs, Says Coalition', *South China Morning Post*, 9 March 2002, EDT4.

63 See Mrs Selina Chow's speech on CE's Policy Address, Hansard HK (17 October 2001) 180.

| | | | |
|---|---|---|---|
| | Alleviating the mortgage repayment burden on owners of negative equity | | HKMA issued a letter to banks indicating that banks may, in dealing with remortgages on loans charged on negative assets, disregard the ceiling for loan amounts. |
| 11/14/2001 | Reducing the fares of various public transport services. | Motion on 11/14/2001 was approved unanimously. | The official's speech: The Government will contact all public transport operators to encourage them to consider it. |
| 11/28/2001 | Reducing water fee and sewerage fee | Motion on 11/28/2001 was approved unanimously. | Budget Speech: to waive water and sewerage charges for one year. |
| 11/28/2001 | Encouraging various utility operators to reduce charges or offer concessions; | Motion on 11/28/2001 was approved unanimously. | Officials' speech: to reflect to the public utilities the consensus of this Council on demanding them to reduce fees or provide concessions. |
| 12/5/2001 | Reducing tuition, medical charges, business registration fees, and vehicle licence and driving licence fees; | Motion on 12/5/2001 was approved unanimously. | Budget Speech: to waive business registration fee for one year; to freeze government fees and charges for one year. |

SOURCE: THE AUTHOR'S COMPILATION IS BASED ON THE FOLLOWING SOURCES: CE'S POLICY ADDRESS IN 2001, HANSARD HK (10 OCTOBER 2001) AND OFFICIALS' SPEECH IN LEGCO, HANSARD HK (14 NOVEMBER 2001); THE FINANCIAL SECRETARY'S SPEECH ON 2001–02 BUDGET, HANSARD HK (7 MARCH 2001).

The ways in which the coalition forced the government to accept its proposals are clearly delineated: first, by seeking consensus amongst the eight constituent parties; second, by negotiating with the FS and CE or with other officials; and, finally, by moving motions urging the government to accept members' proposals. By moving motions with cross-party support, the coalition was able to successfully press the government for more concessions. It would have been unwise, and politically dangerous, for the government to completely disregard the opinion of Legco as a whole, particularly as such measures as fee reductions and freezes generally have widespread popular support. This approach to negotiation proved effective to a certain extent. In fact, despite the criticism of unresolved employment problems and other unacceptable proposals, Councillor James Tien said the coalition was satisfied with the relief measures promised in the budget.[64]

Although the coalition obviously exerted influence when it came to livelihood issues and helping to alleviate the financial burden imposed on the public to some extent, consensus was limited to the 'highest common factor' acceptable to all eight parties.[65] In other words, to achieve cross-party agreement, many more contentious proposals had to be abandoned or at least downgraded. The existence of the coalition did effect changes in the political environment, however. In August 2002, the DAB leader and James Tien were appointed Executive Council (Exco) members by the CE. Both appointments, particularly that of Councillor James Tien, were clearly related to the coalition's influence.[66] With the resignation of Councillor James Tien as the fixed convener and the break-up of the Breakfast Group, its decline seemed inevitable. In the subsequent 2002–03 session, only four suggestions were proposed in the name of the remaining seven-party coalition, only two of which were specific proposals requiring extension of the tax concession.[67]

As a matter of fact, pro-democracy members are more likely to yearn for an active cross-party coalition, as the pro-Beijing political parties and groups have more opportunities to communicate with and get positive and exclusive responses from the government. In view of the potential influence of cross-party coalitions, the government has consistently sought to disintegrate alliances amongst legislators.

64 'Government Tended to Disintegrate the Eight-Party Coalition' (n 56).

65 Hansard HK (2 April 2003) 5085.

66 Legislative Council Secretariat, 'Background brief for the special meeting of Panel on Manpower on 23 November 2010' (LC Paper No. CB(2)343/10-11(02), 2011) 1.

67 Legislative Council Secretariat, 'Background brief for the special meeting of Panel on Manpower on 4 January 2011' (LC Paper No. CB(2)680/10-11(01), 2011) 2.

The government's strategy can clearly be seen at work during deliberations on other financial proposals such as the Work Incentive Transport Subsidy Scheme (WITSS). The WITSS was launched in October 2011 to replace, and expand, the transport subsidy scheme introduced in 2006.[68] Although the new scheme covered many more employees from low-income families than did the original scheme, Legco passed a motion requesting the government to apply a means test based on a household or individual basis and to provide a transport subsidy to part-time workers.[69] On the eve of voting in the Finance Committee, Councillor Lee Cheuk Yan from the Confederation of Trade Unions succeeded in canvassing about 35 members to adjourn the vote on the scheme.[70] However, some members from FTU and the Professional Forum changed their minds after Secretary for Labour and Welfare Matthew Cheung made partial concessions to several pro-Beijing legislators during negotiations.[71] Accordingly, the *ad hoc* cross-party coalition convened by Councillor Lee collapsed within hours. It appears that the government would rather provide concessions to pro-Beijing members alone than negotiate with a powerful coalition.[72]

### *Examination of Other Financial Proposals*

In addition to budget proposals, most other financial proposals, such as those concerning capital investments, civil service remuneration, loan funds and social welfare expenditure, also require the approval of the Finance Committee. Furthermore, the Finance Committee also receives periodic reports on the progress of public works and projects from the executive.

As Table 4.5 shows, from 1998 to 2013, the Finance Committee voted on 1,106 non-budget financial proposals. Of these proposals, eight were negatived by the Finance Committee, 17 were withdrawn by the government and seven were adjourned. 127 were voted on with a division, which means that there was some controversy associated with them and, accordingly, some legislators wished to record their voting behaviour. Even approved proposals did not always have smooth passage through the Finance Committee, with some approved only with government amendments.[73]

68 'Transport Subsidy Funding Attempt Takes a New Twist', *South China Morning Post*, 17 February 2011, EDT2.

69 '交津允兩讓步 通過在望 (WITSS is Expected to Pass with Two Government Concessions)', *Ming Pao Daily News*, 17 February 2011, A03.

70 Interview with President Jasper Tsang on 22 July 2011.

71 CE's Policy Address in 2001, Hansard HK (10 October 2001) 29.

72 Ibid.

73 Discussion on item PWSC(2002–03)95, Finance Committee, 'Minutes of Meeting Held on 16 May 2003' (LC Paper No. FC136/02-03, 2003).

TABLE 4.5 *Result of non-budget financial proposals, 1998–2013*

| Session | Passed* | Negatived | Withdrawn | Adjourned | Total | Division requested |
|---|---|---|---|---|---|---|
| 1998–2000 | 193 | 3 | 8 | 0 | 204 | 27 |
| 2000–2004 | 292 | 3 | 7 | 2 | 304 | 33 |
| 2004–2008 | 261 | 0 | 1 | 0 | 262 | 29 |
| 2008–2012 | 273 | 2 | 1 | 3 | 279 | 27 |
| 2012–2013 | 55 | 0 | 0 | 2 | 57 | 11 |
| Total | 1074 | 8 | 17 | 7 | 1106 | 127 |

* The number under this category excludes those resubmitted proposals.
SOURCE: THE AUTHOR'S CALCULATION BASED ON MINUTES OF THE FINANCIAL COMMITTEE OF LEGCO (1998–2013).

Of the eight negatived proposals, six were voted down before 2008, including two related to transport issues, one aiming to retain a supernumerary post and the remaining three concerning a home starter loan scheme, the ex-gratia allowances arising from clearances and operational expenses for University Grants Committee-funded institutions. The two remaining negatived proposals were vetoed in 2011. One aimed to provide funding to the higher education sector, and was voted down because the government did not comply with members' requirement to freeze tuition fees,[74] and the other concerned the financial implications of Hong Kong hosting the Asian Games in 2023.[75] The government revised and resubmitted three of the eight negatived proposals, two of which were eventually carried by the Finance Committee.

Of the 17 withdrawn proposals, 12 were resubmitted and eventually approved, and some were returned to subcommittees or panels. Although proposals were withdrawn for a variety of reasons, most were withdrawn for failing to satisfy members of the Finance Committee. On 15 January 1999, for example, the Administration withdrew a new item proposed by the Civil Engineering Department after the Chairman of the Finance Committee advised that 'the proposal should be discussed at greater length at the relevant Panel' on the ground that members' request for more detailed information had

74 Discussion on item FCR(2011–12)55, Finance Committee, 'Minutes of Meeting Held on 9 December 2011' (LC Paper No. FC87/11-12, 2011).

75 Discussion on item FCR(2010–11)54, Finance Committee, 'Minutes of Meeting Held on 14 January 2011' (LC Paper No. FC116/10-11, 2011).

not been satisfied.[76] In another instance, it was suggested that a proposal concerning computerisation of the offices of the Hong Kong Police Force be resubmitted after the government had briefed the Panel on Security.[77]

Deliberation on financial proposals other than budget proposals is conducted not only by the Finance Committee, but also by relevant subcommittees and panels. As Table 4.6 shows, to date more than 30 per cent of financial proposals have been discussed by the ESC or PWSC and then recommended to the Finance Committee. Panels undertake even more careful deliberations before proposals are put forward in Finance Committee meetings. This committee system facilitates the effective scrutiny of the progress of public works and projects by Legco, prevents overspending and controls expenditure on government posts.

### *Collapsed Levies*

In addition to the revenue proposals in budgets, the government also proposes other levies and makes taxation proposals from time to time. In the past, some of these have been related to taxation reform, for example, the proposals for a

TABLE 4.6 *Proportions of non-budget financial proposals with recommendation of subcommittees, 1998–2013*

| Session | Financial proposals with recommendation of subcommittees | Financial proposals deliberated by finance committee | Perc. |
|---|---|---|---|
| 1998–2000 | 75 | 204 | 36.76 |
| 2000–2004 | 118 | 304 | 38.81 |
| 2004–2008 | 111 | 262 | 42.37 |
| 2008–2012 | 84 | 279 | 30.11 |
| 2012–2013 | 15 | 57 | 26.32 |
| Total | 403 | 1106 | 36.44 |

SOURCE: THE AUTHOR'S CALCULATION BASED ON MINUTES OF THE FINANCIAL COMMITTEE OF LEGCO (1998–2013).

76 Discussion on item FCR(98–99)64, Finance Committee, 'Minutes of Meeting Held on 15 January 1999' (LC Paper No. FC119/98-99, 1999).

77 Discussions on item FCR (98–99)83, Finance Committee, 'Minutes of Meeting Held on 12 March 1999' (LC Paper No. FC156/98-99, 1999).

Goods and Services Tax (GST) and Boundary Facilities Improvement Tax (BFIT), whilst others have concerned policy changes, for example, the Employees Retraining Levy on foreign domestic helpers (FDHs).

The GST was recommended as a new revenue source in 2002 by the Advisory Committee on New Broad-based Taxes, which was appointed by the then Financial Secretary in May 2000.[78] At the time, Hong Kong had just come out of a deep economic recession, and the government had reported successive operating deficits since the 1998–99 financial year.[79] According to the Advisory Committee, a GST could be adopted over the longer term to raise additional revenue to help resolve Hong Kong's structural fiscal problem.[80] In July 2006, the government published a consultation document considering several alternative ways of broadening the tax base, which recommended the GST as the most viable option.[81] There was considerable debate about the need to broaden the tax base and the regressive nature of a GST,[82] and the consultation document sparked a series of demonstrations against the proposed tax.[83] On 19 October 2006, Councillor Yeung Sum moved a motion against the GST's introduction, which was carried by Legco.[84] Given the strong public opposition to the tax, the government announced in its Interim Report in December 2006 that it would proceed no further with it.[85]

The introduction of the BFIT constituted another government attempt to broaden the tax base. It would have levied a departure tax on land and sea passengers, with the resulting revenue used to finance the improvement of boundary facilities.[86] Public discussion of a land and/or sea departure tax was

78 Advisory Committee on New Broad-Based Taxes, 'Report of the Advisory Committee on New Broad-Based Taxes' (2002) <http://www.fstb.gov.hk/tb/en/docs/btreport.pdf>, accessed 20 October 2011, 25.

79 See the Financial Secretary's speech on 2000–2001 Budget Bill, Hansard HK (7 March 2001) 3881.

80 Advisory Committee on New Broad-Based Taxes (n 78).

81 The Consultation Document was entitled 'Broadening the Tax Base, Ensuring Our Future Prosperity. What's the Best Option for Hong Kong?' [Web Page] (2006), <http://www.taxreform.gov.hk/eng/doc_and_leaflet.htm>, accessed 20 October 2011.

82 Shu Hung Tang, 'A Critical Review of the 2006 Consultation Document on Broadening the Tax Base in Hong Kong', *Asia-Pacific Journal of Taxation*, 10 (2006) 38.

83 Richard Cullen and Richard Simmons, 'Tax Reform and Democratic Reform in Hong Kong: What Do the People Think?', *British Tax Review*, 6 (2008) 671–672.

84 Hansard HK (19 October 2006) 479.

85 Financial Services and the Treasury Bureau, 'Public Consultation on Tax Reform Interim Report', <http://www.taxreform.gov.hk/eng/pdf/interim.pdf>, accessed 20 October 2011.

86 Legislative Council Secretariat, 'Background Brief' (LC Paper No. CB(1) 2114/02-03, 2003).

long-standing, and as early as 10 November 1999, Councillor Lau Kong Wah, a DAB member, moved a motion to oppose the levying of a land departure tax.[87] The vote was very close, but the motion was ultimately negatived. In June 2003, the government then introduced the BFIT Bill to Legco, where it immediately encountered opposition from the major political parties, including DAB, DP and HKPA.[88] Anticipating the failure of the Bill, on 22 October 2003 the FS issued a statement announcing that the government would proceed no further with the BFIT at the current juncture, given that 'the public [was] not yet ready to accept this tax'.[89]

Both of the aforementioned proposals came within the purview of tax reform by the government with the aim of overturning the budget deficit, although the reasons for their demise differ. The prospect of a GST sparked a wave of public protest on the streets of Hong Kong, and political parties from across the political spectrum expressed hostility to the taxation proposal.[90] In the case of the BFIT, in contrast, despite the opposition of the major political parties, there was no strong opposition from the general public. In fact, according to a poll conducted by the University of Hong Kong, 61 per cent of Hong Kong residents agreed to the imposition of a BFIT starting from the 2003–04 financial year.[91] Having the final say over taxation proposals, however, the major political parties of Legco had a decisive impact upon the government's decision to withdraw the BFIT proposal. The decisive role of the major political groups in Legco is also found in the case of the Employees Retraining Levy (also known as the Foreign Domestic Helper Levy).

The Employees Retraining Levy commenced in 1992.[92] In February 2003, the CE in Council approved a recommendation that the employers of FDHs be

87 One of reasons for the opposition on land and sea departure tax by the DAB was that, departure tax implied the notion of 'two countries' which was inconsistent with the concept of 'one country, two systems', Hansard HK (10 November 1999) 1053.

88 '三大黨反對 民建聯促撤邊境稅(BFIT Opposed by Three Major Political Parties)', *Ming Pao Daily News*, 25 September 2003, A10.

89 See the statement on 'Hong Kong's Economy and the Management of Public Finances' by the FS in Legco, Hansard HK (22 October 2003) 455.

90 Cullen and Simmons (n 83) 673.

91 For the result of the poll, see The Public Opinion Programme at the University of Hong Kong, 'HKU POP site Releases the Findings of the Budget Follow-up Survey and the Latest Figures on People's Ratings of the CE Tung Chee-hwa, the CS Donald Tsang Yam-kuen and the FS Antony Leung Kam-chung', [web page] (9 April 2002), <http://hkupop.hku.hk/english/archive/release/release34.html>, accessed 20 October 2011.

92 House Committee, 'Report of the Subcommittee on Employees Retraining Ordinance (Amendment of Schedule 3) Notice 2008' (LC Paper No. CB(2)264/08-09, 2009) 1.

subject to the Levy with effect from 1 October 2003.[93] Owing to an application for judicial review against the Levy's imposition by a number of FDHs, use of the Levy by the Employees Retraining Board was initially suspended.[94] However, the application was dismissed by the CFI, with its decision further upheld by the Court of Appeal in 2006.[95]

In July 2008, with the approval of the CE in Council, the Employees Retraining Ordinance (Amendment of Schedule 3) Notice 2008 (Amendment Notice hereafter) was gazetted to suspend the Levy for two years with effect from August 2008, which meant that the Levy might be imposed again after August 2010. Legco subsequently established a subcommittee to deliberate on the proposed Amendment Notice under the negative vetting procedure. Legislators were split over the suspension period. Those in the democratic camp and some independents contended that the Levy on FDHs should be abolished entirely, a measure that a number of pro-labour legislators in the pro-Beijing camp opposed.[96] Members proposed four amendments seeking to suspend the Levy for different periods of time.[97] Councillor Regina Ip's amendment seeking to abolish the Levy indefinitely was supported by most members of the subcommittee, and was subsequently adopted as its proposed amendment.[98] Despite the government's objection, the Legco President then approved Councillor Ip's amendment.[99] On 11 November 2008, the government abandoned the Amendment Notice and issued the No. 2 Amendment Notice, which proposed suspending the Levy for five years, as suggested by DAB members.[100] Councillor Ip's amendment to the No. 2 Amendment Notice was finally vetoed by 28 to 28, with the government's compromise proposal thus taking effect.

This is a typical case of the government making a compromise to secure enough votes in Legco. As the issue involved little political dispute,

---

93 Ibid.

94 Legislative Council Secretariat, 'Report of the Subcommittee on Employees Retraining Ordinance (Amendment of Schedule 3) Notice 2008' (LC Paper No. CB(2)264/08-09, 2009) 1.

95 *Julita F Raza and Others v Chief Executive in Council and Others* [2005] 3 HKLRD 561.

96 See House Committee (n 92) 3–4.

97 Ibid., 4.

98 Ibid.

99 President's Ruling on Proposed Resolutions to Amend the Employees Retraining Ordinance (Amendment of Schedule 3) (No. 2) Notice 2008 Proposed by Hon Mrs Regina IP LAU Suk-yee and Hon LEE Wing-tat (8 December 2008).

100 Ibid., 11.

cooperation across the political spectrum was able to exert a substantial influence on the government's decision.

### *Means of Scrutinising Budget and Taxation Issues*

It is evident that Legco lacks adequate 'proactive powers'.[101] Members are unable to propose expenditure increases, a limitation that is said to prevent members from pleasing voters by forcing the government to hand out goodies. However, it has also eliminated the possibility of putting forward proposals for the allocation of resources for policies that the government is reluctant to support. Another disadvantage that members face is that Appropriation Bills take the form of a bundled package, meaning that members must be highly cautious in using their veto power to block them. Even those members who have voted against budget bills in the past are not generally aiming to vote down the entire bill, but rather to express their discontent and embarrass the FS.

Nevertheless, the utilisation of powers to increase expenditure or to veto financial proposals is not necessary required for Legco to have an impact. The rise of the eight-party coalition in 2001 proves that legislators can make a substantial impact when they engage in cross-party cooperation. 'Anticipated reactions', or 'anticipated opposition', have become a major avenue for Legco members to squeeze concessions from the government without voting down or moving amendments to budget proposals. In addition, Legco committees, including subcommittees (PWSC and ESC) and panels, play a crucial role in shaping the final form of non-budget financial proposals. On the one hand, the deliberation of subcommittees and panels lightens the workload of the Finance Committee and allows specialisation in policy issues. On the other, it offers opportunities for the government to react promptly to potential controversy.

However, cross-party coalitions and effective committee work depend on the interaction between political groups within Legco and relations between those political groups and the executive. Owing to the government's explicit hindrance and the difficulty in practice of reaching consensus across the political divide, cross-party cooperation in Legco is on the decline. In addition, since the anti-Guangzhou-Shenzhen-Hong Kong Express movement and filibuster of 2010, the internal operation of committees, particularly that of the Finance Committee, has faced the challenge of growing polarisation.

---

101 For 'proactive powers', see Cox and Morgenstern, 'Latin America's Reactive Assemblies and Proactive Presidents', 172.

## *Ex Post* Scrutiny: The Public Accounts Committee

The importance of PACs to financial scrutiny in Westminster-style parliaments is well recognised.[102] These committees have been described as the 'ultimate institutional judge' in the *ex post* scrutiny of regularity, propriety and value for money.[103] Recent studies and observations of PACs highlight their 'non-partisanship' and 'non-policy' orientation as significant features conducive to their effectiveness.[104] According to a report issued by the Commonwealth Parliament Association, an 'ideal committee' is relatively small and adequately resourced. Moreover, it holds open hearings, publishes formal and substantive reports, and establishes a procedure with the government for following up on its work.[105] Although the composition and power of PACs vary by institutional arrangements and constitutional provisions, the effectiveness of their work is ultimately dependent on the extent to which the government accepts and implements their recommendations. Therefore, this section considers the record of Legco's PAC in monitoring public money, and analyses the factors that facilitate and hinder its work.

Similar to the organisation of many other Legco committees, the PAC system in Hong Kong mirrors the structure and practical rules of the British parliament. The PAC of the House of Commons was established—as early as 1857 as an independent audit agency of the legislature tasked with overseeing government accounts.[106] In subsequent years, its objectives came to include not only regularity, but also economy, effectiveness and efficiency.[107] These objectives are also valued by the Legco PAC, which is responsible for considering the Audit Commission reports issued by the Director of Audit, and making further

102 Joachim Wehner, 'Principles and Patterns of Financial Scrutiny: Public Accounts Committees in the Commonwealth', *Commonwealth & Comparative Politics*, 41 (2003) 21.

103 The CPA Parliamentary Financial Scrutiny Workshop, 'Parliamentary Financial Scrutiny: The Role of Public Accounts Committees (PACs)' (Commonwealth Parliamentary Association, World Bank Institute, and La Trobe University, 2006) <http://www.agora-parl.org/sites/default/files/pacs.pdf>, accessed 20 October 2011.

104 For 'non-partisanship' and 'policy neutrality', see (n 102) 25; for 'non-policy', see David Mcgee, 'Strengthening Financial Scrutiny', *53rd Commonwealth Parliamentary Conference* (New Delhi, India, 21–30 September 2007).

105 See Commonwealth Parliamentary Association (n 103) 10.

106 Premchand (n 1) 150.

107 The Committee of Public Accounts of the House of Commons, 'Holding Government to Account: 150 Years of the Committee of Public Accounts' (House of Commons, 2007) <http://www.parliament.uk/documents/upload/PAC%20History%20booklet%20pdf%20version_P1.pdf>, accessed 20 October 2011.

investigations into cases of waste and inefficiency and cases in which officials have failed to collect all revenue and payments due to the government.[108]

### *Objectives of the PAC*

Established in 1978, the PAC is one of Legco's Standing Committees.[109] Its meetings have been open to the public since 1984.[110] It generally comprises seven members, who are appointed by the Legco President in accordance with the election procedure established by the House Committee.[111] In practice, the membership of the PAC roughly corresponds to the distribution of Legco, and is thus representative of the major political groups.

The functions discharged by Legco in the colonial period remain effective under the RoP, which stipulates that the PAC shall consider the Report of the Director of Audit:[112]

(a) on the accounts of the Government;
(b) on such other accounts required to be laid before the Council as the committee may think fit; and
(c) on any matter incidental to the performance of his duties or the exercise of his powers as the committee may think fit.

In addition, it also considers Director of Audit reports dealing with value for money (VFM).[113]

Each year, the Director of Audit submits one report on the regular audit and two reports on VFM to the President of Legco. The PAC then selects and investigates any serious irregularities or shortcomings highlighted in these reports.[114] Within three months of the Director of Audit submitting audit reports, the PAC issues a report containing its conclusions and recommendations.[115] Government minutes in response to the PAC report should then be issued within three months of the PAC report's publication.[116] Although the

108 Miners and Tang (n 36) 140.

109 Ibid.

110 Ibid.

111 RoP, Rule 72(3).

112 RoP, Rule 72 (1).

113 RoP, Rule 72(2).

114 Public Accounts Committee, 'PAC Report No. 30' (1999) <http://www.legco.gov.hk/yr99-00/english/pac/report/pac-r30.pdf>, accessed 1 June 2014, 5.

115 RoP, Rule 72(10).

116 Public Accounts Committee (n 114), Appendix 2 entitled 'Paper presented to the Provisional Legislative Council by the Chairman of the Public Accounts Committee at the

recommendations contained in the PAC report do not have binding power, the government must report on its progress in rectifying the problems identified therein if it has accepted the recommendations or provide explanations in the case that no changes are forthcoming. In sum, the main tasks of the PAC are to point out the lessons learnt from past experience, to comment on the performance of public officers, and, ultimately, to enable the administration to strengthen its control over the expenditure of public funds.[117]

#### *Relation between Audit Commission and PAC*

The PAC's work begins with and is based on the reports of the Audit Commission. Therefore, the quality of these reports and consideration of whether the PAC receives sufficient assistance from the Audit Commission must be given due weight in assessing the PAC's impact.

The Director of Audit has the power to demand access to the documents or records of any government department under Section 9 of the Audit Ordinance (Cap 122) and to require any public officer to provide an explanation. However, the scope of the Audit Commission's work was limited by an agreement achieved between the government and PAC in 1998, which lays out the scope of government audits and a set of guidelines and procedures for VFM audits.[118] This agreement revised and was based on the VFM Audit Guidelines tabled in Legco by the Chairman of the PAC in November 1986.[119] According to these Guidelines, the Director of Audit shall not comment on the policy decisions of Exco or Legco except when those decisions have an effect on the public purse.[120] However, in practice, it is difficult for the Director to completely avoid commenting on policy decisions when he or she is attempting to point out waste and the possible reasons for it. Some audit reports have indeed attracted criticism for containing too many comments on public policies such as government policies on the water supply and power capacity.[121] Therefore, although

---

meeting on 11 February 1998 on Scope of Government Audit in the Hong Kong Special Administrative Region—"Value for Money Audits"'.

117 Public Accounts Committee, 'PAC Report No. 36' (2001) <http://www.legco.gov.hk/yr00-01/english/pac/reports/pac-r36.pdf> accessed 1 June 2014, appendix 4 entitled 'Introductory Remarks by Chairman of the Public Accounts Committee, Councillor Eric LI Ka-cheung, at the First Public Hearing of the Committee on Monday, 7 May 2001'.

118 See Eric Li's address in the Provisional Legco, Hansard HK (11 February 1998) 15.

119 'Guidelines of Value for Money Audit' (n 116).

120 Ibid.

121 See '審計署長不是法官 (The Audit Commissioner is not A Judge)', *Ming Pao Daily News*, 27 November 1999, C09; '質疑中電多收費觸及港府決策 審計署招來"越權"批評 (Watchdog is Criticised for Excess of Power)', *Sing Tao Daily*, 22 October 1999, A13.

the Audit Commission is an independent body within the government and holds the government accountable for public finances, its non-policy orientation determines that its contributions are largely restricted to the technical and specialised aspects of those finances.

The PAC, in contrast, has a stronger and more active role to play. It is authorised to conduct thorough investigations of any subjects mentioned in the Commission's reports and, further, to provide recommendations and require follow-up actions, in the process inevitably commenting on government policy decisions from time to time. Furthermore, Audit Commission reports are not the sole basis of PAC reports.[122] On rare occasions, PAC members reject the Commission's reports. For instance, in the case of the use of the Trade and Industry Department Tower,[123] the PAC backed the government property agency,[124] with the Chairman of the PAC stressing that the Committee discharged its functions independently and was not simply a rubber stamp.[125]

### *Composition of the PAC*

As Table 4.7 shows, there were two pro-democracy members, two pro-Beijing members and three independents on the PAC in Legco's first and second terms. The composition changed in its third term (2004–08) when three pro-Beijing members entered the PAC, and the number of independents was reduced to two, with a non-professional member serving as the Chairman. The 2012–13 session saw further changes, with the PAC now comprising four pro-Beijing members and three pro-democracy members. These changes in composition were accompanied by a cleavage within the Committee. Prior to 2004, it had never occurred to a PAC member to publicly express dissent from a PAC report.[126] However, the publication of the first PAC report of the 2004–08 Legco was accompanied by controversy over both the content of the report and the practices of the Committee. Some pro-democracy PAC members expressed their dissent from the PAC report, which failed to condemn the then officer of the land authority.[127] At the same time, the new Chairman, Councillor Philip Wong, known to be a pro-Beijing member from the Commercial Sector, tried to

122 The Public Accounts Committee's Procedure of Legco.

123 'Lawmakers disagree with audit body's report', *South China Morning Post*, 10 July 2008, EDT2.

124 Ibid.

125 '審計署報告 帳委會不同意 (PAC Disagreed with Audit Report)', *Hong Kong Economic Times*, 10 July 2008, A24.

126 '主席委員不咬弦 帳委會損威信 (PAC Split over Report)', *Ming Pao Daily News*, 24 February 2005, A13.

127 Ibid.

TABLE 4.7 *Political orientation of PAC members, 1998–2013*

| Year | Pro-democracy | Pro-Beijing | Independent | Total |
|---|---|---|---|---|
| 1998–2000 | 2 | 2 | 3* | 7 |
| 2000–2004 | 2 | 2 | 3* | 7 |
| 2004–2008 | 2 | 3* | 2 | 7 |
| 2008–2012 | 3 | 2* | 2 | 7 |
| 2012–2013 | 3 | 4* | 0 | 7 |

Note: An Asterisk designates that the Chairman is included.
SOURCE: THE AUTHOR'S CALCULATION BASED ON THE MEMBERSHIP OF THE PAC ON LEGCO WEBSITE.

prevent his fellow members from convening a press conference to explain the PAC report, even though it was customary to convene such conferences for the PAC.[128] In response to such controversy, the former Chairman, Councillor Eric Li pointed out that the authority and power of the PAC would be weakened if members split over the report.[129]

The publicly exposed cleavage within the PAC has indeed undermined its authority. Although the RoP does not require unanimity amongst members in PAC decisions,[130] unanimous cross-party decisions allow the PAC to demonstrate its impartiality and lack of political motivation. Furthermore, such long-standing practices as calling a press conference to provide explanations for a PAC report should be modified only on very solid grounds. It seems that the composition and chairmanship of the PAC in recent years have affected the Committee's level of autonomy in terms of neutrality and professionalism.

### *PAC Scrutiny of Public Expenditure*

#### Public Hearings

It is usual practice for the PAC to hold public hearings calling officials or any other parties concerned to give evidence. In addition, another important function of public hearings is to afford those concerned an opportunity to explain

128 Jimmy Cheung, 'No Need for Briefing, Says Chairman', *South China Morning Post*, 24 February 2005.

129 Ming Pao Daily News (n 126).

130 See RoP, Rule 72 (3). According to the RoP, the matters of the PAC shall be decided by the majority of the PAC, and the chairperson or the member presiding has the casting vote.

TABLE 4.8 *Public hearings held by PAC, 1998–2013*

| Legco term | No. of subjects examined and given public hearings by PAC | No. of subjects in the audit report | Percentage of subjects given public hearings by PAC |
|---|---|---|---|
| 1998–2000 | 33 | 56 | 58.93 |
| 2000–2004 | 47 | 82 | 57.31 |
| 2004–2008 | 21 | 75 | 28.00 |
| 2008–2012 | 24 | 77 | 31.17 |
| 2012–2013 | 7 | 18 | 38.89 |
| Total | 132 | 308 | 42.86 |

SOURCE: THE AUTHOR'S CALCULATION BASED ON THE MINUTES OF THE PAC AND DIRECTOR OF AUDIT'S REPORTS (1998–2013) <WWW.LEGCO.GOV.HK AND HTTP://WWW.AUD.GOV.HK/ENG/PUBPR_ARPT/RPT.HTM>.

and defend themselves, an opportunity seldom offered by the Audit Commission.

As Table 4.8 shows, from 1998 to 2013, 132 subjects in Audit Commission reports (amounting to 42.86 per cent of all subjects therein) were examined and given a public hearing by the PAC, with a sharp decline in the number of such subjects seen since 2004. In the 2004–08 Legco sessions, the percentage of subjects subjected to a public hearing plunged to 28 per cent. However, this decline was accompanied by a marked increase in the average number of public hearings per subject, indicating that the PAC conducted a more in-depth investigation of each subject during these years, as shown in Table 4.9. There were 1.3 and 1.26 public hearings per subject in Legco's first and second terms, respectively, with that number rising to 2.33 in its third term. Overall, the PAC has reduced the number of subjects examined and conducted more detailed examinations of each subject in the years since 2004.

From 1998 to 2004, only one subject, namely, the Harbour Fest event, was given four public hearings, although more serious cases have arisen in the years since. For example, during Legco's third term, the PAC held 12 public hearings to investigate issues concerning the Hong Kong Tourism Board and six concerning the development of a site at Sai Wan Ho.[131]

It is unclear whether the growing number of public hearings per subject has enhanced the effectiveness of the PAC. However, its focus on particular issues

131 The author's calculation based on the Legco website.

TABLE 4.9 *The average number of public hearings per subject, 1998–2013*

| Year | No. of public hearings | No. of subjects given public hearings by the PAC | The average no. of public hearings per subject |
|---|---|---|---|
| 1998–2000 | 43 | 33 | 1.30 |
| 2000–2004 | 59 | 47 | 1.26 |
| 2004–2008 | 49 | 21 | 2.33 |
| 2008–2012 | 39 | 24 | 1.63 |
| 2012–2013 | 19 | 7 | 2.71 |
| Total | 209 | 132 | 1.58 |

SOURCE: THE AUTHOR'S CALCULATION BASED ON THE MINUTES OF THE PAC.

has certainly drawn greater public attention through media reports. In fact, almost every PAC report arouses considerable public concern about public expenditure, although it is worth considering whether the PAC has adopted a consistent standard for its selection of subjects for examination over the years.

## Investigative Power: Controversy Surrounding Grand Promenade Event

Rule 72(8) of the RoP stipulates the PAC's independence and investigative power as follows.

> The chairman or the committee may invite any public officer, or, in the case of a report on the accounts of or relating to a non-government body or organisation, any member or employee of that body or organisation, to give information or any explanation or to produce any records or documents which the committee may require in the performance of its duties; and the committee may also invite any other person to assist the committee in relation to any such information, explanation, records or documents.

Furthermore, as one of Legco's three Standing Committees, the PAC may order the attendance of witnesses under Section 9 of the Legislative Council (Power and Privilege) Ordinance. Once an attendance order has been issued by the PAC, it is an offence for the person called to decline to attend meetings or answer questions.[132] In practice, however, Legco's ability to exercise these powers has been challenged to varying degree.

Since 1998, the PAC has summoned the appearance of two witnesses. In 2005, a summons was issued ordering former Director of Buildings Mr Leung Chin Man to attend a public PAC hearing, and another was issued in 2013 ordering Mr Timothy Tong, former Commissioner of the Independent Commission against Corruption, to give evidence and produce all relevant papers, books, records or documents in his possession or under his control. The following paragraphs discuss the former case in detail as an illustration of the PAC's investigative power.

An Audit Commission report released in November 2005 prompted queries over a 2001 grant of bonus land for the luxury Grand Promenade project at Sai Wan Ho. The report raised concerns over whether the decision to grant this land had exposed the general revenue to a loss. The PAC proceeded to organise public hearings to hear evidence on the report's findings,[133] and the CE appointed an Independent Committee of Inquiry (ICI) to inquire into the matter.[134]

The PAC decided to invite Mr Leung, the aforementioned former Director of Buildings, to attend the public hearings and provide information and explanations. However, from the outset, Mr Leung declined to attend on the ground that he had sought a judicial review of the Audit Commission report on 28 November. Under instructions from his superior, Mr Leung attended one PAC meeting, but refused to answer any questions. As a result, the PAC made a resolution to summons Mr Leung under the Legislative Council (Powers and Privileges) Ordinance, after which he attended five public hearings and answered questions.

In February 2006, the PAC issued PAC Report No. 45, which lashed out at the Lands Department and Architectural Services Department using such severe wording as 'unacceptable', 'great dissatisfaction' and 'grave dismay' in its conclusions.[135] The matter became more complex when the government-appointed ICI published its report on 9 May 2006. The ICI report concluded

132 Legislative Council (Powers and Privileges) Ordinance, s 17.

133 Public Accounts Committee, 'PAC Report No. 45' (2005) <http://www.legco.gov.hk/yr05-06/english/pac/reports/pac_rpt_45.htm>, accessed 1 June 2014, Chapter 1.

134 Independent Committee of Inquiry on the Sai Wan Ho Development on Land Lot No. 8955 (ICI on Sai Wan Ho), 'Report of the Independent Committee of Inquiry on the Sai Wan Ho Development on Land Lot No. 8955', [web document](2006) <http://gia.info.gov.hk/general/200605/09/P200605090093_0093_13713.pdf>, accessed 1 June 2014.

135 PAC Report No. 45 (n 133).

that, although discretion had been wrongly exercised, no blame rested with Mr Leung.[136] On the basis of this report, government officials insisted that the government had not suffered any revenue loss and that there was no conflict between the ICI report and the PAC and Audit Commission reports,[137] and Mr Leung subsequently dropped his application for judicial review.[138] The ICI report immediately gave rise to discontent amongst Legco members. During the 17 May 2006 Legco meeting, the Chairman of the PAC moved a motion to support the conclusions and recommendations of the PAC report.[139] This motion received unanimous support from all 44 members present, excluding the President of Legco who never casts a vote.[140] The Director of Audit also issued a statement backing the PAC report.[141] The existence of the three reports, i.e. those of the Audit Commission, PAC and ICI, caused public confusion.[142] Although the government claimed that it accepted all three reports, the discrepancy between the Audit Commission and PAC reports on the one hand and ICI report on the other was obvious.

This event exposes the embarrassing situation in which the PAC often finds itself. The government's prompt reaction in setting up an independent committee is said to have been a response to the charge of 'government-business collusion'.[143] Even then, Executive Councillor Professor Anthony Cheung Bing Leung admitted that it was uncommon for the government to establish an independent commission immediately after publication of an Audit Commission report.[144] Furthermore, the ICI report actually rejected the conclusion of the Commission's report, and ultimately protected Mr Leung from a possible disciplinary hearing and punishment. Such circumstances inevitably harm the integrity of the accounting system, which rests, first, on collaboration between the internal audit body and external audit committee of the legislature and, second, on follow-up action by the government. In Mr Leung's case, regardless

136 ICI Report on Sai Wan Ho (n 134).

137 See 'Gov't Accepts All PAC Recommendations', [web page] (17 May 2006), <http://news.gov.hk/en/category/infrastructureandlogistics/060517/html/060517en06010.htm>, accessed 20 October 2011.

138 Editorial, 'A Diary of Contradictions', *South China Morning Post*, 7 June 2006, EDT20.

139 See Hansard HK (17 May 2006), 7378–7456.

140 Ibid.

141 '審計署長強出頭　取態不同現分歧 (The Audit Commissioner Expressed Disagreement with Inquiry Committee Report)', *Hong Kong Economic Journal*, 17 May 2006, P02.

142 See 'Wrong But Reasonable', *Sing Tao Daily*, 22 May 2006, F08; Chris Yeung, 'Cracks in the System', *South China Morning Post*, 7 June 2006, EDT20.

143 Yeung, ibid.

144 Ibid.

of the ICI's conclusion, the timing of its establishment disrupted the accounting system.

### PAC Access to Documents and Information

The PAC's power to request government documents is limited. In 2001, during a PAC investigation into delayed closure of the Cheung Sha Wan Abattoir, which resulted in a HK$900 million loss, Secretary for the Environment and Food initially rejected a PAC request for documents in accordance with the government's long-standing principle of keeping the discussion papers of all Policy Groups of the Chief Secretary's Committee (CSC) confidential.[145] Owing to the PAC's persistence, the Secretary did finally agree to provide a copy of the relevant paragraph in the discussion paper and a relevant letter.[146] The PAC was also successful in obtaining, albeit not without difficulty, the relevant minutes and several extracts from the Director of Food and Environmental Hygiene.[147] It is noteworthy that, in order to obtain the materials necessary for its investigation, the PAC was forced to issue an ultimatum to the administration to release the information it needed by a given deadline.[148] Even then, it did not receive the full set of documents it had requested.[149]

Thanks to PAC members' concerted efforts, the mechanism for the disclosure of information saw slight improvement during the PAC's investigation of the 'construction of two bridges'. The PAC deferred its report on this subject owing to the government's refusal to disclose the information it needed.[150] Two meetings were then held between the PAC and the government to address the question of the Committee's access to information.[151] These meetings focused on four categories of government documents:[152]

1. Exco documents
2. Documents of the Policy Groups of the CSC

145 See PAC Report No.36 (n 117), 10–11.
146 Ibid.
147 Ibid., 14.
148 See 'Accounts Watchdog Dismayed over Delay in Abattoir Closure', *South China Morning Post*, 5 July 2001.
149 See '索文件多制肘議員判斷難 帳委會要求無限制供資料 (PAC Requires Information without Limitation)', *Sing Tao Daily*, 5 July 2001, A14.
150 Eric Li's address on Report No.37, see Hansard HK (6 February 2002).
151 Public Accounts Committee, 'PAC Report No. 37' (2002) <http://www.legco.gov.hk/yr01-02/english/pac/reports/pacno37cb2-e.pdf>, accessed 1 June 2014, 90–93.
152 Ibid.

3. Documents of non-governmental and private-sector organisations
4. Documents of organisations that no longer exist, e.g. former municipal councils

During the meetings, the PAC also requested the power to access all information available to the Director of Audit.

The government promised that the public interest would be considered in light of the circumstances surrounding each case.[153] It said it would also consider making the papers of Exco and the CSC or its Policy Groups available to the PAC 'on a case-by-case basis' and 'on a confidential basis'.[154] Further, as requested by the PAC, the government agreed to introduce amendments to the relevant provisions of future works-related contracts that had originally contained confidentiality provisions.[155] However, it refused to disclose the minutes of Exco and the CSC or its Policy Groups or to put the PAC and Audit Commission on an equal footing.[156]

This process of negotiation between the PAC and the government reflects the difficulties that the Committee often encounters in attempting to access information. In the arrangements it agreed for providing information to the PAC, the government merely offered a limited compromise that depends on the circumstances of the case in question, thereby ensuring that the disclosure of information and release of documents remain totally at the government's discretion. These information-related difficulties put the PAC in an awkward position and hinder its ability to effectively scrutinise public expenditure.

### Follow-up Mechanism

As noted, it is quite clear that the PAC's influence ultimately depends on the extent to which the government accepts its recommendations and rectifies any problems in practice. Implementation of PAC recommendations is recognised as an essential element of the government's accountability to the legislature and an important measure of the Committee's usefulness and effectiveness.[157] In the HKSAR, the cycle of accountability is assured through

153 Finance Bureau Government Secretariat, 'Provision of Certain Documents to the Public Accounts Committee' (Financial Circular No. 12/2001, 2001).

154 Ibid.

155 PAC (n 151) 92.

156 Finance Bureau Government Secretariat (n 153); PAC, ibid.

157 'Guidance on Reporting and Follow-up, Parliamentary Oversight—Committees and Relationships~A Guide to Strengthening Public Accounts Committees' (CCAF-FCVI, 2006).

the submission of government minutes within three months of publication of a PAC report. Government submissions are usually followed by PAC comments on whether the government has taken action to implement the Committee's recommendations, which appear in one or two sections of the next PAC report.

It is difficult to determine the exact proportion of PAC recommendations that the government has implemented because the subjects examined by the PAC often comprise diverse range of issues. Some government actions have been taken immediately after publication of an Audit Commission report. For instance, in government minutes submitted to the PAC concerning the grant of land in Discovery Bay and Yi Long Wan, the Lands Department submitted a report showing that it had amended its instructions and carried out a survey in accordance with the recommendations of the Director of Audit.[158] Recommendations concerning efficiency are more likely to be accepted by the administration than others. For example, in one section of PAC Report No. 41 assessing the follow-up action on mechanised street cleaning services taken by the Food and Environmental Hygiene Department (FEHD), the PAC noted that the FEHD had implemented new measures and recommendations,[159] with some of these measures implemented by promulgating Technical Circulars or amending instructions.[160] These are long-term and effective improvements. However, the situation becomes more complex when the recommendations in PAC reports concern organisational structure and/or policy. During a review of the financial performance of the Post Office (PO), for instance, the PO accepted such recommendations as a reduction in the number of delivery rounds and the need for productivity enhancements,[161] but, as far as postal policy and services are concerned, it merely emphasised the complexity of the issues involved and the necessity for further studies.[162] In addition to its general conclusions on a particular subject, the PAC can condemn the public officer concerned or recommend disciplinary action, but doing so could be risky, and

158 'Government Minutes in response to the Report No.43 of the PAC' (February 2005), <http://www.legco.gov.hk/yr04-05/english/pac/minutes/pac_gm_43-e.pdf>, accessed 20 October 2011, 26–28.

159 Public Accounts Committee, 'PAC Report No. 41' (2004) <http://www.legco.gov.hk/yr03-04/english/pac/reports/pac_rpt_41.htm>, accessed 1 June 2014, 4–5.

160 In response to PAC Report No.42, the Drainage Services Department promulgated Technical Circular No.8/2004 to lay down time limit, and the ETWB (Environment, Transport and Works Bureau) promulgated new technical circulars. See Public Accounts Committee, 'PAC Report No.45' (2006) <http://www.legco.gov.hk/yr05-06/english/pac/reports/pac_rpt_45.htm>, accessed 1 June 2014, 4–5.

161 See PAC (n 159) 7–9.

162 Ibid.

would not necessarily prove effective, as the Committee would need to explain how that officer's decisions were related to a loss of public money.

With respect to the progress reports it provides to the PAC, the government did very well in following up on the corporate governance and administration of the English Schools Foundation, on which it submitted four action plans.[163] However, effective mechanisms for urging the administration to implement PAC recommendations within a specified time period and for assessing such implementation remain lacking. Hence, it is no surprise to find that even when the government has announced a completion date, it sometimes manages to ignore recommendations.

Take the relocation of the General Post Office (GPO) as an example. The first examination of this subject took place in 1999. In its Report No. 31, the PAC suggested that the GPO be relocated and set a timetable for following up on the progress of that relocation.[164] The government eventually abandoned the relocation plan in 2004, but in the interim the PAC persistently reviewed the progress on the relocation plan in Report Nos. 33, 35, 37, 39 and 41. A timeline can be constructed as follows. (Italic type added by the author for emphasis)

1999: Relocation of the GPO should be given higher priority, and the government should draw up a timetable and strictly follow it.[165] (Report No. 31)

2000: The government informed the Committee that it was making arrangements for the relocation and set up the earliest possible date to complete the plan.[166] (Report No. 33)

2001: The government provided new minutes showing the progress of the relocation plan.[167] (Report No. 35)

2002: According to the latest plans, the earliest possible completion date for the *reclamation works was 2007*.[168] (Report No. 37)

163 See Government Minutes in response to PAC Report No. 43, 45, 47 and 49 (2005, 2006) <http://www.legco.gov.hk/general/english/pac/reports/rpt_0408.htm>, accessed 1 June 2014.

164 Public Accounts Committee, 'PAC Report No. 31' (1999) <http://www.legco.gov.hk/yr99-00/english/pac/report/pac-r31.pdf>, accessed 1 June 2014, 44–46.

165 Ibid.

166 Public Accounts Committee, 'PAC Report No. 33' (2000) <http://www.legco.gov.hk/yr99-00/english/pac/report/pac-r33.pdf>, accessed 1 June 2014, 19.

167 Public Accounts Committee, 'PAC Report No. 35' (2001) <http://www.legco.gov.hk/yr00-01/english/pac/reports/pac-r35.pdf>, accessed 1 June 2014, 26–27.

168 PAC Report No.37(n 151) 34.

2003: [The government informed the PAC that] the relocation *did not need to be completed before 2009–10* at the earliest to dovetail with the development timetable for the Comprehensive Development Area.[169] (Report No. 39)

2004: [The government informed the PAC that] the project *was no longer economically viable* and would have to be abandoned.[170] (Report No. 41)

The PAC expressed regret about the outcome, and criticised the government for its delay:

> The PAC considers that if the Administration had promptly carried out the relocation exercise in early 1999 as recommended by the PAC, the GPO site might have been released for redevelopment while it still had high capital value. We hope that the Administration will learn a lesson from this case and take expeditious actions to conclude without delay other issues which have been outstanding for quite some time.[171]

The case of the abandoned GPO relocation plan shows that, without binding power, the PAC has no recourse other than to be persistent in urging the government to take action and to express criticism in an attempt to arouse public concern.

### *Impact of the PAC*

The aim of the PAC's work is to complete the following accountability cycle: Audit Commission examination—legislative oversight—administrative response. As an important organ for ensuring checks and balances within Legco during this cycle, the PAC provides a mechanism for supervising the usage of public expenditure, and has thus become a necessary component of financial accountability.

---

169 Public Accounts Committee, 'PAC Report No. 39' (2003) <http://www.legco.gov.hk/yr02-03/english/pac/reports/pac_rpt.htm>, accessed 1 June 2014, 20.

170 See PAC Report No. 41 (n 159), 14: 'The Administration had re-assessed the cost-benefits of the project for the relocation of the General Post Office (GPO). Taking into account the current market conditions and the much-reduced plot ratio of the site, the expected proceeds from sale of the GPO site would not be sufficient to cover the costs for reprovisioning the facilities elsewhere. The project, which included the relocation of the GPO's offices and plants, its Counter/Post Office Box Sections and its Delivery Office, was therefore no longer economically viable and had to be abandoned.'

171 Hansard HK (25 February 2004) 3918–3919.

Its non-partisan nature is a crucial characteristic of the PAC. By keeping the Committee above the political affray, cross-party decisions ensure that it receives support from the whole Council. Although the PAC inevitably comments on policy decisions, its general non-policy approach means that it is accepted by the government as politically non-threatening.[172] The non-partisan and non-policy nature of the PAC, along with its conventional practices, ensure its impartiality. Hence, having a Chairperson with a strong political inclination is not conducive to the authority and autonomy of the PAC.

As we have seen, the PAC has engaged in much more detailed inquiry in recent years, at the expense of fewer subjects being examined. It seems clear that it has been more influential in improving efficiency than in reviewing government policies or improving its organisational structure. However, despite the PAC enjoying a higher level of cross-party cooperation than any other Legco committee, its reports are persuasive rather than decisive in nature. The PAC is thus forced to attract public concern in order to keep issues under review and push the executive into taking action.

### Expenditure Without Legco Approval

Not all financial proposals require prior approval of the Finance Committee or Legco as a whole. For instance, use of the Fiscal Reserve lies outside its remit. This section discusses controversy surrounding use of the Exchange Fund, and how they affect Legco's power to scrutinise public finance.

The Fiscal Reserve Account contains the fiscal surpluses that the Hong Kong government has accumulated over many years. In 1976, this account was transferred to the Exchange Fund, into which all general revenue surpluses were subsequently to be placed as Hong Kong dollar deposits.[173] Since April 1998, Fiscal Reserves have been placed with the Exchange Fund to achieve a higher long-term real rate of return.[174] Accordingly, the Exchange Fund comprises the Fiscal Reserves of the government's General Revenue Account, the monetary base that backs the Hong Kong dollar, the accumulated surplus of the Exchange

---

172 McGee (n 104).

173 Hong Kong Monetary Authority, 'HKMA Background Brief No. 5: Reserves Management in Hong Kong Reserves management in Hong Kong', [web page] (December 2007) <http://www.hkma.gov.hk/media/eng/publication-and-research/background-briefs/bg_brief_5/full_e.pdf>, accessed 1 June 2014, 25.

174 For the history of the Exchange Fund, see ibid.

Fund, and the Land Fund, which were merged with the Exchange Fund in 1998.[175]

Article 113 of the Basic Law stipulates that '[t]he Exchange Fund of the Hong Kong Special Administrative Region shall be managed and controlled by the government of the Region, primarily for regulating the exchange value of the Hong Kong dollar'. In addition, the Exchange Fund Ordinance (EFO) stipulates that the Exchange Fund be maintained under the control of the FS, and used primarily for affecting, either directly or indirectly, the exchange value of the Hong Kong dollar and ensuring the stability and integrity of Hong Kong's monetary and financial systems with a view to maintaining the HKSAR as an international financial centre.[176] Control over the Exchange Fund is to be exercised in consultation with an Exchange Fund Advisory Committee whose members are appointed by the CE.[177] Furthermore, the powers and duties imposed on the FS under the terms of the EFO may be delegated to the Hong Kong Monetary Authority (HKMA).[178]

This mechanism for use of the Exchange Fund empowers the FS to use the huge reserves therein for particular purposes and precludes any need for Legco approval. The result is that the procedure for using the Fund is subject to no scrutiny by outside organs, the legislature in particular. However, as a part of government revenue, the Fiscal Reserves are derived from taxation and/or other revenues collected with the approval of Legco,[179] and it is therefore unusual that the EFO and Basic Law remain silent on the procedure for government access to those reserves.[180] As the powers under the EFO may be delegated to the HKMA, the transparency and accountability of this authority have also become the focus of attention. Since the return of sovereignty to China, there have been at least two occasions on which controversy has broken out over use of the Exchange Fund.

The first occasion was in August 1998. Since October 1997, the Hong Kong dollar had had to contend with widespread speculative selling by a few investment houses. On 4 August 1998, being convinced that these speculators' aim was to undermine the stability of the Hong Kong dollar's exchange value and manipulate interest rates, the FS decided to exercise his power under the EFO and ask the HKMA to draw upon the Exchange Fund to mount a counteroffensive

175 Cullen, Wong, and Civic Exchange, *The Foundations of the Hong Kong Revenue Regime*, 20.

176 Exchange Fund Ordinance, Cap 66, s 3(1) and s 3(1A).

177 Ibid., s 3(1).

178 Ibid., s 5B(1).

179 Private communication with Professor Richard Cullen.

180 Ibid.

in the stock and futures markets.[181] In the course of this action, the HKSAR saw outlay of approximately HK$118 billion.[182] However, at a meeting of the Panel on Financial Affairs, queries were raised about the government's unprecedented move to utilise the Exchange Fund to invest in the stock and futures markets without any discussion in Legco, thereby making it difficult for Legco to perform its role of monitoring the government and controlling public expenditure.[183] The FS ascribed the government's move to the sensitivity of the operation.[184]

The second occasion concerned the purchase of premises for a new HKMA office. In 2001, the HKMA announced that this purchase would be charged to the Exchange Fund, which meant that the Finance Committee's approval would not be required.[185] Members of the Panel of Financial Affairs queried the legality of charging the cost of permanent office accommodation to the Exchange Fund.[186]

From the outset, both the FS and the HKMA asserted that the purchase could indeed be lawfully so charged pursuant to s 6(a) of the EFO, which empowers the FS to approve the number of staff appointments and staff emoluments.[187] However, Legco's Legal Adviser considered the argument about 'staff costs' to be 'untenable', and the Department of Justice also expressed doubt as to whether the cost of accommodation could properly be regarded as a 'staff cost'.[188] The FS then appealed to s 6(b) of the EFO, which empowers the CE to approve any incidental expenditure necessary for the due performance of any duties falling to the FS and Advisory Committee in connection with the operation of the Exchange Fund.[189] This appeal raised fresh legal issues concerning whether the approval power conferred on the CE by s 6(b) could be

---

181 See Hong Kong Government, 'Statement by Financial Secretary' (14 August 1998) <http://www.info.gov.hk/gia/general/199808/14/0814160.htm>, accessed 1 June 2014.

182 HKSAR, 'Hong Kong Year Book' (1998) <http://www.yearbook.gov.hk/1998/ewww/events/index08.htm>, accessed 1 June 2014.

183 See Panel of Financial Affairs of Legco, 'Minutes of the meeting held on 7 September 1998' (LC Paper No. CB(1) 534/98-99, 1998).

184 Ibid.

185 Legislative Council Secretariat, 'Background brief on permanent accommodation for the Hong Kong Monetary Authority' (LC Paper No. CB(1) 169/01-02(05), 2002).

186 Ibid.

187 See Jimmy Ma Yiu Tim, 'Legal Adviser's comments on the Legal Views of the Department of Justice as set out in the Letter of the Administrative Assistant to Financial Secretary' (LC Paper No. LS153/00-01, 2001).

188 Ibid., paras 3, 4.

189 Ibid., para 17.

delegated to the FS. The FS finally sought the CE's approval under s 6(b) of the EFO, but the government's explanations were deemed inconsistent and insufficient. Legco's Legal Advisor pointed out that the intention of s 6(b) was to provide 'a statutory requirement of an independent review at a level senior to the FS' and that 'any approval under section 6(b) [was] to be given by the CE personally'.[190] In this case, the delegation of power by the CE to the FS 'would in effect dismantle the statutory requirement of an independent review at a level senior to the FS'.[191]

Obviously, the procedures for using the Exchange Fund and general revenue differ, despite having the same source, i.e. taxation and other revenues that are subject to Legco oversight. The primary purpose of the Fiscal Reserves, along with other categories of the Exchange Fund, is to maintain the stability of the Hong Kong dollar exchange rate and, more broadly, Hong Kong's currency and monetary system.[192] The FS and HKMA have exercised considerable power in using these huge reserves free from any outside supervision, which has weakened Legco's role in supervising public expenditure and led to executive-legislative tension. On the case of the HKMA's purchase of office premises, DAB Chairman Councillor Tam Yiu Chung comments that, regardless of any legal dispute, the government should have informed Legco of the matter and discussed it with members in advance.[193]

## Conclusion

Sir Erskine May said that 'the role of Parliament in respect of State expenditure and taxation has never been one of initiation',[194] and Hong Kong is no exception. The role of Legco in public finance, like that of most legislatures in the Westminster tradition, is to scrutinise the financial proposals put forward by the executive.

This chapter makes clear that Legco has played an active role in examining budgets and other financial proposals since 1998, as evidenced by the steady increase in the amount of time spent on its deliberation of budget proposals

190 Ibid., paras 16, 17.

191 Ibid., para 17.

192 See the FS's concluding speech on the Second Reading of the Appropriation Bill 2001 in Legco, Hansard HK (4 April 2001).

193 Interview with Mr Tam Yiu Chung on 11 February 2009.

194 See May, Mckay, and Cranmer, *Erskine May's Treatise on the Law, Privileges, Proceedings, and Usage of Parliament.*

over the years and the number of members' questions raised concerning those proposals. As Legco has the final say on public expenditure, the government often has to make concessions by moving amendments or withdrawing proposals in order to secure adequate votes for budget or other financial proposals. This is how the bargaining pattern of 'anticipated reactions' or 'anticipated opposition' works.

The empirical results reported throughout the chapter suggest that the effectiveness of Legco's committee work depends on the level of cross-party cooperation achieved and Legco's ability to reflect, consolidate and condition public opinion. Cross-party cooperation in Legco has witnessed a rise and fall since 1998, from the zenith of the eight-party coalition to the nadir of today's *ad hoc* and very limited such cooperation. Going forward, the growing fragmentation within Legco and the declining neutrality of committee chairpersons may constitute the greatest challenges the legislature faces in seeking to effectively supervise public finance.

CHAPTER 5

# Motions without Legislative Effect

The preceding chapters have explored two traditional functions of the Legislative Council of Hong Kong, namely, law-making power and financial scrutiny. Emipirical studies reveal that the real impact that Legco exerts upon legislation and public finance depends on the effectiveness of committee work and the quality of communication between Legco and the public. Legco has become an arena in which contending powers representing different interests can engage in public debate and influence the making of laws and financial policies. It is worth noting that, in order to deliberate bills and budgets, legislators need to have access to relevant information and ensure that relevant issues are fully debated, which brings us to a third but crucial function of Legco, namely, motion debates.

On the one hand, motion debates offer opportunities for legislators to express their views or expressly call upon the government to take a certain action and, on the other, afford the government knowledge of the degree to which the issues proposed in motions will be supported.[1] Given their absence of legislative effect, motions rarely resulted in significant policy changes in the colonial era.[2] Under the post-colonial Rules of Procedure (RoP), the content of motions proposed by legislators faced fewer restrictions than did members' bills and amendments to bills. Members of Legco have actively taken advantage of this relative lack of restriciton, sometimes arousing controversy, for example, by moving no confidence motions against government officials and introducing motions criticising the Standing Committee of the National People's Congress (NPCSC) or Central People's Government (CPG). Most of these moves have been criticised as an abuse of power or improper expansion of power (see discussion below).

Using data on motions, this chapter explores the factors affecting the introduction of a motion and the determinants of voting results on motions, and assesses the achievement of successful motions. It also discusses in detail a special type of motion, namely, no confidence motions, through case studies.

1 Cheek-Milby, *A Legislature Comes of Age: Hong Kong's Search for Influence and Identity*, 154.

2 Norman John Miners, 'The Transformation of the Hong Kong Legislative Council 1970–1994: From Consensus to Confrontation', *Asian Journal of Public Administration*, 16 (1994), 239–241.

 | DOI 10.1163/9789004276284_006

### Restrictions on Moving a Motion or Amendment to a Motion

Only two motions are normally debated at Legco's Wednesday plenary meetings and hence members sometimes need to win in a ballot. According to Rule 30(3)(c), the President of Legco may return a notice of motion or amendment to the members. Rules 31 and 32 of the RoP stipulate the following restrictions on the content of motions and amendments.

1. Matters with charging effect: motions and amendments with charging effect, that is, in the opinion of the President or Chairman they will dispose of or charge any part of the revenue or public money, shall be moved only by the Chief Executive or a designated officer or member with the CE's written consent;[3]
2. Matters being considered in the legislative procedure: motions and amendments may be ruled out of order if they are the same as the motion intended to have legislative effect, or a bill, notice of which have been given earlier;[4]
3. Matters being considered by committees with inquiry functions: motions and amendments may be ruled out of order if they are the same as any matter being considered by a standing committee or a select committee, or a committee authorised by the Council to conduct an inquiry into that matter;[5]
4. Matters already negatived during the same session: no further motion shall be moved during the current session in relation to the question that has been made a negative decision by the Council; Where the Council has taken an affirmative decision on a specific question, no further motion shall be moved in relation to that question during the current session except a motion to rescind the decision, moved with the permission of the President.[6]

Furthermore, the rules regarding the content of speeches in Rule 41 apply to motions. The Legco President has seldom applied the first restriction of the charging effect to members' motions. Of the members' motions and amendments that received rulings and were recorded between 1998 and 2013,[7] most

---

3 RoP, Rule 31(1).

4 RoP, Rule 31(2).

5 Ibid.

6 RoP, Rule 32.

7 Sources of the President's rulings on members' motions and amendments are mainly under the category of 'President's rulings' on the website of Legco.

were negative, although, with some, it was suggested that certain terms be modified or certain parts removed. The reasoning and principles adopted by the President can be summarised as follows.

1. Influencing the legislative procedure. In her ruling on the motion on 'That this Council should shelve the examination of the National Security (Legislative Provisions) Bill', the President wrote: 'To debate a motion with such focus would amount to depriving the Bills Committee of its proper functions and could cause confusion to the legislative procedure stipulated in RoP'.[8]
2. Accusatory expressions. In ruling on motions concerning the CPG, NPC and NPCSC, the President ruled that 'it was out of order for the Legislative Council to debate a motion involving accusatory expressions against and condemnation of the character of [the] NPCSC or the acts of [the] NPCSC undertaken according to our country's Constitution and the Basic Law, which would be likely to degrade it in the public estimation'.[9]
3. Interference with the independence of the Judiciary. In her ruling on a motion relating to 'introducing legislative amendments to open up community radio stations', the President ruled that 'it is not appropriate to include in the wording of a motion or an amendment, which is to be

8 See President's Ruling on Motions Relating to the Scrutiny of the National Security (Legislative Provisions) Bill Proposed by Hon Albert HO Chun-yan for the Legislative Council Meeting on 21 May 2003 (5 May 2003).

9 The President applied this reasoning in the following five rulings: President's Ruling on Amendments Proposed by Hon Martin LEE Chu-ming to Motion on 'Requesting the Chief Executive to Submit a Supplementary Report to the Standing Committee of the National People's Congress' to be Moved by Frederick FUNG Kin-kee at the Council Meeting of 5 May 2004 (30 April 2004);

President's Ruling on Motion on 'Regretting the Decision of the Standing Committee of the National People's Congress to Rule Out Universal Suffrage in the Years 2007 and 2008' Proposed by Hon Albert HO Chun-yan for Debate at the Legislative Council Meeting on 19 May 2004 (7 May 2004);

President's Ruling on Amendment Proposed by Hon LEE Cheuk-yan to Motion on 'Regretting the Decision of the Standing Committee of the National People's Congress to Rule Out Universal Suffrage in the Years 2007 and 2008' to be Moved by Hon Albert HO Chun-yan at the Legislative Council Meeting on 19 May 2004 (14 May 2004);

President's Ruling on Motion on 'Opposing Interpretation of the Basic Law by the Standing Committee of the National People's Congress' Proposed by Hon LEUNG Kwok-hung for Debate at the Legislative Council Meeting on 11 May 2005 (30 April 2005)

President's Ruling on Motion on 'The 4 June incident' Proposed by Hon LEUNG Kwok-hung for Debate at the Legislative Council Meeting on 16 May 2007 (7 May 2007).

debated by this Council, any anticipation of how a court may rule on a particular case before it, as this could be perceived by the public as an attempt by this Council to interfere with the independence of the Judiciary'.[10]

4. Anticipation of permission granted by the administration. In handling the motion relating to the 1 July march moved by Councillor Lee Cheuk Yan, the President said, 'the Legislative Council should not appeal for people to take part in activities that do not meet such requirements [of laws]'.[11]
5. Questions previously negatived by the Council. The President applied Rule 32(2) to rule out an amendment that contained a statement urging the government to expeditiously implement universal suffrage, considering that the proposed amendment was substantially the same as a question that had previously been decided in the negative by the Council.[12]
6. It is out of order if the amendment exceeds the scope of the original motion.[13]

Of all of the rulings summarised above, the second one, i.e. the ruling on motions relating to the NPCSC, has given rise to the greatest controversy. On 26 April 2004, after considering a report by the Chief Executive (CE) of the HKSAR, the NPCSC made the decision that the election of the third CE in 2007 and of Legco members in 2008 (Legco's fourth term) would not proceed by means of universal suffrage. That decision provoked a strong reaction in the community, particularly amongst those in the pro-democracy camp. Initiatives against the decision included an amendment moved by Councillor Martin Lee Chu Ming and a motion by Councillor Albert Ho Chun Yan. The expressions used in their draft amendment/motion can be found in Table 5.1. The President

---

10 See President's Ruling on the Amendment Proposed by Hon LEUNG Kwok-hung to the Motion on 'Introducing Legislative Amendments to Open Up Community Radio Stations' to Be Moved by Hon James TO Kun-sun at the Council Meeting of 23 January 2008 (21 January 2008);

President's Ruling on Hon Ronny TONG Ka-wah's Proposed Amendment to Hon CHAN Kam-lam's Amendment to the Motion on 'Introducing Legislative Amendments to Open Up Community Radio Stations' to Be Moved by Hon James TO Kun-sun at the Council Meeting of 23 January 2008 (22 January 2008).

11 See President's Ruling on Motion Relating to 'The 1 July March' Proposed by Hon LEE Cheuk-yan for the Legislative Council Meeting on 9 June 2004 (25 May 2004).

12 President's Ruling on Amendments Proposed by Dr Hon YEUNG Sum to Motion on 'Supporting the Middle Class' to be Moved by Dr Hon David CHU Yu-lin at the Council Meeting of 10 December 2003 (9 December 2003).

13 President's Ruling on Councillor Martin Lee's Amendments (n 9).

TABLE 5.1 *President's rulings on members' motion or amendments relating to the NPCSC and CPG*

| Member | Relevant Expressions | President's Rulings |
|---|---|---|
| Martin Lee Chu Ming | the Standing Committee of the National People's Congress (NPCSC) has ***abused its power*** | N(negatived) |
| | that ruling out flatly the respective elections of CE in 2007 and of the Legislative Council in 2008 by universal suffrage not only ***violates the Basic Law*** and ignores Hong Kong people's aspirations for democracy, but also ***seriously damages the 'one country, two systems' and 'Hong Kong's high degree of autonomy'*** | N |
| | that this Council ***strongly condemns*** this and urges the people of Hong Kong to continue striving for democracy and never give up | N |
| Albert Ho Chun Yan | the decision of NPCSC not only does ***not conform to the basic principles of 'one country, two systems' and 'a high degree of autonomy'*** | N |
| | the decision of NPCSC ***completely ignores*** Hong Kong people's general aspirations for democracy | A(approved) |
| | this Council ***expresses regret about and dissatisfaction*** with such decision, and calls upon the people of Hong Kong to continue striving for democracy with all might and never give up. | A |
| Lee Cheuk Yan | as many people also consider that, in making its decision on the constitutional development of Hong Kong without fully consulting the views of the people of Hong Kong, NPCSC has ***violated the basic principle of 'one country, two systems' and done harm to the Hong Kong Special Administrative Region's 'high degree of autonomy'*** | N |
| | and affects the confidence of Hong Kong people in 'one country, two systems' | A |
| Leung Kwok Hung | this Council does ***not accept*** the NPCSC's passing of the draft interpretation in respect of Article 53 of the Basic Law regarding the term of office of the new Chief Executive | N |
| | this Council also urges the NPCSC to withdraw its decision made on 26 April 2004 to rule out the election of the Chief Executive and all Members of the Legislative Council by universal suffrage in 2007 and 2008 respectively in Hong Kong, which ***throttles the rights of the people of Hong Kong to a high degree of autonomy*** and to the full implementation of election by universal suffrage | N |
| Leung Kwok Hung | this Council ***condemns*** the prime culprit of the bloody crackdown on the pro-democracy movement in 1989 | N |

SOURCE: THE AUTHOR'S COMPILATION BASED ON HANSARD HK (BOLD AND ITALIC TYPES ADDED BY AUTHOR FOR EMPHASIS).

subsequently disallowed such 'accusatory expressions' as the NPCSC has 'abused its power', 'violate[d] the Basic Law' and 'seriously damage[d] the "one country, two systems" [structure] and Hong Kong's high degree of autonomy', and she also refused to allow the word 'condemn'. The President ultimately failed to approve Councillor Lee's amendment and permitted Councillor Ho to move only the part of his motion stating that 'the Council expresses regret about and dissatisfaction' with the NPCSC's decision. These rulings aroused serious concern amongst both democrats and the CPG. On the one hand, an official of the CPG Liaison Office in the HKSAR said that any members' motion containing words 'strongly condemn[ing]' the NPCSC or expressing 'regret about and dissatisfaction' with a decision made by the NPCSC was tantamount to challenging the NPCSC and would contravene both the Constitution of the People's Republic of China and the Basic Law.[14] On the other hand, democrats accused the rulings of restricting their freedom of speech and initiation power.[15] They also raised questions about whether Legco would be able to criticise the NPCSC for breaching laws and/or threatening Hong Kong's high degree of autonomy and 'one country, two systems' structure in the future.[16]

In dealing with issues relating to the NPCSC, the then President said there were two considerations: first, whether it was in order for the Council to debate a motion (in the form of an amendment) related to the exercise of the NPCSC's power concerning the HKSAR and, second, if so, whether the terms of the motion were in order.[17] She concluded that 'depending on the specific terms of a proposed motion, it is not entirely impossible for a motion relating to a state organ to be admitted for debate in the Council, provided that it meets the requirements of the relevant instruments and rules'.[18] Nevertheless, the NPCSC has made a decision by virtue of its interpretation of Article 7 of Annex I and Article III of Annex II to the Basic Law, and it is out of order for Legco to debate a motion involving accusatory expressions against the character of the NPCSC, or acts of the NPCSC in accordance with the law, as doing so would be likely to degrade it in the public's estimation.[19]

Based on these considerations, the President of Legco has issued rulings on five motions or amendments regarding the NPCSC. As Table 5.1 shows, the

14 '中聯辦: 立法會議員動議不能挑戰全國人大常委會 (Central Liaison Office: Legislator's Motion Cannot Challenge the NPCSC)', *Xinhua News Agency*, 7 May 2004, <http://www.fmcoprc.gov.hk/chn/zt/zzfz/t94988.htm>, accessed 3 February 2010.

15 '陳景生: 裁決不符香港利益 (Edward Chan King Sang: President's Ruling is Not in the Best Interests of Hong Kong)', *Hong Kong Economic Journal*, 8 May 2004, P06.

16 Ibid.

17 President's Ruling on Martin Lee's amendments (n 9), 5.

18 Ibid., 6.

19 Ibid.

'accusatory expressions' cited in these rulings include accusations that the NPCSC's is violating the principles of 'one country, two systems' and threatening both the Basic Law and the high degree of autonomy that Hong Kong enjoys. Moreover, the table also makes clear that it is considered unacceptable for Legco, as a local legislature, to express its unwillingness to accept a decision made by the NPCSC, the standing organ of the Supreme State Organ. However, in these rulings, the President did not preclude the use of more moderate expressions in motions, such as noting that a given decision 'affect[s] the confidence of Hong Kong people in "one country, two systems"', 'throttles the right of [the] people to…universal suffrage', and 'fully ignore[s] people's aspiration[s]'. Expressions urging the NPCSC to take action were also deemed admissible.

These rulings demonstrate the Legco President's attempts to establish the boundaries of the rights and privileges of Legco members and to strike a balance between members' freedom of speech and respect for the NPCSC. In them, the President consciously emphasised the constitutional role of the NPCSC and the close relationship between this supreme organ of state power and Legco as part of the HKSAR government.[20] In fact, such emphasis may have avoided any direct confrontation between the two legislatures. As Professor Albert Chen has pointed out, the President's ruling on motions regarding the NPCSC is a compromise made in goodwill and shows the self-restraint of power.[21]

In addition to ruling out motions relating to the NPCSC and CPG, Legco Presidents have also ruled out motions or amendments relating to judicial proceedings. In spite of the nature of a procedural decision, the President must consider the constitutional structure and Legco's relationship with other organs such as Hong Kong's Judiciary and national state organs, which may be a pragmatic solution to avoid a constitutional crisis. The principles upon which former rulings were made have become precedents. For example, President Jasper Tsang followed the principles established by his predecessor, President Rita Fan, in dealing with an amendment to appeal directly to the people to encourage them to actively participate in the annual 1 July protest.[22]

20 The then President, Mrs Rita Fan is considered to have made contribution to precluding Article 74 of the Basic Law from applying to members' committee stage amendments, but she is also criticised of prejudice in handling issues relating to NPC and CPG. Interview with Mr Albert Ho Chun Yan on 17 Feb 2009.

21 Albert H.Y. Chen,—國兩制下香港的法治探索 (*Hong Kong's Explorations in the Rule of Law under One Country Two Systems*) (Hong Kong: Zhonghua Shu Ju, 2010), 208.

22 See President's Ruling on Amendment to the Motion on 'Proposal on the Constitutional Reform in Hong Kong' Moved by Councillor Albert Chan Wai Yip on 17 June 2009 (17 June 2009).

## Determinants of Result of Members' Motions

Table 5.2 shows the results of motions moved by members between 1998 and 2013. Legco's first term recorded the lowest pass rate: 66.67 per cent. Since then, the pass rate has held steady at more than 70 per cent. Over the whole period, the average pass rate of the 809 motions moved stands at around 70 per cent, which provides a startling contrast with the extremely low pass rate for Committee Stage Amendments (CSAs), with just four per cent of the 485 CSAs proposed between 1998 and 2013 passing.[23] Of course, there are major differences between bills and motions in terms of content and effects. With respect to content, as a means of expressing opinions and sparking public debate, motions usually contain general terms and proposals for a specific policy, and rarely using wording as precise as that in bills. In contrast to the wording of members' CSAs, that of motions is more likely to be accepted by the majority of Legco members and less likely to face objections from the government, unless legislators advocate opposing a government policy by proposing a motion. With respect to effects, a successful motion does not necessarily lead to the formulation of decisions with legislative effect, and members cannot compel the government to immediately implement a motion. In these circumstances, members, pro-Beijing members in particular, may have fewer misgivings about voting for motions. By contrast, members' CSAs become law once they are passed. Therefore, it is unsurprising that members may support an issue raised in a motion, but then vote it down when it appears in a member's CSA.

There has been a growing number of amendments to motions, as shown in Table 5.3. In Legco's first term, members proposed 0.8 amendments per motion, whereas the years since 2004 have seen more than two per motion on average. Furthermore, the success rate of amendments has steadily increased over the years, reaching 60 per cent in Legco's fourth term.

The proportion of motions passed with amendments has also increased over the years. As Table 5.4 shows, amongst successful motions, the proportion of those with amendments increased from 30 per cent in Legco's first term to 84 per cent in its fourth term. In the first session of the fifth term (2012–13), 89.29 per cent of successful motions passed with amendments. These amendments ranged from substantive modifications to original motions to relatively slight amendments to expressions. In either case, being subject to debating and voting, amendments essentially provided members with an additional means of promoting meaningful debate and formulating statements or consensus that may gain more support in Legco.

---

23 See Chapter 3 in this book.

TABLE 5.2 *Result of motions moved by members, 1998–2013*

| Year | Negatived | | Passed | | Withdrawn | | Total | |
|---|---|---|---|---|---|---|---|---|
| | Freq. | Per cent | Freq. | Per cent | Freq. | Per cent | Freq. | Per cent |
| 1998–2000 | 40 | 32.52 | 82 | 66.67 | 1 | 0.81 | 123 | 100 |
| 2000–2004 | 57 | 26.76 | 156 | 73.24 | 0 | 0 | 213 | 100 |
| 2004–2008 | 62 | 28.18 | 158 | 71.82 | 0 | 0 | 220 | 100 |
| 2008–2012 | 52 | 25.74 | 150 | 74.26 | 0 | 0 | 202 | 100 |
| 2012–2013 | 23 | 45.10 | 28 | 54.90 | 0 | 0 | 51 | 100 |
| Total | 234 | 28.92 | 574 | 70.95 | 1 | 0.12 | 809 | 100 |

SOURCE: THE AUTHOR'S CALCULATION BASED ON HANSARD HK (1998–2013).

TABLE 5.3 *Amendments to members' motions, 1998–2013*

| Year | Amendments proposed | Amendments passed | Amendments pass rate | Amendments proposed per motion |
|---|---|---|---|---|
| 1998–2000 | 98 | 28 | 28.57 | 0.8 |
| 2000–2004 | 206 | 90 | 43.69 | 0.97 |
| 2004–2008 | 459 | 212 | 46.19 | 2.09 |
| 2008–2012 | 636 | 383 | 60.22 | 3.15 |
| 2012–2013 | 267 | 126 | 47.19 | 5.24 |

SOURCE: THE AUTHOR'S CALCULATION BASED ON HANSARD HK (1998–2013).

TABLE 5.4 *Passed members' motions, 1998–2013*

| Year | Passed without amendments | | Passed with amendments | | Total | |
|---|---|---|---|---|---|---|
| | Freq. | Perc. | Freq. | Perc. | Freq. | Perc. |
| 1998–2000 | 57 | 69.51 | 25 | 30.49 | 82 | 100 |
| 2000–2004 | 91 | 58.33 | 65 | 41.67 | 156 | 100 |
| 2004–2008 | 50 | 31.65 | 108 | 68.35 | 158 | 100 |
| 2008–2012 | 24 | 16.00 | 126 | 84.00 | 150 | 100 |
| 2012–2013 | 3 | 10.71 | 25 | 89.29 | 28 | 100 |

SOURCE: THE AUTHOR'S CALCULATION BASED ON HANSARD HK (1998–2013).

TABLE 5.5 *Members' motions by the sponsors' constituencies, 1998–2013*

| Year | FC | | GC | | EC | | Total | |
|---|---|---|---|---|---|---|---|---|
| | Freq. | Perc. | Freq. | Perc. | Freq. | Perc. | Freq. | Perc. |
| 1998–2000 | 53 | 43.09 | 53 | 43.09 | 17 | 13.82 | 123 | 100 |
| 2000–2004 | 90 | 42.25 | 105 | 49.30 | 18 | 8.45 | 213 | 100 |
| 2004–2008 | 88 | 40 | 132 | 60 | – | – | 220 | 100 |
| 2008–2012 | 96 | 47.52 | 106 | 52.48 | – | – | 202 | 100 |
| 2012–2013 | 25 | 49.02 | 26 | 50.98 | – | – | 51 | 100 |
| Total | 352 | 43.51 | 422 | 52.16 | 35 | 4.33 | 809 | 100 |

SOURCE: THE AUTHOR'S CALCULATION BASED ON HANSARD HK (1998–2013).

### *Introduction of Motions*

This section describes the activities of motion movers returned by different constituencies. As Table 5.5 shows, although Functional Constituencies (FCs) have retained half the seats in Legco since the first Legco election, FC members moved 43.51 per cent of motions on average from 1998 to 2013, whilst members of Geographical Constituencies (GCs) moved 52.16 per cent on average. Since the 2004 Legco election, there have been an equal number of GC and FC seats owing to the dismantling of the Electoral College (EC). In Legco's third term (2004–08), 60 per cent of motions were moved by GC members, who accounted for 50 per cent of Legco members. In its fourth term, Legco has seen a rise in the proportion of motions moved by FC members, from 40 per cent in the third term to 47.52 per cent in the fourth. It seems that FC members have been more active in moving motions since 2008. In fact, there has been little change in the number of motions moved by the major political groups, such as the Liberal Party (LP), Democratic Alliance for the Betterment and Progress of Hong Kong (DAB) and Alliance (called the Professional Forum since 2008). However, the FC seats obtained by democrats decreased from seven in the 2004–08 sessions to just four in the 2008–12 sessions, which means that new pro-Beijing or independent members have joined Legco. In addition, other new blood has been brought into FCs, including Councillors Paul Tse, Lam Tai Fai and Chan Kin Por. These new FC members have been very active in policy debates. At the same time, a number of formerly silent FC members have become more active. For instance, Councillor Philip Wong from the Commerce Sector moved five motions in the 2008–12 sessions after having moved only one between 1998 and 2008. It is clear that FC members feel under increased pressure, possibly because

TABLE 5.6 *Members' motions by the nature of the issues controlling for the sponsors' constituencies, 1998–2013*

| Nature of the Issue | FCS | | GCS | | EC | | Total | |
|---|---|---|---|---|---|---|---|---|
| | Freq. | Perc. | Freq. | Perc. | Freq. | Perc. | Freq. | Perc. |
| People's livelihood | 136 | 41.98 | 176 | 54.32 | 12 | 3.70 | 324 | 100 |
| Economy and development | 87 | 61.27 | 44 | 30.99 | 11 | 7.75 | 142 | 100 |
| Constitutional and political affair | 17 | 18.09 | 76 | 80.85 | 1 | 1.06 | 94 | 100 |
| Environmental and conservation | 21 | 35.00 | 35 | 58.33 | 4 | 6.67 | 60 | 100 |
| Other motions | 29 | 76.32 | 8 | 21.05 | 1 | 2.63 | 38 | 100 |
| Tax, fees and budget | 12 | 44.44 | 14 | 51.85 | 1 | 3.70 | 27 | 100 |
| Human rights | 7 | 21.88 | 25 | 78.13 | 0 | 0 | 32 | 100 |
| Home affair | 8 | 42.11 | 8 | 42.11 | 3 | 15.79 | 19 | 100 |
| Public service | 10 | 52.63 | 8 | 42.11 | 1 | 5.26 | 19 | 100 |
| Justice, legal service and legislation | 8 | 42.11 | 11 | 57.89 | 0 | 0 | 19 | 100 |
| Financial policy | 10 | 62.50 | 6 | 37.50 | 0 | 0 | 16 | 100 |
| Broadcasting | 3 | 33.33 | 6 | 66.67 | 0 | 0 | 9 | 100 |
| Security | 4 | 40.00 | 5 | 50.00 | 1 | 10.00 | 10 | 100 |
| Total | 352 | 43.51 | 422 | 52.16 | 35 | 4.33 | 809 | 100 |

SOURCE: THE AUTHOR'S CALCULATION BASED ON HANSARD HK (1998–2013).

of ongoing criticism of their poor performance in participating in Legco business. Furthermore, the uncertain future of FCs may also motivate FC members to improve their performance, and hence the public's perception of them.

Table 5.6 examines the nature of the issues that motions have been concerned with. It can be seen that livelihood issues have accounted for the greatest number, followed by issues related to the economy and development, constitutional and political affairs, and the environment and conservation, in that order.

Despite their general inclination towards inactivity, FC members have moved more motions concerned with the economy and development (61.27 per cent), financial policy (62.5 per cent) and public services (52.63 per cent) than their GC counterparts, as shown in Table 5.6. In addition, they have moved most of those falling in the 'Other motions' category (76.22 per cent), which mainly includes motions of thanks and motions moved by committee Chairpersons to report to the whole Council on behalf of committees or subcommittees. It is evident from the table that members of GCs are more focused on issues concerning constitutional and political affairs (80.85 per cent), human rights (78.13 per cent) and livelihood (54.32 per cent). Compared to FC members, they moved fewer motions regarding economic and development (30.99 per cent) and financial policy (37.5 per cent) issues.

In sum, FC members are less active in moving motions than GC members, and pay more attention to economic affairs than to livelihood issues. The issues of greatest concern to GC members, in contrast, are fundamental rights, constitutional and political affairs, and livelihood issues. However, it seems that FC members have begun to feel under pressure to improve their performance and the public's perception of them. Finally, new members, particularly those who transferred from FCs to GCs in the last Legco election, seem to adopt a different approach from those who have served in FCs for a long time.

### *Separate Voting Mechanism*

This section examines the impact of the Separate Voting Mechanism (SVM) on the voting results of motions. It can be seen from Table 5.7 that from 1998 to 2013, of the 234 members' motions that were negatived, 87 were blocked because of the SVM. Between 1998 and 2008, the proportion of motions negatived because of the SVM increased from 35 per cent to 45.16 per cent. Although Legco's fourth term saw a decrease in both the numbers and percentage of motions negatived by the SVM, 37.18 per cent of motions on average were blocked by the mechanism between 1998 and 2013. These findings demonstrate that the SVM has become an important blocker of members' motions.

Under the SVM, motions may be blocked by members of FCs or GCs. The further analysis in Tables 5.8 and 5.9 indicates that FC and GC members negatived 58 and 28 motions, respectively. Of the 58 motions negatived by FC members, 37 concerned livelihood issues. These members blocked 23 motions proposed by pro-Beijing members, 34 by pro-democracy members and one by an independent, as shown in Table 5.8. In addition to motions concerning livelihood issues, FCs members also blocked pro-Beijing members' motions relating to District Councils reform and human rights and environmental and conservation issues. These results suggest that the nature of the issues concerned is a more influential factor than the motion mover's political orientation in the voting behaviour of FC members.

With respect to motions negatived by GCs, Table 5.9 shows that all had been moved by pro-Beijing members or independents. Motions of thanks for a CE policy address were the most commonly negatived by GC members.

TABLE 5.7 *Proportion of motions negatived by SVM of negatived motions, 1998–2013*

| Term | No. of motions negatived by SVM | | Total no. of negatived motions | |
|---|---|---|---|---|
| | Freq. | Perc. | Freq. | Perc. |
| 1998–2000 | 14 | 35.00 | 40 | 100 |
| 2000–2004 | 22 | 38.60 | 57 | 100 |
| 2004–2008 | 28 | 45.16 | 62 | 100 |
| 2008–2012 | 14 | 26.92 | 52 | 100 |
| 2012–2013 | 9 | 39.13 | 23 | 100 |
| Total | 87 | 37.18 | 234 | 100 |

SOURCE: THE AUTHOR'S CALCULATION BASED ON HANSARD HK (1998–2013).

TABLE 5.8 *Motions negatived by FCs by the nature of the issues controlling for the sponsors' political orientation under SVM, 1998–2013*

| Nature of the issues | Moved by pro-Beijing members | Moved by pro-democracy members | Moved by independents | Total |
|---|---|---|---|---|
| Constitutional and political affair | 1 | 1 | 0 | 2 |
| Human rights | 1 | 0 | 0 | 1 |
| Tax, fees and budget | 3 | 0 | 0 | 3 |
| Environmental and conservation | 1 | 1 | 0 | 2 |
| Justice, legal service and legislation | 0 | 4 | 0 | 4 |
| Economy and development | 0 | 4 | 0 | 4 |
| People's livelihood | 16 | 20 | 1 | 37 |
| Public service | 0 | 1 | 0 | 1 |
| Home affair | 0 | 1 | 0 | 1 |
| Broadcasting | 0 | 1 | 0 | 1 |
| Other motions | 0 | 1 | 0 | 1 |
| Security | 1 | 0 | 1 | 1 |
| Total | 23 | 34 | 1 | 58 |

SOURCE: THE AUTHOR'S CALCULATION BASED ON HANSARD HK (1998–2013).

TABLE 5.9 *Motions negatived by GCs by the nature of the issues controlling for the sponsors' political orientation under SVM, 1998–2013*

| Nature of the issues | Moved by pro-Beijing members | Moved by independent | Total |
|---|---|---|---|
| Constitutional and political affair | 0 | 1 | 1 |
| Tax, fees and budget | 1 | 0 | 1 |
| Environmental and conservation | 1 | 0 | 1 |
| Economy and development | 3 | 1 | 3 |
| People's livelihood | 5 | 2 | 7 |
| Financial policy | 1 | 0 | 1 |
| Human rights | 1 | 0 | 1 |
| Other motions (motions of thanks) | 11 | 1 | 12 |
| Total | 23 | 5 | 28 |

SOURCE: THE AUTHOR'S CALCULATION BASED ON HANSARD HK (1998–2013).

The following conclusions can be drawn from these findings.

1. The SVM has become a major obstacle to the passage of members' motions. To date, FC members have employed the SVM more frequently than GC members, and thus benefited more from the mechanism, generally blocking motions that they do not favour regardless of the support of the simple majority of Legco.
2. Most motions negatived with recourse to the SVM are related to livelihood issues. The next most common types are motions of thanks and motions concerning the economy and development.
3. FC members use the SVM to block motions concerned with livelihood issues, whilst their GC counterparts use it primarily to express discontent with the CE and his Policy Address by blocking motions of thanks.
4. The voting results of members' motions show that the nature of the issues involved is a more influential factor than the sponsors' political orientation.

### *Political Orientation and the Nature of the Issues*

The preceding section examines how members of the two types of constituencies use the SVM to achieve their goals. This section further explores

TABLE 5.10 *Pass rate of members' motions by the nature of the issues controlling for the sponsors' political orientation, 1998–2013*

| Nature of issue | Moved by pro-Beijing members | Moved by pro-democracy members | Moved by independents |
|---|---|---|---|
| Constitutional and political affair | 87.50 | 8.75 | 66.67 |
| Financial Policy | 87.50 | 71.43 | 100.00 |
| Human rights | 60.00 | 62.96 | – |
| Tax, fees and budget | 73.33 | 83.33 | – |
| Environmental and conservation | 94.29 | 76.47 | 100.00 |
| Justice, legal service and legislation | 100.00 | 42.86 | – |
| Economy and development | 95.10 | 71.43 | 78.95 |
| People's livelihood | 81.51 | 68.79 | 76.19 |
| Public service | 60.00 | 54.55 | 100.00 |
| Home affair | 88.24 | 100.00 | 0.00 |
| Broadcasting | – | 66.67 | – |
| Other motions | 52.17 | 87.50 | 71.43 |
| Security | 85.71 | 100.00 | – |
| Total | 84.57 | 55.59 | 78.79 |

SOURCE: THE AUTHOR'S CALCULATION BASED ON HANSARD HK (1998–2013).

the determinants of the passage of members' motions, including their sponsors' political orientation and the nature of the issues concerned.

Table 5.10 reports the pass rate of motions concerning various issues according to the sponsers' political orientation. The respective pass rate of motions moved by pro-Beijing members (84.57 per cent) and by independents (78.79 per cent) is much higher than that of motions moved by pro-democracy members (55.59 per cent). This result is unsurprising considering the pro-Beijing camp's dominance of Legco. The wide gap in the pass rates of motions moved by democrats and pro-Beijing members extends to most types of the issues, but is particularly severe when it comes to constitutional and political affairs, and economic and development issues.

Of the motions regarding constitutional and political affairs moved by democrats, just 8.75 per cent were passed. In stark contrast, 87.5 per cent of those moved by pro-Beijing members were carried by Legco. Other types of motions that appear to be influenced by the sponsor's political orientation include those related to economic and development issues, as well as environmental and conservation, justice, legal service and legislation, and livelihood issues, as shown in Table 5.10.

With respect to motions regarding tax, fees and budget issues, security issues, and other issues (mainly motions of thanks and committee reports), however, the pass rate of those moved by democrats exceeds that of those moved by the pro-Beijing camp. As GC members employ the SVM primarily to negative motions of thanks, which are more likely to be moved by pro-Beijing members, such motions have a low success rate. The SVM is also responsible for the lower pass rate of motions concerning tax, fees and budget-related issues moved by pro-Beijing members. Of the four negatived motions sponsored by pro-Beijing members in Table 5.10, three called for a reduction in fees and charges and were defeated by FC members and one called for a fuel duty reduction and was negatived by GC members. With regard to security-related motions, one of the five motions moved by a DAB member was defeated by FC members using the SVM, which led to the overall low pass rate given the limited number of motions concerned with security. It is clear that the SVM has become a key means of defeating motions moved by pro-Beijing members, particularly when FC members object to those motions.

### *Government's Response to Successful Motions*

To examine the way in which the government has responded to successful motions, this section analyses 36 progress reports provided by the government selected from the 2006–07 session. These reports can be categorised as follows.[24]

1. Negative responses (four cases):
   (1) The government denies its responsibility for the issues raised and indicates it will encourage the relevant organisations to take action.
   (2) The government remains of the view that the member's proposal is not an appropriate or effective means of taking action.
   (3) It is difficult to further consider the member's proposals in view of the lack of relevant supporting documents or evidence.
   (4) The government has reservations over certain proposal items.

24 The author's calculation is based on Hansard HK (2005–06).

2. Neutral responses (eight cases)
   (1) The government will review international practices before considering the necessity of regulating the issue by law, and will make reference to those practices when it tables the regulation concerned to Legco within a given period;
   (2) The government has an open stance on the issues raised and will consult the public extensively before deciding on appropriate policy and arrangements.
   (3) The government summarises and reiterates its current policies and measures, and announces plans for consultation, study and review.
   (4) The government has not at this stage come to any conclusion on the issues concerned.
3. Positive responses (24 cases)
   (1) The government has decided to cease relevant proceedings or revise current arrangements at members' request (2 cases).
   (2) The government has been making an effort or taken corresponding measures on the issues raised, and will continue to improve that effort/measures. It will also consult the public and conduct timely reviews (11 cases).
   (3) The government will take into account and make reference to members' suggestions. It will also consult the public and Legco, and conduct a policy review (4 cases).
   (4) The issues raised are in accordance with established government policy. The government has been taking action in the past few years and will continue to monitor and review the issues. It will also seek the views of the community and make reference to the relevant overseas experience (6 cases).
   (5) The process of drafting the relevant law has already begun (1 case).

The majority of the government's responses (24 out of 36) fall into the positive category. Members' suggestions in successful motions are rarely met with an outright refusal. However, government officials tend to respond by reiterating the current policy and promising future reviews. Even in positive replies, the government rarely gives assurance that it will take swift action on the issues raised. Of the 24 positive replies above, only eight included timetables for action. Such an outcome may result not only from the government's reaction, but also from the wording in the motions. It is unnecessary for the government to produce a report containing specific measures to respond to a motion calling for something to be 'enhanced' in general terms. The content of most motions is couched in such general terms, which makes them more likely to be accepted by both other members and the government, although members can specify their requirements more clearly if they wish.

A comparison between two motions concerning the 2007 budget bill may be illustrative in demonstrating the importance of the terms used. The two motions in question passed on 10 and 24 January 2007, respectively. Both urge the government to use the fiscal reserves appropriately to alleviate the public's living burden. The motion passed on 10 January contained a general statement of members' requirements. In its reply, the government reiterated that the measures requested had been introduced in the budget speech. The 24 January motion, in contrast, outlined 14 specific measures. Accordingly, in its response, the government provided more detailed and comprehensive information.

In addition to the stress on current policy, it is noteworthy that the government places great emphasis on public consultation and reviews. Uncertain replies are generally related to an ongoing consultation or review plan. Although many motions urge the government to take specific actions or legislate on a particular issue, members find it difficult to exert strong and immediate pressure on the government. However, notwithstanding the absence of any binding power, a successful motion reflects consensus amongst Legco members and the general public and should therefore be taken seriously by the government.

## No Confidence Motions

Some motions require special attention because they are clear expressions of 'no confidence' in principal officials, often urging these officials to accept responsibility. The term 'no confidence motion' in Legco is similar to a 'motion of censure' or vote of no confidence in the British Parliament, which declares 'That this House has no confidence in Her Majesty's Government' and normally includes words indicating the particular matter on which the opposition wishes to censure the government.[25] In Britain, if a censure motion is carried, the government is obliged to resign or seek the dissolution of Parliament.[26] However, this convention is not directed at the conduct of Ministers, either

25 Blackburn and Kennon, *Griffith & Ryle on Parliament: Functions, Practice and Procedures*, 484–485.

26 Modern practice since 1895 suggests dissolution rather than resignation. The censure motion is usually mentioned along with 'vote of confidence'. The government may say in advance that it regards a particular vote as one of confidence. A government defeat in either motion may lead to the resignation of the government or dissolution, because the government lost the support of majority of parliament. See Blackburn and Kennon, ibid, 60–61 and 484–485.

individually or collectively.[27] Notwithstanding use of the term of 'no confidence', a no confidence motion in Hong Kong is unlikely to share the particular nature of a censure motion in the British Parliament. Censure resolutions in the US Congress, in contrast, some of which use the phrase 'loss of confidence' or are described as no confidence votes,[28] share greater similarity with no confidence motions in Hong Kong. For example, there are no constitutional provisions or specific legal effect for no confidence votes in either jurisdiction, and both are critical of officials (including Presidents in the US).[29] Notwithstanding doubts over the propriety of Congressional censure of public officials, the introduction of censure resolutions has become accepted Congressional practice accepted in both houses of the US Congress.[30]

Similar doubts have been raised over the use of no confidence motions in Legco. Some commentators have argued that the Basic Law makes no provision for no confidence motions and that such motions deprive the HKSAR Government of the power to nominate principal officials and the CPG of the power to appoint such officials.[31] Despite these doubts, pro-democracy members of Legco have moved eight motions of no confidence since the return of sovereignty to China, including three moved between 1999 and 2003 and another five moved between 2012 and 2013, as shown in Table 5.11.

In the earlier period, votes of no confidence were moved against the Secretary for Justice (in 1999), the Chairperson of the Housing Authority (HA) and Director of Housing (in 2000), and the Financial Secretary (in 2003). The first motion of no confidence in the then CE was moved in April 2012. Shortly after Mr Leung Chun Ying's assumption of office as CE on 1 July 2012, two motions of no confidence in him were moved, and the Secretary for Development and Secretary for Education were the subject of another motion of no confidence in the same year. Of the eight no confidence motions moved,

---

27 May, Mckay, and Cranmer, *Erskine May's Treatise on the Law, Privileges, Proceedings, and Usage of Parliament*, 330.

28 Such resolutions officially express an opinion concerning an executive officer using the terms of 'confidence', 'censure', 'condemnation' and 'resignation', see Jack Maskell and Richard S. Beth, '"No Confidence" Votes and Other Forms of Congressional Censure of Public Officials' (RL34037, Congrssional Research Service, 11 June 2007) <https://www.hsdl.org/?view&did=739550>, accessed 2 January 2015.

29 Ibid.

30 Ibid.

31 Weiyun Xiao, '关于香港特别行政区基本法的几个问题 (Three Problems About the Basic Law of Hong Kong Special Administrative Region)', 法学杂志 (*Law Science Magazine*), 2 (2005), 8.

TABLE 5.11 *No confidence motions moved at Legco's plenary meetings, 1998–2013*

| Motion | Date | Mover | Voting Result | Resignation (Y/N) |
|---|---|---|---|---|
| Vote of no confidence in the Secretary for Justice | 11 Mar 1999 | Margaret Ng | N | N |
| Vote of no confidence in the Chairman of the HA and the Director of Housing | 28 June 2000 | Fred Li | P | Y (Chairman of the HA) |
| Vote of no confidence in the Financial Secretary | 7 May 2003 | Margaret Ng | N | Y |
| Vote of no confidence in the Chief Executive | 19 April 2012 | Tanya Chan | N | N |
| Vote of no confidence in the President of Legislative Council | 11 July 2012 | Wong Yuk Man | Not dealt with | N |
| Vote of no confidence in the Secretary for Development and the Secretary for Education | 14 Nov 2012 | Wong Yuk Man | N | N |
| Vote of no confidence in the Chief Executive | 12 Dec 2012 | Wu Chi Wai | N | N |
| Vote of no confidence in the Chief Executive | 16 Oct 2013 | Kwok Ka Ki | N | N |

SOURCE: THE AUTHOR'S CALCULATION BASED ON HANSARD HK (1998–2013).

only those against the HA Chairperson and Director of Housing passed. A vote of no confidence in the President of Legco had not been dealt with by the end of the most recent Legco term, and the other six were negatived.

### *No Confidence Motions in Early Days of the HKSAR*

The vote of no confidence in the then Secretary for Justice, Ms Elsie Leung, in 1999 was aimed at her decision not to prosecute Ms Sally Aw Sian, Chairperson of the newspaper group that publishes the *Sing Tao Daily* and *Hong Kong Standard*. The motion also questioned the role of the Secretary for Justice in seeking clarification from the NPCSC on the right of abode ruling made by the Court of Final Appeal.[32] On 18 March 1998, three employees of the *Hong Kong Standard* were charged with conspiring with Ms Aw to inflate the

32 Margaret Ng's speech on no confidence motion in the Secretary for Justice, Hansard HK (11 March 1999).

paper's circulation figures,[33] but Ms Aw was not prosecuted. The decision not to prosecute was criticised for violating the principle of equality before the law because Ms Aw happened to be a family friend of the then CE and a member of the Chinese People's Political Consultative Conference.[34] Secretary Leung's position further worsened when she offered an explanation based partly on the public interest.[35] Before Legco met to debate the motion, the government mounted an extensive lobbying campaign against it,[36] and the motion was ultimately defeated by 29 votes to 21, with eight abstentions. Although Ms Secretary Leung did not offer her resignation, her standing and authority as Secretary for Justice were undoubtedly damaged.[37]

The second motion of no confidence moved by Legco derived from a series of scandals concerning the construction of public housing and Home Ownership Scheme flats, which collectively became known as the 'short piling' scandal. From 1999 to 2000, a number of public housing-related building problems were uncovered, arousing serious public concern.[38] On 3 November 1999, Councillor Leung Yiu Chung moved a motion expressing the Council's disappointment with the HA's performance and requesting the government to overhaul its composition. Both FC and GC members rejected this motion. Meanwhile, the HA set up two investigative panels in September 1999 and January 2000, although these remedial measures did not please many Legco members. On 20 March 2000, a motion was passed by the Legco Panel on Housing requesting the CE to appoint a statutory committee to undertake a review of the operations of the entire construction industry and to follow up on the investigations of the cases of Tin Chung Court, Tin Shui Wai and Yuen Chau Kok.[39] Subsequently, the two HA investigative panels published reports

---

33 Ibid.

34 Ibid.

35 Anne S.Y. Cheung and Albert H.Y. Chen, 'The Search for the Rule of Law in the Hong Kong Special Administrative Region, 1997–2003', in Wong Yiu-Chung (ed.), *"One Country, Two Systems" in Crisis: Hong Kong's Transformation Since the Handover* (Lanham: Lexington Books, 2004), 74–75.

36 Chen, 'Hong Kong's Legal System in the New Constitutional Order: The Experience of 1997–2000', 243.

37 Ibid.

38 The Select Committee on Building Problems of Public Housing Units of Legco, 'First Report of the Select Committee on Building Problems of Public Housing Units' (2003) <http://www.legco.gov.hk/yr02-03/english/sc/sc_bldg/reports/rpt_1.htm>, accessed 10 September 2011, 1–2.

39 Panel on Housing, 'Minute of meeting held on 20 March 2000' (LC Paper No. CB(1) 1870/99-00, 2010), 9–10.

in March and May, respectively, which were followed by the appointment of an Investigation Panel on Staff Discipline by the Secretary for Housing in June 2000.[40] Legco was still not satisfied, however, and on 9 June 2000 Councillor Fred Li of the Democratic Party (DP) gave notice of a motion of no confidence in HA Chairperson Ms Rosanna Wong and Director of Housing Mr Tony Miller. Since Legco had first put the no confidence motion on the agenda, Ms Wong had offered to resign on many occasions, but her resignation had been rejected by the then CE.[41] She finally tendered her resignation on 24 June 2000 when she felt that she no longer enjoyed the confidence of the community, despite the strong persuasion to stay by the CE.[42] Her decision to resign was welcomed by Legco members, but did not affect the no confidence motion debate on 28 June.[43] The motion passed by 39 to 9 votes, with six abstentions. Its passage was quite significant, as it constituted the first time for Legco to pass a no confidence motion against a senior public service figure and senior civil servant, even though some legislators expressed certain reservations about the involvement of Mr Miller, who ultimately chose not to resign.

The third no confidence motion was related to a suspected conflict of interest. In 2003, then Financial Secretary Mr Antony Leung failed to declare his purchase of a luxury car just as he was about to raise the first registration vehicle tax in the budget.[44] He offered a sincere apology, but insisted that his mistake was purely due to negligence. Mr Leung also donated HK$380,000 to charity, twice the amount of the tax discrepancy, to compensate for the oversight.[45] On 10 March, he offered to resign over the brewing scandal, but his resignation was refused by then CE Mr Tung Chee Hwa. Mr Tung recognised that Mr Leung had breached the code for principal officials under the accountability system, but insisted that what he had done amounted only to gross negligence, not to corruption.[46] Democrats were unconvinced by either Mr Tung's

40 '房局查涉短樁案員工 知產權署長任小組主席 (Director of Intellectual Property Department Chaired the Investigation Panel on Staff Discipline set up by the Secretary for Housing)', *Hong Kong Daily News*, 14 June 2000, A05.

41 '王易鳴政治壓力下辭職 (Rosanna Wong Resigned under Political Pressure)', *Ming Pao Daily News*, 25 June 2000, A02.

42 Ibid.

43 Ibid.

44 Editorial, 'Mr Leung is Discredited, so Let Him Go, Mr Tung', *South China Morning Post*, 8 May 2003, P10.

45 Jermain T.M. Lam, 'Ministerial System in Hong Kong: A Strengthening of the Executive Leadership', *Asian Perspective*, 28 (2004), 206.

46 'ICAC Complaint Lodged over Antony Leung's Car', *South China Morning Post*, 17 March 2003.

defence or Mr Leung's explanation.[47] On 9 April, Councillor Yeung Sum of the DP moved a motion to appoint a Select Committee to investigate the purchase of a personal vehicle by the Financial Secretary. Although this motion was vetoed, a motion of no confidence in the Financial Secretary was proposed by an independent Councillor Margaret Ng on 7 May. It was defeated by 31 to 22 votes, with two abstentions. Despite the voting results, the Financial Secretary's 'credibility took a beating with the revelations',[48] and the newly introduced accountability system was also damaged by the CE's decision to refuse Mr Leung's resignation.[49] About two months later, the Financial Secretary formally submitted his resignation to the CE, which was finally accepted on 16 July when Mr Tung's government was in the midst of its worst crises to date, namely, the SARS outbreak, Article 23 legislation and the aftermath of the large-scale protest march on 1 July.

These three motions of no confidence differed in their consequences, public reactions, and impact on the accountability system. Then HA Chairperson Ms Wong offered her resignation even before voting on the no confidence motion began, whilst the former Financial Secretary eventually stepped down despite the motion's defeat. Hence, it is difficult to draw any conclusion concerning the correlation between the result of a no confidence motion and the resignation of a government official. It seems to be public confidence and the political situation that ultimately determine whether an official stays or goes. In the Antony Leung case, as one commentator said, 'even though he escaped a formal censure with the help of pro-government legislators, he will not be able to stare people in the eye as he discharges his duties'.[50] In addition, the introduction of the Principal Officials Accountability System (POAS) in 2002 may have provided the institutional motivation for Mr Leung's resignation.[51]

### *Recent Development of No Confidence Motions*

The rank of the officials censured by motions of no confidence since 2012 is obviously higher than previously. The most recent such motions included three votes of no confidence against the CE, one against the President of Legco and one against two principal officials.

The first vote of no confidence in the CE was moved by Councillor Tanya Chan, who expressed her distrust of then CE Mr Donald Tsang. A series of

47 Lam (n 45).

48 See 'Mr Leung is Discredited, so Let Him Go, Mr Tung' (n 44).

49 Ibid.

50 Ibid.

51 Lam (n 45), 207.

scandals involving Mr Tsang were exposed in 2012. In the first, it was revealed that he had accepted hospitality from several businessmen without declaring a potential conflict of interest.[52] Mr Tsang was then accused of granting a licence to Digital Broadcasting Corporation Hong Kong Ltd (DBC) and subsequently renting an apartment from the major shareholder of DBC at a low price.[53] The vote of no confidence in the President of Legco resulted from the President's decision to curtail debate on the Legislative Council (Amendment) Bill 2012.[54]

The expressions of no confidence in the Secretary for Development and Secretary for Education, which were debated in a single motion, had different motivations. The accusations against Secretary for Development Mr Paul Chan involved several instances of alleged misconduct, whilst Secretary for Education Mr Eddie Ng was accused of implementing a national education policy that arousing strong public antipathy.[55]

The first motion of no confidence in current CE Mr Leung Chun Ying was aimed at his 'integrity problem' during the CE election campaign. Mr Leung had fiercely attacked another CE candidate, Mr Henry Tang, in a televised debate over unauthorised building works on Mr Tang's house. However, shortly after Mr Leung was elected, unauthorised building works were also discovered at his residence.[56] The second vote of no confidence in Mr Leung was motivated by a series of incidents, including his refusal to issue a free television licence to Hong Kong TV and his performance in the aftermath of a fatal ferry crash off Lamma Island.[57] The CE was also criticised for creating divisions in society and failing to fulfil his election promises.[58] It is noteworthy that both votes of no confidence in the CE cited Mr Leung's low popularity rating as evidence of his incompetence in the top job.

The more frequent use of no confidence motions in recent years reflects the growing conflict between the government and the pro-democracy camp within Legco. In contrast to the votes of no confidence seen in the early days of the HKSAR, recent years have seen a shift in focus from expressions of dismay at the personal misconduct of government officials in particular incidents to the

---

52 Hansard HK (19 April 2012), 8516, 8521.

53 Ibid., 8516, 8517–8518.

54 'Vote of no confidence in the President of the Legislative Council' (LC Paper No. CB(3) 916/11–12, 2012).

55 Hansard HK (14 November 2012), 1925.

56 Hansard HK (12 December 2012), 3735.

57 Hansard HK (16 October 2013), 708–712.

58 Ibid.

general incompetence of government officials, as seen particularly in the votes of no confidence in the current CE.

### *Propriety of Introducing a No Confidence Motion*

There has been considerable debate over the propriety of introducing a no confidence motion in Legco. Professor Xiao Weiyun, one of the drafter of the Basic Law, has argued that such introduction contravenes the Basic Law.[59] He insists that neither Article 64 nor Article 73 of the Basic Law, which stipulate the accountability of the government to Legco and the functions of Legco, respectively, includes the power to move a no confidence motion.[60] Professor Xiao believes that such power is not conducive to an executive-led system and has essentially served to expand Legco's power.[61] In this sense, he distinguishes a no confidence motion from a regular motion concerning the public interest.[62] Professor Xiao's arguments are widely accepted by other mainland academics. For example, Dr Wang Yu argues that the CE's nomination power and CPG's appointment power for principal officials under Article 48(5) of the Basic Law have been derogated by the debating and voting on no confidence motions in Legco,[63] and Professor Cheng Jie regards these motions as a specific manifestation of Legco's expansion of power.[64] The latter scholar furthermore sees POAS, which was implemented in 2002, as providing an institutional basis for no confidence motions, with principal officials' accountability to the CE shifting to accountability to Legco.[65]

These critics pose two essential questions: (1) whether the introduction of a no confidence motion is consistent with the Basic Law, namely, the question of constitutionality, and (2) whether Legco has expanded its power by moving such motions. The second question is subordinate to the first in nature.

With respect to the question of constitutionality, the arguments of most critics rely primarily on the absence of express constitutional provision for no confidence motions. However, the absence of such a provision is not necessarily indicative of the unconstitutionality of the practice. Furthermore, Article 73(6) of the Basic Law empowers Legco to debate issues concerning the

59 Xiao (n 31).

60 Ibid.

61 Ibid.

62 Ibid.

63 Yu Wang, "一国两制" 宪法精神研究 (*A Study of the Spirit of the Constitution Concerning 'One Country Two Systems'*) (Guangzhou: Guangdong People's Press, 2008), 204–205.

64 Jie Cheng, '香港宪制发展与行政主导体制 (Constitutional Development and the Executive-Dominated System in Hong Kong)', 法学 (*Legal Science*), 1 (2009), 48–49.

65 Ibid.

public interest. It is clear that debating the conduct of officials and the CE and expressing a lack of confidence in their performance is relevant to the public interest, and there is no substantial difference between regular motions and motions of no confidence, neither of which has a specific legal effect. A successful vote of no confidence in officials or the CE places neither under a legal obligation to step down, and is also unlikely to derogate the CE's power to nominate and the CPG's power to appoint principal officials under Article 48(5). Accordingly, there is no legal basis to the claim that introducing a no confidence motion is inconsistent with the Basic Law or that Legco has expanded its power by doing so.

The real influence of a no confidence motions is more properly viewed from the political angle than the legal angle. The impeachment procedure outlined in Article 73(9) provides a device for Legco to officially censure the CE for a serious breach of law or dereliction of duty. However, the Basic Law lacks any express procedure for officially censuring officials for misconduct or for censuring the CE for behaviour that falls short of qualifying for an impeachment proceeding. Under the circumstances, a no confidence motion in Legco is similar in nature to such censures, notwithstanding the absence of any legal effect.

The battle over no confidence motions between legislators and government officials is often described as a battle over legitimacy and a public mandate.[66] The real political pressure to resign that is exerted upon officials has its origins in public opinion, namely, popular distrust of the government. Given the absence of any strong external accountability to the public on the part of the executive under the existing political system, debates over no confidence motions may offer a safety valve to release the pressure arising from public outcry over scandals or failures of duty involving government officials,[67] and may also stimulate discussion of reforms to the accountability system.[68] The introduction of no

66 Ma, *Political Development in Hong Kong: State, Political Society, and Civil Society*, 130.

67 In the case of the no confidence motion in the chairperson of Housing Authority and Director of Housing, at first the HA made an attempt to deal with the incident through internal investigation, and the government then would took disciplinary action or legal action. However, all of the measures rarely involved the leadership of the HA as well as the Housing Department which exactly were required to be held accountable for the building blunders due to their failures in supervision. Accordingly, the passage of the no confidence motion carried a message that what the public expect was not only a government with bureaucratic accountability to a certain extent, but also a more accountable government in the sense of political accountability.

68 A good example is the motion debate on no confidence against the chairperson of Housing Authority and Director of Housing. In that case, there was a view that the two posts should be treated separately in that the chairperson of Housing Authority could be perceived as a political appointee and a sort of Minister, whilst the Director of Housing

confidence motions may embarrass government officials and the CE by censuring their conduct. However, the malfunction of the executive-led system actually derives from almost every aspect of the governance system,[69] and can hardly be resolved by emphasising the constitutional power of the executive or restraining the legislature from proactively exercising its power.

## Motion for Adjournment of the Council

A motion for adjournment of the Council is another special type of motion that is moved 'when for any sufficient reason it is not desired to formulate a motion in express terms for the purpose of debating an issue or issues'.[70] Such a motion is neither subject to any specific action (distinct from ordinary motions) or limited by wording restrictions (distinct from members' questions).[71] Any member or designated public officer attending a Council meeting may move a motion to adjourn the Council for the purpose of debating an issue or issues. According to Rule 16 of the RoP, adjournment motions can take place in two situations:

1. to move such motion between two items of business with the permission of the President, if the President is satisfied that the adjournment is for the purpose of discussing a specific issue of *urgent public importance* [Rule 16(2)]; and
2. to move such motion at the conclusion of all the business on the Agenda of the Council for the purpose of raising any issue concerning *public interest*, with a view to eliciting a reply from a designated public officer [Rule 16(4)]. (Italic type added by the author for emphasis)

---

was supposed to be an apolitical civil servant. See Leong Che Hung's speech at the Legco meeting, Hansard HK (28 June 2000), 9246.

69 As Professor Anthony Cheung points out, the executive-led system has not functioned successfully over the years and there has been the process of 'hollowing-out' of executive power. In Tung Chee haw's era, this hollowing-out process resulted from several components, including institutional incompatibility, policy performance shortfalls, politics-bureaucracy disjunction and withdrawal of local and central government trust. Amongst these components, the incompatibility between the Basic Law's institutional arrangements and the changing political environment is considered as the fundamental cause. See Anthony Cheung, 'Executive-Led Governance or Executive Power "Hollowed-out"—the Political Quagmire of Hong Kong', *Asian Journal of Political Science*, 15 (2007) 21, 24.

70 RoP, Rule 16(1).

71 Cheek-Milby (n 1).

With respect to an adjournment motion that requires a reply from a designated public officer, members need to give notice of the issue in writing to the Clerk not less than seven clear days before the meeting, provided that the President waives the notice.[72] The time limit on a single adjournment debate in the RoP increased from one hour to one-and-a-half hours in May 2008.

There are distinct requirements for the introduction of both types of adjournment motions. Adjournment motions under Rule 16(2), namely, those moved between two items, do not require seven days' notice but must be of urgent public importance. The public importance requirement makes it more difficult for this type of adjournment motion to obtain the President's approval than motions moved at the conclusion of all business on the agenda under Rule 16(4). The results of adjournment motions between 1998 and 2013 are listed in Table 5.12.

Adjournment motions moved under Rule 16(4) need only satisfy the requirement of being of the 'public interest', which has a very broad meaning. After members give notice of such a motion, the House Committee (HC) discusses and recommends its decision to the President. Even if the HC does not accede to members' requests, members can still seek the President's decision. The President might still allow the introduction if he/she believes that the HC's decision was politically motivated and therefore should be overturned.[73] Furthermore, in cases in which no notice is given and no HC meetings are held, the President will try to seek members' views, particularly those of the major political parties, in making a decision on whether the notice should be waived.[74]

From 1998 to 2013, the President refused to waive the notice of one adjournment motion moved under Rule 16(4). In that case, Councillor Albert Ho had proposed an adjournment motion to debate the Court of Final Appeal's decision to request an interpretation of the Basic Law from the NPCSC regarding the controversy over diplomatic immunity from debt litigation involving the Democratic Republic of the Congo.[75] Of the 23 motions tabled in Legco during this period, 13 were passed and 10 had not been voted on at the expiry of the one-and-a-half-hour limit imposed under Rule 16(7), as shown in Table 5.12.

---

72 RoP, Rule 16(5).

73 Interview with President Rita Fan on 1 December 2010.

74 In the case of Councillor Yeung Sum's motion for adjournment to debate March on 1 July 2003, through collecting members' views, the President finally waived the notice, Hansard HK (3 July 2003), 8378–8379.

75 The President's Ruling on Albert HO Chun-yan's Application for Moving a Motion for the Adjournment of the Council (14 June 2011).

TABLE 5.12 *Result of motions for adjournment debate, 1998–2013*

| Legco Term | Moved under Rule 16(2) | | | | Moved under Rule 16(4) | | | | | Total |
|---|---|---|---|---|---|---|---|---|---|---|
| | Negatived by the President | Negatived by the Council | P | Total | Negatived by the President | Negatived by the Council | Not Voted | P | Total | |
| 1998–2000 | 0 | 0 | 0 | 0 | 0 | 0 | 0 | 0 | 0 | 0 |
| 2000–2004 | 0 | 1 | 0 | 1 | 0 | 0 | 0 | 2 | 2 | 3 |
| 2004–2008 | 4 | 4 | 0 | 8 | 0 | 0 | 2 | 4 | 6 | 14 |
| 2008–2012 | 7 | 6 | 0 | 13 | 1 | 0 | 7 | 5 | 13 | 26 |
| 2012–2013 | 3 | 0 | 0 | 3 | 0 | 0 | 1 | 2 | 3 | 6 |
| Total | 14 | 11 | 0 | 25 | 1 | 0 | 10 | 13 | 24 | 49 |

SOURCE: THE AUTHOR'S CALCULATION BASED ON HANSARD HK (1998–2013).
Note: P, Passed.

In contrast to adjournment motions moved under Rule 16(4), more stringent requirements are imposed on those moved between two items of business (often two motions) under Rule 16(2). To guarantee impartiality, Ms Rita Fan, President of Legco from 1998 to 2008, applied two principles in deciding what constitutes a matter of 'urgent public importance'. These principles have been followed by her successor, President Jasper Tsang. For example, in President Tsang's ruling on an application to move a motion for adjournment of the Council proposed by Councillor Leung Kwok Hung on 27 January 2010, he ruled:[76]

> I had made reference to the rulings of the former President on Members' applications for moving the same type of motion debates, and noted that the former President had established in a number of rulings the following two principles for consideration, namely:
> (a) if the debate is not carried out at the Council meeting specified by the Member concerned, whether there will be any *irreversible consequences*, and
> (b) if the issue is not debated at that Council meeting, whether the Council will not debate the issue in the foreseeable future. [Italic type added by the author for emphasis]

76 The President's Ruling on the Application for Moving a Motion for the Adjournment of the Council by Hon LEUNG Kwok-hung (22 January 2010).

According to former President Fan, the first principle concerning 'irreversible consequences' is the primary consideration that must be taken into account when making a decision about whether there is any urgency to move an adjournment motion under Rule 16(2).[77] If a motion does not satisfy the 'irreversible consequences' criterion, then it should be proposed by means of an ordinary motion, which may require notice and be placed on the ballot. Hence, her application of the principle of 'irreversible consequences' set a precedent for future Legco Presidents' rulings on 'urgent' adjournment motions.

The President rarely makes decisions on the terms of adjournment motions, as they are usually proposed without formulating express terms. However, in recent years, President Tsang has considered Rule 16(1) of the RoP together with the existing requirements for the introduction of adjournment motion in two cases. Rule 16(1) reads as follows.

> When for any sufficient reason it is not desired to formulate a motion in express terms for the purpose of debating an issue or issues, a motion that the Council do now adjourn may be moved for the purpose of such a debate.

In December 2012, Councillor Leung Kwok Hung proposed an adjournment motion which called for mainland dissidents' relatives Liu Xia and Li Wangling to be released from house arrest and for a full investigation of the murder of fellow dissident Li Wangyang.[78] President Tsang ruled that Leung's motion was inadmissible under Rule 16(1) because of such express terms as 'cease' [停止], 'investigate fully' [徹查] and 'unjust sentence' [冤案], which were indicative of a particular leaning. In addition, he ruled that the urgency of the issue had not been sufficiently established.[79] Another motion proposed by Councillor Leung raised the question whether the CE should provide an explanation to the public and be questioned by Legco members over the allegations made by Mr Lew Mon Hung in the iSun Affairs magazine.[80] In this ruling, President Tsang did not even specify the terms he considered to be out of order under Rule 16(1).

---

77 Interview with Councillor Rita Fan on 1 December 2010.

78 The persons named in the motion are political dissenters and their family members in mainland China, see the President's Ruling on the Application for Moving a Motion for the Adjournment of the Council by Hon LEUNG Kwok-hung (11 December 2012) (only in Chinese).

79 Ibid.

80 President's Ruling on the Application for Moving a Motion for the Adjournment of the Council by Hon LEUNG Kwok-hung (29 January 2013) (only in Chinese).

President Tsang's rulings in both cases raise the serious question of whether a motion for adjournment of the Council can include express terms indicative of a particular leaning, which is a new restriction that was never applied by his predecessor in similar cases.

Between 1998 and 2013, the President of the day negatived 10 motions for adjournment of the Council under Rule 16(2), as shown in Table 5.12. However, even those that were permitted under Rule 16(2) failed to pass Legco.

The limitations on motions for adjournment debates imply that they serve special purposes. Both types of debates discussed above, but particularly those moved between two items of business, may substantially modify the original agenda of Legco decided by the President and announced to all participants in advance. In making decisions on such motions, the President must safeguard members' right to debate issues concerning the public interest on the one hand and ensure the smooth operation of Council meetings on the other. In practice, the average pass rate of adjournment motions is much lower than that of ordinary motions without legislative effect, which may be connected with the nature of the issues contained therein. Most adjournment motions proposed by members are related to constitutional and political affairs or livelihood issues, which are the most controversial types of the issues in ordinary motions. Hence, very few adjournment motions are put to a vote and passed.[81]

## Conclusion

The content of members' motions without legislative effect are subject to fewer restrictions than that of private member's bills and member's CSAs. The President in the 1998–2008 sessions rarely made controversial rulings. The only exceptions were her rulings on the disallowance of several accusatory expressions concerning the NPCSC and CPG in motions and amendments. It is noteworthy that her successor, President Tsang, imposed a new restriction on the content of members' motions in interpreting Rule 16(1), although it remains open to question whether that restriction constitutes a sound restriction on members' freedom of speech.

Motion debates have become a crucial channel for discussing public policy and achieving consensus in Legco. During these debates, political groups can present policy initiatives, review existing policies and urge the executive to improve policy implementation or legislation. In contrast to the low degree of

81 According to the author's calculation based on Hansard HK, seven subjects were related to constitutional and political affairs and ten were related to transport and housing.

participation by pro-Beijing political groups in moving CSAs to government bills, the pro-Beijing camp is more active in moving motions. Increasing numbers of amendments to motions have been proposed and passed over the years. The analysis of motions for adjournment in the preceding section highlights the core function of motion debates, that is, to secure legislators' right to fully debate issues relating to the public interest. Motion debates enhance members' ability to effect policy in terms of reflecting and conditioning public opinion. The ongoing debate over the propriety of introducing no confidence motions indicates that motions can serve as a multi-purpose weapon by which legislators hold the government accountable, although the process of exploring ways of using that weapon is usually accompanied by a competition for power and a public mandate between the legislature and executive.

CHAPTER 6

# Questions

Questions in the British Parliament are used to 'seek information or to press for action', and they 'oblige Ministers to explain and defend the work, policy decisions and actions of their Departments'.[1] Since their first use in 1721, questions in Parliament have undergone significant and striking changes, including the introduction of 'Prime Minister's Questions'.[2] Although the major function of questions remains unchanged, they now serve such specific purposes as seeking attention, harrying the government, and releasing the tensions and passions caused by deep divisions of opinion.[3]

Questions in the Hong Kong legislature (Legco) play a similar role to those in the British Parliament, namely, allowing legislators to seek information from the government, although that role did not become prominent until the 1960s.[4] The most important related change prior to 1997 was the introduction of a monthly question time by Governor Patten in 1992. This innovation made the executive branch more accountable to the legislature, although severe restrictions were imposed on the subject and length of questions that could be asked.[5] In post-1997 Legco, questions to the CE are raised during the CE's question-and-answer sessions, which usually take place four or five times a year. With the exception of Rule 25 governing the content of questions, the rules regulating questions to the government do not apply to the CE's question-and-answer sessions, thereby distinguishing questions to the CE from questions to government officials. This chapter discusses the restrictions on the nature and content of questions, and analyses those put questions to the government and those put to the CE.

1 House of Commons Information Office, 'Parliamentary Questions', [web document] (August 2010), <http://www.parliament.uk/documents/commons-information-office/p01.pdf>, accessed 1 July 2014.

2 Ibid.

3 Philip Norton, 'Questions and the Role of Parliament', in Mark N. Franklin, Philip Norton, and Study of Parliament Group. (eds.), *Parliamentary Questions* (Oxford: Clarendon Press, 1993) 197–199.

4 Cheek-Milby, *A Legislature Comes of Age: Hong Kong's Search for Influence and Identity* 156.

5 The subject matter was determined by the Governor and was limited to topics that had been addressed by the Governor in his opening comments, see Cheek-Milby, ibid., 156, 291.

 | DOI 10.1163/9789004276284_007

### Notice and Number of Questions

Rule 22(1) of the RoP provides that a question should be addressed 'to the Government on the work of the Government, and either seeking information on such matter or asking for official action with regard to it'. With the exception of urgent questions, notice of a question to the government should be given no later than seven clear days before the meeting at which an answer is required.[6] Following the increase in Legco seats in the 2012 election, the number of questions that may be asked at one meeting was increased from 20 to 22 in 2013.[7] Of the 22 questions permitted, only six can seek oral replies, with the remainder able to solicit written replies alone.[8] Hence, opportunities to seek oral replies are more precious to members. In addition, the President may permit members to ask urgent questions without notice on the grounds of urgency and/or public importance, provided that he/she is satisfied that sufficient private notice has been given to the government.[9] Another restriction is that each member may ask no more than two questions or one oral question at one meeting, excluding questions asked by another member with the original mover's consent.[10] Moreover, the President may allow a member to ask an additional question if he/she is satisfied that that question is an important one of public concern.[11] Supplementary questions are often raised to elucidate an answer to a particular question, but the President may disallow a supplementary question if it is unrelated to the original question or infringes Rule 22 (on the nature of questions) or Rule 25 (on the content of questions).

### Content of Questions

Rule 25 provides restrictions on the content of questions to the government and the CE. In summarising these restrictions in Table 6.1, reference was made to Erskine May's categories of rules regulating the content of questions in the British Parliament[12] because Legco has retained most such rules, with the exception of those relating to the royal family and royal prerogatives.[13]

6 RoP, Rule 24(2).
7 RoP, Rule 23(2).
8 RoP, Rule 23(3).
9 RoP, Rule 24(4).
10 RoP, Rules 24(3), 24(3)(A), 26(6) and 26(6A).
11 RoP, Rule 24(3A).
12 May, Mckay, and Cranmer, *Erskine May's Treatise on the Law, Privileges, Proceedings, and Usage of Parliament* 346–353.
13 For restrictions on questions in the British Parliament, see May, ibid., 347.

TABLE 6.1 *Restrictions on content of questions*

| Restriction | Related rules |
|---|---|
| Personal reflections | Rule 25(1)(a): A question shall not include the names of persons, or statements which are not strictly necessary to make the question intelligible.<br>Rule 25(1)(j): A question shall not be asked about the character or conduct of any person mentioned in Rule 41(7) (Contents of Speeches) and a question shall not be asked about the character or conduct of any other person except in his official or public capacity. |
| Factual basis | Rule 25(1)(b): A question shall not contain a statement which the Member who asks the question is not prepared to substantiate. |
| Argument and disorderly expressions | Rule 25(1)(c): A question shall not contain arguments, inferences, opinions, imputations or epithets, or tendentious, ironical or offensive expressions. |
| Secret | Rule 25(1)(f): A question shall not seek information about a matter which is of its nature secret. |
| Reflection on Judicial decision | Rule 25(1)(g): A question shall not reflect on the decision of a court of law or be so drafted as to be likely to prejudice a case pending in a court of law. |
| Accessible documents or ordinary works of references | Rule 25(1)(k): A question shall not be asked seeking information which can be found in accessible documents or ordinary works of reference. |
| Questions already answered | Rule 25(1)(l): A question which has been fully answered shall not be asked again during the same session. |
| The same subject matter | Rule 25(3): The President may rule a question out of order if the question is substantially the same as that of any matter raised in another earlier question, notice of which has been given earlier for the same Council meeting, raised in an earlier motion or a bill, notice of which has been given earlier for a specific Council meeting, or being considered by a standing committee or a select committee or a inquiry committee. |

TABLE 6.1 *Restrictions on content of questions* (cont.)

| Restriction | Related rules |
|---|---|
| Miscellaneous | Rule 25(1)(d): A question shall not contain independent questions or be so complex that it cannot reasonably be answered as a single question.<br>Rule 25(1)(i): A question shall not be asked whether statements in the press or of private individuals or private concerns are accurate.<br>Rule 25(1)(h): A question shall not be asked for the purpose of obtaining an expression of opinion, the solution of an abstract legal question, or the answer to a hypothetical proposition. |

SOURCE: THE AUTHOR'S COMPILATION BASED ON THE ROP.

If a question violates the rules in Table 6.1 or Rule 22 (on the nature of questions), alteration may be required to prevent the President from ruling the question out of order.[14] Similar restrictions on personal reflection, disorderly expressions and reflection on judicial decisions can be found in Rule 41, which regulates the content of speeches and also applies to motion debates. However, the restrictions on the content of questions in the RoP are distinct from those on the content of motions. First, the restriction on arguments in a question indicates that questions cannot be used as a device to prompt debate or express opinions. Second, there must be a necessity to use questions to obtain information, that is, the information cannot be available in readily accessible documents or ordinary works of reference such as annual reports. Third, questions must be drafted in a clear manner, and should not be overly complex or contain several independent questions. Finally, the content of questions should fall within the responsibility or capacity of government officials. Hence, questions asked to confirm the accuracy of statements in the press or made by private individuals may be ruled out of order.

These peculiar restrictions on the content of questions highlight the major purpose served by asking questions and distinguish them from motions or any other Legco functions.

14 RoP, Rule 25(2).

The President of Legco occasionally makes rulings on the content of questions. For example, on 30 September 1998, in a supplementary question, Councillor Andrew Wong queried the Secretary for Security on the total number of applications for permission to intercept communications that the CE and authorised persons had approved since 1 July 1997.[15] The Secretary refused to answer the question on the ground that the answer would involve confidential information.[16] Councillor Wong then sought the President's ruling on the matter. The then President said that she would not forbid Mr Wong from raising such a supplementary question because she did not know whether the figures involved were actually confidential. At the same time, she noted that:

> 'very often, the speaker of the legislature was unable to rule whether the answer sought related to confidential information without the support of other relevant argument or information; as such, the confidentiality or otherwise of the information could only be judged by the minister speaking on behalf of the government'.[17]

Accordingly, the President concluded in the case of Wong's question that, in the absence of sufficient information, the confidentiality of the information sought could be judged only by the official concerned.[18]

The President has also made decisions during the CE's question-and-answer sessions. On 14 January 1999, for example, Councillor Sin Chung Kai raised a question about the opening up of the local fixed network market and mentioned the name of Mr Li Ka Shing, the wealthiest businessperson in Hong Kong.[19] The President ruled that, subject to paragraph (a) of Rule 25, the CE or any other public officer 'should not answer a question on a particular person or a particular event',[20] but noted that she hoped the CE would 'answer on principle'.[21] Councillor James To expressed doubt that 'the Rules of Procedure state that if it is necessary to mention names, names must be mentioned', and further pointed out that the issue of whether to answer a question 'is [a free choice] of the Chief Executive and there is no need for guidance'.[22] However, the President rejected Councillor To's points.

15 Hansard HK (30 September 1998).
16 Ibid.
17 Ibid.
18 Ibid.
19 Hansard HK (14 January 1999).
20 Ibid.
21 Ibid.
22 Ibid.

It seems that it is difficult for the President to make rulings on members' questions because controversy often arises unexpectedly during the course of asking and answering questions. More importantly, even if the President allows controversial questions, officials have discretion over whether or not to provide an answer.

## Questions to the Government

The number of questions has remained stable over the years with the exception of the 1998–99 Legco session, which started in July, rather than October, and thus held more meetings than other sessions, as shown in Table 6.2. Supplementary questions are usually raised after officials have given answers to original oral questions. As Table 6.2 shows, between 1998 and 2013, five to six supplementary questions on average were raised for each principal question. As the total time limit is one to one-and-a-half hours,[23] Legco may spend about 20 minutes on each original question and its supplementary questions.[24] In some cases, written replies may be submitted later in answer to supplementary questions that require detailed information.

With respect to members' performance in asking questions, the Catholic Monitors on Legislative Councillors points out in their annual reports that, as far as the number of questions per member is concerned, pro-democracy members are more diligent than non-democrats, and directly elected members are more diligent than FC members.[25]

With respect to the government departments that are asked to give replies to members' questions, they appear to carry different answer-related burdens. Table 6.3 lists the six principal officials in the order of the number of questions they were asked in the 2002–03 session and 2007–08 sessions. Owing to the reorganisation of government policy bureaux in 2007, the number of such bureaux increased from 11 to 12 in the 2007–08 session, and many of their policy areas differed from those of their predecessors. That said, the most 'popular' policy areas question-wise remained food, health, welfare, housing, transport, the

23 House Rules, Rule 7(a).

24 The President would remind the members that only one supplementary question could be asked when the question has taken 16 to 18 minutes.

25 See Catholic Monitors on Legislative Councillors, 'Annual Reports' (1998–2013) Catholic Monitors on Legislative Councillors, (<http://www.legco-monitors.org> accessed 10 September 2011.

TABLE 6.2 *Number of questions per session, 1998–2013*

| Year | No. of oral questions | No. of supplementary questions | Average no. of supplementary questions per question | No. of written questions | Total |
|---|---|---|---|---|---|
| 1998–1999 | 206 | 1290 | 6.26 | 585 | 2081 |
| 1999–2000 | 154 | 992 | 6.44 | 449 | 1595 |
| 2000–2001 | 159 | 986 | 6.20 | 451 | 1596 |
| 2001–2002 | 153 | 952 | 6.22 | 436 | 1541 |
| 2002–2003 | 160 | 1006 | 6.29 | 455 | 1621 |
| 2003–2004 | 155 | 909 | 5.86 | 457 | 1521 |
| 2004–2005 | 155 | 977 | 6.30 | 454 | 1586 |
| 2005–2006 | 156 | 1003 | 6.43 | 442 | 1601 |
| 2006–2007 | 167 | 951 | 5.69 | 470 | 1588 |
| 2007–2008 | 167 | 895 | 5.36 | 471 | 1533 |
| 2008–2009 | 154 | 826 | 5.36 | 443 | 1423 |
| 2009–2010 | 163 | 916 | 5.62 | 457 | 1536 |
| 2010–2011 | 178 | 847 | 4.76 | 472 | 1497 |
| 2011–2012 | 181 | 841 | 4.64 | 479 | 1501 |
| 2012–2013 | 145 | 907 | 6.25 | 473 | 1525 |

SOURCE: THE AUTHOR'S COMPILATION BASED ON ANNUAL REPORTS OF LEGCO (1998–2013).

environment, education and economic development. It is noteworthy that in the 2002–03 session, the six most popular policy bureaux gave replies to 74.3 per cent of all questions, whilst in the 2007–08 session, they answered 63.62 per cent. The decrease indicates that the reorganisation may have eased the burden on each bureau to some extent.

Two noteworthy practices can be observed: 1) concentrating on the same subject by asking questions concerning different aspects of that subject and 2) asking the same questions or follow-up questions in subsequent meetings. With regard to the first practice, 14 questions were asked about the chaos of the new airport during the 1998–99 session, some of them by individual members at the same meeting. In another case in 2003, four members belonging to different political camps reached agreement on asking oral questions about Hong Kong Harbour Fest at the same meeting. The subjects of the four questions concerned selection of the event organiser, marketing, the government's role,

TABLE 6.3 *Top six policy bureaux in selected sessions*

| 2002–2003 | | | 2007–2008 | | |
|---|---|---|---|---|---|
| **Officials** | **No.** | **Perc.** | **Officials** | **No.** | **Perc.** |
| Secretary for the Environment, Transport and Works | 122 | 19.84 | Secretary for Food and Health | 100 | 15.67 |
| Secretary for Health, Welfare and Food | 101 | 16.42 | Secretary for Transport and Housing | 93 | 14.58 |
| Secretary for Housing, Planning and Lands | 70 | 11.38 | Secretary for Commerce and Economic Development | 57 | 8.93 |
| Secretary for Security | 66 | 10.73 | Secretary for Labour and Welfare | 55 | 8.62 |
| Secretary for Economic Development and Labour | 50 | 8.13 | Secretary for the Environment | 51 | 7.99 |
| Secretary for Education and Manpower | 48 | 7.8 | Secretary for Education | 50 | 7.83 |
| Total | 457 | 74.3 | Total | 406 | 63.62 |

SOURCE: THE AUTHOR'S CALCULATION BASED ON LEGCO WEBSITE, LIST OF QUESTIONS RAISED BY MEMBERS AT THE LEGCO MEETINGS, 2002–03 AND 2007–08.

and event arrangements and ticket sales.[26] With respect to the second practice, legislators often shift to another perspective on a given question to achieve more by asking it. For instance, Councillor James To asked questions about the commencement date of the Interception of Communications Ordinance in two consecutive years, namely, 1998 and 1999. In answering him the first time round, the government expressed a negative attitude towards publicising the Ordinance's commencement date. In his question the next year, Councillor To further focused on the principles the government relied on in deciding the commencement dates of ordinances passed by the legislature.[27] This question concerned the constitutional relation between the executive branch and the legislature in the promulgation of laws. By exerting constant pressure on the government and attracting the public's attention, this practice is conducive to keeping a given issue under review.

### Chief Executive's Question-and-Answer Session

According to Legco's House Rules, questions to the CE are normally confined to specified topics of which he notifies the Council in advance.[28] Questions may be raised over the CE's policy address or concerning topics that the CE wishes to address with the Council. As Table 6.4 shows, the CE usually holds question-and-answer sessions three to five times a year, including a session dedicated to questions concerning his policy address. Four CE question-and-answer sessions have been held every year since 2002–03, except for the 2005–2006 session, which saw five such sessions. The extra session in 2005–06 resulted from an agreement achieved in January 2006 between Legco and the CE to increase the time limit to one-and-a-half hours and add an extra session for specific topics.[29] However, such an extra session was not held again until the 2011–12 session. A convention has been established concerning the time limit and frequency of the CE's question-and-answer session, although such arrangements technically fall the CE's discretion under the RoP.

26 '下周立會提 4 項質詢 (Four Questions Raised Next Week)', *Ming Pao Daily News*, 31 October 2003, A10.

27 Hansard HK (10 November 1999) 1066.

28 House Rules, Rule 4.

29 Hansard HK (12 January 2006) 3856. It is noted that year 2005–06 is the first term of the then CE, Mr Donald Tsang. This fact may help to understand his active attitude to the Legco.

TABLE 6.4 *CE's question-and-answer sessions, 1998–2013*

| Frequency | Session |
|---|---|
| 3 | 1998–1999, 1999–2000, 2000–2001, 2001–2002 |
| 4 | 2002–2003, 2003–2004, 2006–2007, 2008–2009, 2009–2010, 2010–2011 |
| 5 | 2005–2006, 2011–2012, 2012–2013 |

SOURCE: THE AUTHOR'S COMPILATION BASED ON ANNUAL REPORTS OF LEGCO (1998–2013).

The topics of the CE's addresses depend on the focus of the government's work and the economic and/or political situation at the time. Each address normally covers a wide range of subjects, making it difficult to rule legislators out of order for deviating from topics they have been notified of before the question-and-answer sessions. Sometimes the Legco President draws a line under the topic of questions. For instance, during the question-and-answer session held on 30 March 2006, the government's new work plan for the March 2006 to June 2007 period was announced. The wide-ranging nature of that plan made it very difficult for members to ask irrelevant questions. Another extreme example is what occurred during the session held on 18 May 2006. The CE had just addressed the impact of the national government's Outline of the Eleventh Five Year Plan for National Economic and Social Development on the Hong Kong economy and expected legislators to focus on it. Instead, most of the questions raised concerned local issues such as the function of the District Councils, the problems of Hong Kong's aging population and the minimum wage; very few concerned the Outline.[30]

Questions to the CE rarely solicit specific figures, which are an important target of questions to the government, particularly of written questions. Open questions provide more opportunities for the CE to explain his thoughts on his policy address and on various important policies. If the CE handles them well, the question-and-answer sessions can serve as a kind of publicity campaign, publicising government policy and burnishing the government's public image. Hence, in contrast to questions to the government, legislators obtain less specific and useful information during these sessions. However, the open questions involved do carry the risks that the CE will be asked 'surprising' or embarrassing questions, the answer to which may accidentally trigger a

30 Hansard HK (18 May 2006).

political storm. For instance, at the CE's question-and-answer session on 14 May 2009, Councillor Margaret Ng asked then CE Mr Donald Tsang: 'Can you tell the people categorically whether or not you support the vindication of the 4 June incident?'[31] After close questioning, the CE finally came out with an astonishing remark: 'My opinion represents the opinion of Hong Kong people as a whole'.[32] The democrats in Legco were so outraged by this remark that they walked out in protest, and the CE was placed in an awkward position. His opinion poll rating dropped significantly in the second half of May, and the decline was believed to relate to his inappropriate remark.[33]

## Conclusion

Symbolic importance is attached to 'question time', as it provides an opportunity for officials and the CE to be regularly questioned in public by elected representatives. For the CE and officials, it constitutes a good opportunity to explain existing policies, to gauge Councillors' reactions to upcoming policies and/or to improve the public perception of officials. The downside is that they have to face a bit of heckling and may make inappropriate remarks under pressure that risk tarnishing previous achievements.

For Legco members, question time is primarily reserved for the purposes of seeking information, pressing the government for commitments about or a stance on particular policies, and pushing for government action. It has been reported that an answer to a single question can cost over HK $10,000.[34] By providing legislators with information under its control and organising that information, the government facilitates legislators' policy research.

However, those people who value the free flow of information and government transparency may often feel disappointed with question time because officials enjoy extremely broad discretion in deciding whether to satisfy legislators' requests. The grounds for refusal include issues of confidentiality and a

31 Hansard HK (14 May 2009) 7812.

32 Ibid.

33 Dr Robert Ting-Yiu Chung's commentary on the popularity figures of CE Donald Tsang and the HKSAR Government, see The University of Hong Kong Public Opinion Programme, 'HKU POP site releases the latest popularity figures of CE Donald Tsang and the HKSAR Government, Press Release on 26 May 2009' [web page] (26 May 2009), <http://hkupop.hku.hk/english/release/release663.html>, accessed 1 June 2014.

34 '官員游說嘆為觀止 政壇回憶錄 (Stunning Lobbies by Officials)', *Sing Tao Daily*, 18 January 2001, A10.

lack of 'time and manpower', amongst other reasons.[35] In many cases, no specific reasons are given beyond repeated statements about existing policies. Embarrassing officials may succeed in attracting public attention, but is very unlikely to lead to an immediate change in policy unless the public is mobilised to exert great pressure on the government. Generally speaking, question time is best viewed as a channel through which legislators keep particular topics under review. It thus plays a complementary role in checking the government.

Whilst the outcomes of posing questions depend largely on the cooperation of government officials, legislators also share responsibility for maximising the positive impact of questions. A review of Hansard shows that many of the questions raised by legislators concern trivial topics and are overly concentrated on petty district-related issues. For instance, an oral question on 3 May 2000 asked whether the government would take measures to ensure that audiences switched off their mobile phones and pagers before the commencement of films and theatre performances, and a written question on 20 November 2002 concerned the opening hours of the public toilets in Victoria Park. Although these issues are not irrelevant to the public interest, it is doubtful whether they need to be raised during Legco's question time or addressed to principal officials. Whilst it is necessary for legislators to give due weight to voters in their constituencies, it is also important that they carefully consider how best to take advantage of the precious opportunity that questions afford and how to most effectively use the resulting information whose provision costs considerable time and public money.

35 See Councillor Cheung Man Kwong's question about associate degree, Hansard HK (14 May 2008) 7221.

CHAPTER 7

# Investigation Power

## *Legislative Council (Powers and Privileges) Ordinance*

The investigation power of Legco mainly derives from the Legislative Council (Powers and Privileges) Ordinance (PPO), section 9 of which reads as follows.

(1) The Council or a standing committee thereof may, subject to sections 13 and 14, order any person to attend before the Council or before such committee and to give evidence or to produce any paper, book, record or document in the possession or under the control of such person.
(2) The powers conferred by subsection (1) on a standing committee may be exercised by any other committee which is specially authorized by a resolution of the Council to exercise such powers in respect of any matter or question specified in the resolution.

These provisions ensure that the Council and its three Standing Committees, namely, the Finance Committee, Public Accounts Committee (PAC) and Committee on Members' Interests, have the power to order the attendance of witnesses or order any person to produce any document. Section 9(2) further provides that other committees may be authorised to exercise such powers by a Legco resolution.

The PPO was enacted in 1985 and remains in force. Since the return of sovereignty to China, Article 73(10) of the Basic Law provides the constitutional basis for Legco's summons power. It prescribes that Legco has the power to summon, as required when exercising powers and functions defined in other sub clauses of Article 73, the persons concerned to testify or give evidence. The following section discusses the significance of Legco's summons power by reviewing the drafting history of the PPO and analysing the application of and challenges to that Ordinance.

### Drafting History of the 1985 Legislative Council (Powers and Privileges) Ordinance

The enactment of the PPO in 1985 had profound significance for Legco and the constitutional development of Hong Kong at a time of transition. The Legislative Council (Powers and Privileges) Bill (the Bill hereafter) was proposed in

 | DOI 10.1163/9789004276284_008

May 1985 shortly after ratification of the Sino-British Joint Declaration. Moreover, in September 1985, elected members were to enter Legco for the first time. The then Chief Secretary outlined the major considerations involved in introducing the Bill to Legco, which can be summarised as follows.[1]

1. The inherent powers and privileges derived from the present status of colonial Legco must be codified to smoothen the transition.
2. It is necessary to provide members of Legco with powers and privileges for when Hong Kong moves towards representative government.
3. The power of the new Legco President must be clearly vested as the Governor will cease to be the President.
4. The recent activities of the standing and select committees prove the necessity for codification.

Obviously, these points focused on the coming transitional period during which Legco would include more elected members, which would mean that 'consensus politics may come under some pressure'.[2] Furthermore, in the opinion of unofficial members, both during the transition period and in the future, Legco 'must be able to exercise its judgement and authority as decision makers and representatives of the people'.[3] Such considerations imply that the Bill was aimed not only at consolidating and codifying scattered powers and privileges in Standing Orders, other ordinances and existing norms, but also at enhancing the policy influence and monitoring role of Legco by conferring statutory powers upon it. Hence, in terms of its implications for constitutional development and political structure, it is fair to say that this Bill was of the 'first importance'.[4]

The Bill triggered widespread public debate. The government was initially criticised for pushing the Bill through without any prior consultation with the public or community organisations, including the Law Reform Commission, Bar Association or Law Society.[5] Furthermore, considerable doubts were raised over whether the Bill introduced new powers or merely codified existing law, as the government claimed.[6] The Hong Kong Affairs Society expressed its

---

1 Hansard HK (15 May 1985).

2 Ibid.

3 See Ms Maria Tam's speech on the resumption of the second reading of the Bill, Hansard HK (15 May 1985) 1217. Ms Tam was the convenor of the ad hoc group of Legco dealing with the Bill.

4 Margaret Ng, 'Bill of First Importance', *Hong Kong Standard*, 17 May 1985.

5 'Bill is Better Dead Than Read', *South China Morning Post*, 10 June 1985.

6 'Powers Bill Needs Scrutiny', *Hong Kong Standard*, 3 June 1985.

concern over the additional powers over ordinary citizens the Bill afforded Legco and the lack of any system of control over those powers.[7] On 3 June 1985, the government moved a set of amendments in response to public submissions, including the deletion of the offences of intentional disrespect and defamatory and unauthorised publications, which were considered 'the most controversial of [the] new offences' (Clauses 17 and 20),[8] and the amendments to Clause 24 which originally provided that the Council, President and any officer of the Council would not be subject to the jurisdiction of any court.[9] These were substantial amendments. Meanwhile, the government and Ms Maria Tam, the convener of an ad hoc group dealing with the Bill, explained that there would be very little danger of abuse of power by the President or Legco under the ultimate control of an elected legislature in the future.[10]

Notwithstanding these amendments, an appeal was made to the government to defer the final reading of the Bill. A number of organisations and interested parties, including the Hong Kong Affairs Society, Meeting Point, the Journalists Association, the Hong Kong Christian Council, district board members, law students and pressure groups, urged the government to defer the Bill.[11] Members from the Hong Kong Forum insisted that the revised Bill failed to control the threats to the freedom of expression and the checking of power even though it seemed 'less unacceptable than the original one'.[12]

No critics denied the necessity for Legco to be vested with certain powers to exercise its functions properly. Rather, the criticism of the original Bill focused on whether the exercise of such powers and privileges was placed under effective control. The crux of the controversy, as revealed by Ms Tam, was finding a way to strike a balance between 'legislating for an effective and strong Legco

---

7 Ibid. With regard to the political discussion groups of the time, they emerged in 1980s and included the Meeting Point (MP) (founded 1983), the Hong Kong Affairs Society (1984), the Progressive Hong Kong Society (1984), the Hong Kong Forum (1984) and the Association for Democracy and People's Livelihood (1986). These political groups were 'embryonic political parties' and 'represented a movement of political participation from below in a period of liberalization, decolonization and democratization, the harbingers of the party movement in the 1990s'. See Ma, *Political Development in Hong Kong: State, Political Society, and Civil Society*, 137.

8 See (n 6).

9 Ibid.

10 'Longer Delay Still Won't Please Everyone—Tam', *South China Morning Post*, 27 June 1985.

11 'Critics All Out to Hold Up Powers Bill', *Hong Kong Standard*, 15 June 1985.

12 Robert S.K. Lee, Bill Poon, S.Y. Ng and C.Y. Cheung, 'Threats in Original Bill Still Linger', *South China Morning Post*, 26 June 1985.

and accommodating the concerns of the public and the media over their freedoms'.[13]

After the handover, several amendments were made to the terminology of the Ordinance in 1997 and 2003 and to the Adaptation of Laws Bill in 2000.[14] According to section 13 of the PPO, only the President of Legco has the power to excuse persons from answering questions or producing documents if such questions or documents are of a private nature and do not affect the subject of the inquiry. However, section 14(2) provides the CE with a veto right over the attendance of a witness if his/her evidence relates to correspondence concerning any naval, air force matter or other military matter or any other matter relating to the security of Hong Kong or to the responsibilities of the Central People's Government otherwise than with respect to the administration of Hong Kong by its own government. The Basic Law that was drafted after the enactment of the PPO empowers the CE to decide, in light of security and vital public interests, whether government officials or other personnel in charge of government affairs should testify or give evidence before Legco or its committees (Article 48(11)). The content of Article 48(11) is regarded as expanding the scope of the right of veto given to the CE under section 14(2) of the PPO.[15] Article 48(11) has been incorporated into Rule 80 of the RoP which stipulates the attendance of witnesses and has become the primary restriction on Legco's summons power (as discussed below).

## How Legco Uses Its Investigation Power under the PPO

The power to summon witnesses has attracted more attention than the other powers stipulated in the PPO. Figure 7.1 shows the number and results of motions or resolutions that invoked summons power under the PPO from 1985 to 2013.

In the colonial era, following the Ordinance's enactment in 1985, Legco members moved eight motions for the purpose of establishing a Select Committee (SC) or authorising a Panel to investigate issues. Seven of these motions were passed, and one was withdrawn because the government agreed to set up a Commission of Inquiry. Five SCs or Panels were afforded summons

13 See Maria Tam's speech (n 3).

14 Chief Secretary for Administration's Office, 'Legco Brief for Adaptation of Laws Bill 2000', (CSO/ADM CR 11/3231/97(00) Pt. 4, 2000).

15 See *Cheng Kar Shun and Leung Chi Kin v the Honourable Li Fung Ying and Others* [2009] HKEC 1587, para 158.

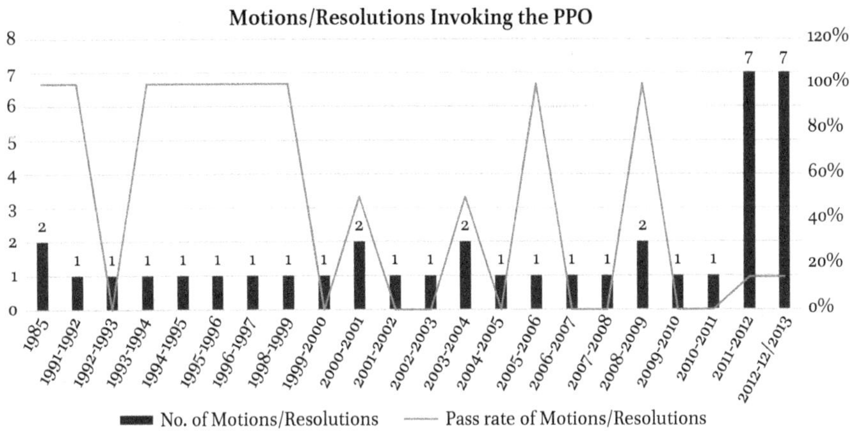


FIGURE 7.1 *Motions/Resolutions Invoking the PPO, 1985–2013*
SOURCE: THE AUTHOR'S CALCULATION BASED ON HANSARD HK (1985–2013).

power under the terms of the Ordinance, four of which ordered witnesses to appear.[16] The 1992–97 period was relatively active, with members using their summons power to investigate a wide range of issues, including the departure of senior civil servants, the arrangements for Legco elections, a landslip disaster and labour disputes. This active period corresponds with changes to the composition of Legco in the 1990s, namely, the appearance of directly elected members in 1991 and the growth in their number of seats in 1995. In this regard, one consideration in the introduction of the PPO at the drafting stage, that is, 'Hong Kong moves towards the representative government',[17] proved forward-looking for the operation of Legco in the transitional period.

The situation becomes more complicated after the 1997 return of sovereignty. As Figure 7.1 shows, between the 1998–99 and 2010–11 sessions, a total of 16 resolutions were moved for the purpose of authorising some SCs, Panels or Subcommittees to exercise powers under section 9 of the PPO, only six of which passed. This is quite a low pass rate relative to that before 1997. Each application of the powers afforded by the PPO has become the focus of public attention. For example, four SCs were set up to, respectively, investigate the commencement of the operations of the new Hong Kong International Airport in 1998, the building problems in the construction of public housing units in 2001, the handling of the SARS outbreak by the government and the Hospital Authority in 2003 and the post-service work of former Director of Buildings

16 The author's calculation based on Hansard HK.

17 See Hansard HK (15 May 1985).

Mr Leung Chin Man in 2008. In addition, a Subcommittee was established in 2008 to examine the issues arising from Lehman Brothers-related minibonds and other structured financial products. The PAC also passed a resolution to summon Mr Leung to testify in 2005.[18] In most cases, the officials or other individuals or bodies concerned chose to attend the hearings or produce papers, despite their reluctance to do so. In some cases, the officials concerned were under orders from their supervisors to cooperation with Legco.

The results in Figure 7.1 illustrate the relatively cautious attitude of Legco members towards invoking their summons power from 1998 to 2011. There are several possible explanations for such caution.

First, the investigations often involved the conduct of officials or a review of government policies, which have the potential to provoke heated discussions of the accountability system. Pro-Beijing members must consider the potential threat to the government's authority and the political consequences of any strike against the CE's 'cabinet'. Similar considerations are involved in these members' assessment of votes of no confidence in government officials.

Second, investigations conducted by SCs involve a lengthy process, numerous witnesses and public hearings, and considerable expenditure, which renders legislators very cautious about forming them. For instance, the aforementioned SC on the Building Problems of Public Housing Units spent more than three years examining the related issues, during which time it summoned a total of 85 witnesses, held 56 public hearings and 14 in camera hearings, in addition to numerous scheduled meetings, spending millions of dollars in the process, as shown in Table 7.1 below.

Finally, another critical reason for such caution is that only issues catching public attention are likely to be added to the agenda of a Select Committees or other committee with summons power. Resolutions seeking information on a single issue, for example, generally attract little public attention. For instance, from 1998 to 2011, Legco negatived four resolutions whose only aim was to request papers, records and other documents from the government or officials. All six of the successful cases, in contrast, involved matters of considerable public interest. For example, one of these cases was the aforementioned PAC resolution to summon the former Director of Buildings, a case that also involved defending the authority of Legco (discussed in Chapter 4). The other five cases covered issues with potentially serious social consequences, and therefore attracted widespread public attention and media coverage, which in turn exerted considerable pressure on legislators, particularly popularly

18 See discussions in the section of 'The Ex Post Scrutiny: The Public Accounts Committee' in Chapter 4.

TABLE 7.1 *Select committees/subcommittees carrying out investigation function, 1998–2013*

| Committee | Date of resolution passed | Time spent (month) | No. of public hearing | No. of hearing in camera | No. of witness |
|---|---|---|---|---|---|
| SC on New Airport | 29/7/1998 | 6 | 31 | – | 27 |
| SC on public housing | 7/2/2001 | 23 | 43 | 4 | 53 |
| | | –* | 13 | 10 | 32 |
| SC on SARS | 29/10/2003 | 10 | 30 | – | 77** |
| Subcommittee on Lehman event | 12/11/2008 | 43 | 70 | 36 | 62 |
| SC on post-service work | 10/12/2008 | 24*** | 23 | – | 24 |
| SC on Mr Leung Chun Ying's involvement in the West Kowloon Reclamation Concept Plan Competition | 29/2/2012 | 4 | 6 | – | 17 |

Source: The author's compilation based on the following reports:
Report of the Legislative Council Select Committee to Inquire into the Circumstances Leading to the Problems Surrounding the Commencement of the Operation of the New Hong Kong International Airport at Chek Lap Kok since 6 July 1998 and related issues (2004);
First Report and Second Report of the Select Committee on Building Problems of Public Housing Units;
Report of the Select Committee to inquire into the handling of the Severe Acute Respiratory Syndrome outbreak by the Government and the Hospital Authority (2004);
Report of the Subcommittee to Study Issues Arising from Lehman Brothers-related Minibonds and Structured Financial Products (2012);
Report of the Select Committee to Inquire into Matters Relating to the Post-service Work of Mr Leung Chin-man (2010); and
Report of the Select Committee to Study Mr Leung Chun-ying's Involvement as a Member of the Jury in the West Kowloon Reclamation Concept Plan Competition and Related Issues (2012).
All are available at: www.legco.gov.hk.

* The SC deferred the publication of the part concerning Tin Chung Court incident because Tin Chung Court incident was in relation to a pending criminal jury trial in mid-October 2002 when the Select Committee was deliberating on its draft report, see Legislative Council Select Committee on Building Problems of Public Housing Units, 'First Report of the Select Committee on Building Problems of Public Housing Units January 2003', (2003) <http://www.legco.gov.hk/yr02-03/english/sc/sc_bldg/reports/rpt_1/m_1.pdf> accessed 1 June 2014, para 1.22.

** Of the 77 witnesses, three gave witness statements and one submitted written evidence.

*** The Committee ceased its work from July 2009 to November 2009 because two witnesses applied for judicial review against the orders of the Select Committee.

elected members and those in parties concentrating on direct elections. A typical case is the establishment of the Subcommittee to Study Issues Arising from Lehman Brothers-related Minibonds and Structured Financial Products S (Lehman incident hereafter). In October 2008, the House Committee of Legco defeated a motion suggesting the establishment of a SC to investigate the issues arising from the Lehman incident. However, this incident had led to massive losses for tens of thousands of investors[19] and, arguably more importantly, had shaken consumer confidence in the financial markets and stability of the financial system. During the course of seeking compensation for their losses, investors gradually recognised the decisive role that DAB had played in voting down the motion to establish a SC. On 12 November 2008, about 200 investors protested at DAB headquarters, chanting slogans and displaying placards, with three women actually kneeling in front of the party vice-chairwoman to beg for help.[20] Furthermore, DAB received a petition with 1,850 signatures from investors asking the party to reverse its decision.[21] The party eventually bowed to public pressure and subsequently voted for a resolution to invoke the PPO to establish a Subcommittee to investigate the Lehman incident. This case clearly indicates that the political groups in Legco, particularly those with ambition to gain more seats in GCs, have to take public opinion into account and try to avoid attracting a negative public image if they want to secure voter support.

The 2011–13 sessions have seen a sharp increase in the number of motions invoking the PPO in Legco, with the number recorded in the two sessions exceeding the total number recorded in the previous 14 years. This increase is related to the CE election campaign in 2012 that involved various political forces and led to cleavage within the pro-Beijing camp. Five out of the seven motions moved during the 2011–12 session were directed at the then CE Mr Donald Tsang or then CE candidate (later then CE-elect) Mr Leung Chun Ying, who attracted one and four, respectively. The only one that saw success was the motion moved to investigate Mr Leung's involvement as a member of the jury in the West Kowloon Reclamation Concept Plan Competition.

---

19 The Hong Kong Monetary Authority announced that they received 21,734 Lehman-Brothers-related complaint cases until November 26, 2010. It is generally thought that not all affected cases were reported to HKMA and the real number of affected people may be therefore larger than 21,734. See HKMA, 'Progress of the HKMA's investigations in Lehman-Brothers-related cases', [web page] (2010), <http://info.gov.hk/hkma/eng/press/2010/20101126e4.htm>, accessed 10 September 2011.

20 Ambrose Leung and Fanny W.Y. Fung, 'Legco Likely to Pass Bill on Minibond Investigation', *South China Morning Post*, 11 November 2008, EDT4.

21 Ibid.

Mr Leung's assumption of office on 1 July 2012 was accompanied by a wave of motions invoking the PPO. From December 2012 to December 2013, Legco members moved six motions in plenary meetings calling for the establishment of SCs or authorising powers under s 9(1) of the PPO. Four of these were moved against Mr Leung himself or one of his loyal supporters, and the other two were directed at the Executive Council's decision to refuse a domestic free television programme service licence. All six were negatived by Legco, although the PAC was granted the summons power to order the former Commissioner of the ICAC to appear before the Committee.

The sharp increase in the number of proposals invoking the PPO coincided with the fiercer political division in Legco since the 2012 CE election, not only between the pro-Beijing and pro-democracy camps, but also within the pro-Beijing camp.

Table 7.1 shows the length and number of public hearings held by SCs or Subcommittees carrying out Legco's investigation function under the auspices of the PPO. The investigation of the Subcommittee on the Lehman incident lasted 43 months, with 70 public hearings and 36 hearings in camera and 62 witnesses invited to appear. The SCs on public housing problems and the post-service work of the former Director of Buildings spent approximately two years each on the respective investigations and on producing reports, whereas those inquiring into the handling of the SARS outbreak and issues concerning the new airport lasted ten and six months, respectively. The investigation of the SC on CE Leung's involvement in the West Kowloon Reclamation Concept Plan Competition lasted a comparatively brief four months. The number of witnesses invited by these SCs or Subcommittees to attend public or in camera hearings ranged from 17 to 77. It is clear that these were rather meticulous and comprehensive investigations, being long in duration, having a high frequency of hearings and calling a considerable number of witnesses.

## Significance of Investigation Power under the PPO

Although only a few of the cases invoking the PPO have been successful, summons power granted by the Ordinance has quite significant implications for the operation of Legco for several reasons.

First, calling for an investigation under the terms of the PPO has proved to be an effective channel through which legislators can obtain information in order to discharge their functions. Members regularly encounter difficulties in accessing information, so this is not insignificant.[22] A successful resolution or

22 See discussions in section of the PAC of Chapter 4 in this book.

motion with authorisation to use PPO-invoked places the government, individuals or organisations under an obligation to produce documents and/or to give evidence. In some cases, legislators have managed to obtain documents or engage in face-to-face discussions with officials just by warning that they might invoke the PPO. In 2006, for example, officers of both the Link Real Estate Investment Trust (Link REIT) and the administration refused to attend a meeting of the Panel on Housing until the Panel warned in two consecutive years that it would consider exercising summons power conferred by the PPO.[23] Another example occurred in 2008. Legislators had criticised the delays in completing a theme park on Ma Wan Island and requested that the Development Bureau disclose its agreement with the developer to explain the delay.[24] Following the government's refusal on many occasions to provide the relevant documents, Councillor Lee Wing Tat announced his intention to invoke the PPO force it to do so.[25] Shortly thereafter, a Development Bureau official contacted Councillor Lee and expressed willingness to discuss the issue with him, and Councillor Lee ultimately withdrew his motion.[26]

Second, given its constitutional role, Legco has played an indispensable role in promoting a more effective accountability system than that afforded by the inquiry commissions appointed by the government. The importance of this role was amply demonstrated during the review of the SARS crisis. Three investigation committees or panels were set up for the purpose of examining and reviewing the work of the government in the handling of SARS outbreak: the SARS Expert Committee appointed by the CE (Expert Committee), the SARS Review Panel appointed by the Hospital Authority Board (Review Panel) and the Legco Select Committee on SARS (SC on SARS). The reviews differed with respect to membership, terms of reference, the conclusions reached and public reactions to the final reports. These differences are analysed in detail in the following.

---

23 '蘇慶和允到立會解畫 避談租務 (Victor So Promised to attend Legco but No Explanation for Tenancy Matters)', *Hong Kong Economic Times*, 13 March 2007, A27. See also Panel on Housing, 'Background brief on divestment of Housing Authority's retail and car-parking facilities', (LC Paper No. CB(1)562/06-07(05), 2007).

24 Helen Wu, 'Lawmakers Condemn Delays in Theme Park's Construction', *South China Morning Post*, 12 June 2008, CITY4; '李永達暫撤特權動議停索馬灣公園資料 (Lee Wing-Tat Temporarily Withdrew Resolution Asking Information on Ma Wan Theme Park)', *Sing Tao Daily*, 19 June 2008, A14.

25 Ibid.

26 Ibid.

1. Terms of reference: The main scope of the inquiry of the Review Panel was to examine the Hospital Authority's management of the outbreak including its coordination with the Department of Health.[27] It was more of an internal review than the other two. The investigation by the Expert Committee covered the entire healthcare system and was thus wider in scope than that of the Review Panel.[28] Neither committee addressed issues of accountability, unlike the SC on SARS, which focused on 'the performance and accountability of the Government and the Hospital Authority and their officers at [the] policy-making and management levels' in handling the SARS crisis.[29]
2. Conclusion of the review: All three reports made recommendations for improvements to the public healthcare system and for the handling of future epidemic outbreaks. However, there was a marked difference between them in their evaluation of the executive's performance. The Expert Committee concluded that 'the epidemic in Hong Kong was handled well', and nobody was 'deemed to be culpable of negligence, lack of diligence or maladministration'.[30] By contrast, the report of the Review Panel raised the criticism of the hospitals, government departments and officials involved, including the Director of Health.[31] The Legco report described the performance of the Secretary for Health, Welfare and Food and the Director of Health as 'not satisfactory in the handling of the SARS outbreak',[32] and also criticised the Chairman of the Hospital Authority and other key medical officials.
3. Public reactions: The Review Panel's report was welcomed by medical experts, patients' rights groups and the representative of the Medical Sector in Legco, but attracted strong objections from government officials.[33]

---

27 Hospital Authority Review Panel, 'Report of the Hospital Authority Review Panel on the SARS Outbreak', (September 2003), <http://www.ha.org.hk/sars/ps/report/reviewpanel_c.pdf>, accessed 1 June 2014, para 1.3.

28 SARS Expert Committee, 'SARS in Hong Kong: from Experience to Action', [web document] (2 October 2003), <http://www.sars-expertcom.gov.hk/english/reports/reports/files/e_chp1.pdf>, accessed 1 June 2014, para 1.3.

29 Select Committee on SARS, 'Report of the Select Committee to Inquire into the Handling of the Severe Acute Respiratory Syndrome Outbreak by the Government and the Hospital Authority', (July 2004), <http://www.legco.gov.hk/yr03-04/english/sc/sc_sars/reports/ch1.pdf>, accessed 1 June 2014, para 1.6, Chapter 1.

30 SARS Expert Committee (n 28) para 17.2.

31 Hospital Authority Review Panel (n 27).

32 Select Committee on SARS (n 29), Chapter 15.

33 Teddy Ng, 'Report into Disease Receives Welcome', *The Standard*, 17 October 2003, B02.

> The Expert Committee was accused of failing to name the officials responsible for the crisis.[34] Although the report issued by the SC on SARS named the responsible officials, some SARS victims and their families criticised it for failing to suggest any punishment for these officials.[35] Some frontline medical staff also considered the Legco report to be 'unfair',[36] and the Chairman of the Hospital Authority insisted that the Authority had made no mistakes.[37] The release of the SC report placed considerable political and public pressure on the officials concerned, leading to Secretary for Health, Welfare and Food Yeoh Eng Kiong and then Hospital Authority Chairman Leong Che Hung offering their resignations.[38] SARS victims also urged the other officials named in the Legco report to step down.[39]

The foregoing analysis shows that, despite their detailed and professional recommendations for the improvement of the public healthcare system, neither the Review Panel nor Executive Committees met the requirements of accountability owing to the limitations in their terms of reference. By contrast, Legco's constitutional role as an external monitor rendered the SC on SARS investigation more responsive to the question of responsibility. Furthermore, the work of this SC received ongoing support from legislators through other means. For instance, the release of the SC on SARS report was followed by a motion debate on the report on 7 July 2004, which further 'condemn[ed] the former Director of Health, Dr Margaret Chan Fung Fu-chun'. Legco's investigation and subsequent debate placed information on the SARS outbreak in the public domain and stimulated an in-depth public debate on the issue that ultimately led to the resignation of two high-ranking officials.

### Challenges to the PPO: Cheng Kar Shun Case

The power to summon witnesses to testify before Legco and produce documents has become the most powerful weapon at Legco members' disposal as

34 Teddy Ng, 'SARS Report Anger', *The Standard*, 3 October 2003, B01.

35 Elaine Wu, Chandra Wong and Mary Ann Benitez, 'Yeoh Must Go, Say SARS Victims', *South China Morning Post*, 7 July 2004, EDT1.

36 Sylvia Hui, 'Doctors Claim SARS Report Was "Unfair"', *The Standard*, 9 July 2004, B03.

37 Mary Ann Benitez, Klaudia Lee and Elizabeth Lo, 'Hospitals Chief: We Made No Mistake', *South China Morning Post*, 9 July 2004, EDT1.

38 Hui (n 36).

39 Gary Cheung, Ravina Shamdasani and Martin Wong, 'Victims Say More Heads Should Roll Over Virus', *South China Morning Post*, 9 July 2004, EDT3.

they go about fulfilling their various functions, and accordingly has encountered a number of challenges from the persons concerned and from defenders of the executive-led government.

The greatest challenge to Legco's summons power to date was the case of *Cheng Kar Shun and Leung Chi Kin v the Honourable Li Fung Ying and Others*, which originated in the 'Leung Chin Man incident'.[40] Mr Leung Chin Man is a retired senior civil servant. During his government career, serving first as the Director of Buildings and then as Permanent Secretary for Housing, Planning and Lands, controversy broke out over the sale of the Hung Hom Peninsula public housing estate in 2004.[41] The deal between the government and the developer aroused suspicion amongst members of the public who viewed it as a 'cut-price' sale that gave 'windfall profit[s]' to the developer, a joint venture between Sun Hung Kai Properties and a subsidiary of New World Development.[42] In January 2007, Mr Leung retired from the Civil Service and, in August 2008, was named Deputy Managing Director and Executive Director of New World China Ltd, the subsidiary concerned.[43] Given his previous involvement in the dispute concerning the Hung Hom Peninsula development, this appointment was met with a public outcry.[44] Moreover, as Mr Leung had obtained prior government approval to take up a job within three years of leaving the Civil Service, the policies and arrangements governing the post-service work of directorate civil servants were also thrown into doubt. Notwithstanding the cancellation of Mr Leung's employment contract with New World China, Legco passed a resolution to appoint a SC to inquire into his post-service work and related matters,[45] including whether there were any loopholes in the existing system for processing former directorate civil servants' applications for approval to take up post-retirement work and whether Mr Leung's New World appointment constituted 'deferred reward' for his handling of the Hung Hom Peninsula development when he was in

---

40 *Cheng v Li* (n 15).

41 Peggy Sito and Sandy Li, 'Cut-price Sale of Flats on Harbour Stirs Anger', *South China Morning Post*, 10 February 2004, EDT1.

42 Ibid. Panel on Housing passed a motion at the meeting on December 6 2004 to recommend that Legco set up a select committee to inquire into the Government's sale of Hung Hom Peninsula. See Panel on Housing, 'Minutes of meeting held on December 6 2004', (LC Paper No. CB(1) 1218/04-05(04), 2004). But panel members changed their mind and agreed to postpone the discussion of its proposal for appointing the select committee, see *Cheng v Li* (n 15) para 13.

43 See *Cheng v Li*, ibid., paras 14–15.

44 Ibid., paras 14, 16.

45 Ibid., para 18.

government.[46] Legco authorised the SC to exercise the power conferred by s 9(1) of the PPO.

In July 2009, the SC ordered Mr Cheng Kar Shun and Mr Leung Chi Kin, the Managing Director and Executive Director of New World China Land Ltd, respectively, to give evidence and produce documents. On 10 July 2009, both men applied for leave to apply for a judicial review against the orders of the SC.[47] The court granted such leave, but the grounds of the application were limited to two issues: (1) the power of the SC to make the relevant orders upon a proper interpretation of Article 73(10) of the Basic Law, and thus the constitutionality of the relevant provisions of the PPO,[48] and (2) the question of whether the SC had acted outwith its remit under the resolution.[49] The application was eventually dismissed.

On the first ground, the court rejected the applicants' argument that the power to order witnesses is vested only in the Council, not in its committees, and thus that s 9(2) of the PPO is unconstitutional.[50] The court held that the Basic Law, as a constitutional instrument, 'must not be read with a literal, technical, narrow or rigid approach' and 'must be given a purposive interpretation, which fully takes into account the context and purpose of the relevant provisions'.[51] Hence, the term 'Legislative Council' in Article 73 could be construed to mean 'Legco functioning as a full body or the Council functioning through committees, as the individual context may require'.[52]

With respect to the provisions in the PPO, on the one hand, the Basic Law 'does not condescend on particularity', and its wording is 'large and general'.[53] On the other, the Ordinance 'is a piece of specific legislation' and 'contains many definitions and fine details';[54] '[t]he absence of these definitions and

46 See the summary by Albert H.Y. Chen, 'Constitutional Developments in Autumn 2009', *Hong Kong Law Journal*, 39 (2009) 752.

47 See *Cheng v Li* (n 15) para 27.

48 Ibid.

49 Ibid.

50 See Chen (n 46) 753.

51 See *Cheng v Li* (n 15) para 103. The leading cases decided by the CFA which supported this approach to the interpretation of the Basic Law include *Ng Ka Ling v Director of Immigration* (1999) 2 HKCFAR 4, and *Director of Immigration v Chong Fung Yuen* (2001) 4 HKCFAR 211, see Chen (n 46) 753.

52 See Chen, ibid.

53 Ibid.

54 See *Cheng v Li* (n 15) para 161.

details in the constitutional document does not render those provisions only found in the legislation *ultra vires* the constitutional document'.[55]

In deciding the proper interpretation of Article 73(10) of the Basic Law, the court made reference to Article 48(11) of that Law, and pointed out that the Basic Law itself contemplates the possibility of persons giving evidence before a Legco committee.[56]

As the Basic Law does not create a new legislature out of a vacuum,[57] it declared, both as a matter of history and practice 'many of the powers and functions set out in article 73 were and are exercised to varying extent[s] not only by the Council as a full body, but also at [the] committee level'.[58] The summons power is 'a power ancillary to and parasitic on those substantive powers and functions' in Articles 73(1) to (9), and it is 'legitimate to think' that such power 'may also be exercised by the committee in appropriate circumstances',[59] the court emphasised in its ruling.

With reference to the proper interpretation of the Basic Law, the court held that, as a 'living instrument', it 'must be interpreted flexibly to meet the challenge[s] of the time',[60] and further that '[t]he advantages of giving a select committee the power to summon witnesses are obvious and hardly require repetition'.[61] Furthermore, as the work of a SC is always 'under the supervision of the full body of Legco', and Legco is ultimately accountable to the people of Hong Kong,[62] the court in this case was reluctant 'to impose [a] straitjacket on the Legislative Council as to how it may go about its business'.[63]

On the second ground of the challenge, the court first dealt with the question of its own jurisdiction over the matter. The court claimed that it had jurisdiction to consider the constitutional validity of Legco's practice 'in going about its business' but that 'the jurisdiction must be exercised with great restraint'.[64]

With regard to the case in question, the court pointed out that the PPO provides 'a build-in mechanism to deal with a witness' objection to answer[ing]

55 Ibid.

56 See Chen (n 46) 754.

57 See *Cheng v Li* (n 15) para 123.

58 Ibid., para 108.

59 Ibid., para 146. See also Chen (n 46) 754.

60 See *Cheng v Li* (n 15) paras 197–198.

61 Ibid., para 198.

62 Ibid.

63 Ibid., para 99. See also Chen (n 46) 755.

64 See *Cheng v Li* (n 15) para 220.

questions or produc[ing] papers'[65] and that the PPO makes it 'plain that all these matter are to be dealt with "in-house"'.[66] As the counsel to the respondents submitted, an application should be entertained by the court only if it is a 'clear-cut case of *ultra vires* or of an abuse or misuse of the power to order [the] attendance of witnesses'.[67] With regard to the factual basis of the challenge, the court rejected the second ground.

The *Cheng v Li* case may be taken to have achieved a proper balance between the powers of the government branches in the exercise of Legco's summons power. First, the court exhibited judicial deference to the internal workings of Legco, declining to interfere with those workings and exercising its remaining jurisdiction with considerable restrictions. As Professor Albert Chen has pointed out, the judge upheld the validity of the existing norms governing the operation of Legco and respected the continuity of Legco.[68] Furthermore, this case and another constitutional case dealing with the powers and operations of the legislature and judicial scrutiny of its internal workings, namely, *Leung Kwok Hung v President of Legislative Council and another*,[69] are together regarded as 'having paved a jurisprudential foundation for judicial deference to the views of the legislature in matters of constitutional interpretation affecting the internal operation of Legco and the effective performance of its constitutional functions'.[70] Second, the Secretary for Justice and counsel for the government in this case defended the constitutional role of Legco in scrutinising public policies and supervising the government and its officers, and accepted the power of its committees to summon witnesses.[71] The balance amongst the executive branch, judiciary and legislature corresponds to the constitutional roles assigned under the Basic Law, namely, judicial independence and the executive and legislature both checking each other and coordinating their activities.[72]

65 Ibid., para 228.

66 Ibid., paras 229–230.

67 Ibid., para 236.

68 Chen (n 46) 759.

69 *Leung Kwok Hung v The President of The Legislative Council of The Hong Kong Special Administrative Region and Another* [2007] 1 HKLRD 387.

70 Chen (n 46) 759.

71 See *Cheng v Li* (n 15) paras 193–194.

72 Basic Law Drafting Committee, 'Progress report of the Sub-group on Political System' in the Secretariat of the Basic Law Drafting Committee of the HKSAR (ed.), *A Compilation of Documents of the Third Plenary Session of the Basic Law Drafting Committee of the HKSAR of the PRC* (1986), <http://ebook.lib.hku.hk/bldho/articles/BL0020.pdf>, accessed 1 June 2014, 32.

## Conclusion

In adopting a flexible and purposive interpretation of the Basic Law, the court in the *Cheng v Li* case upheld the constitutionality of s 9 of the PPO, which confers summons power on Standing Committees and authorises Legco to delegate that power to other committees. It further declared that the meaning of Article 73(10) is clear and plain and contains no further restrictions on the summons power except for the phrase 'as required when exercising the above-mentioned powers and functions' in Articles 73(1)–(9).

In fact, the most substantial restriction on Legco's summons power arises from Article 48(11) of the Basic Law, which empowers the CE to grant immunity to officials or other persons in charge of government affairs, relieving them from having to testify or produce documents. The CE's decision to do so, however, must be made on the grounds of security and vital public interest.[73] This article of the Basic Law is generally regarded by proponents of the executive-led system as evidence of dominance of the executive branch over the legislature.[74] However, as the court pointed out in *Cheng v Li*, Article 48(11) proceeds on the premise that, in the absence of any CE veto, officials are 'compellable' by Legco or its committees to testify or give evidence.[75] The article should thus be read as providing for exceptional circumstances regarding the attendance of officials rather than manifesting the priority afforded the executive in the constitutional framework.

A notable shift has occurred in the use of summons power by legislators over time. In the early days of the HKSAR, Legco as a whole showed considerable self-restraint and caution by exercising that power only when matters of great public concern arose. In contrast to the government's internal inquiries, investigations conducted by Legco committees generally enjoy credibility with the public, which has enhanced Legco's role in ensuring accountability. However, since the 2011–12 session, notwithstanding the growing number of motions to invoke the PPO, their success rate has been extremely low.

73 Article 48(11) of the Basic Law provides that the CE can decide 'in light of security and vital public interests, whether government officials or other personnel in charge of government affairs should testify or give evidence before the Legislative Council or its committees'.

74 Wang and Gu argue that Article 48(11) vests the CE with the priority in investigative power and enhances the executive-led system, see Shucheng Wang and Minkang Gu, '香港立法会调查权界限分析 (an Analysis of the Investigation Power of the Legislative Council of Hong Kong)', *Global Law Review*, 6 (2010) 149.

75 See (n 15) paras 139, 142.

In addition to motions proposed by pro-democracy members expressing discontent with the governing team, those with less profound political implications but a greater potential impact on the general public failed to gain support from the pro-Beijing camp. Instances of resolutions concerning such issues include resolutions targeting the collection and transfer to third parties customers' personal data by Octopus Holdings Lted, Exco's decision concerning the issuing of licences for domestic free television programme services and tariff adjustments by Hong Kong's two power companies. It is clear that the pro-Beijing camp as a whole has tended to avoid invoking its summons power in recent years, which is a sign of greater cooperation between this camp (or Legco as a whole) and the government, and thus of gradual decline in the system of checks and balances.

CHAPTER 8

# Conclusion

The constitutional design of the Basic Law establishes the Legislative Council's (Legco) independence from the executive branch and its crucial role as one of the HKSAR's three government branches under the separation of powers, thereby providing the basic framework for the legislature's autonomy. Similar to other legislatures following the Westminster tradition, Legco plays a less proactive role in the policymaking process, serving more as a reactive actor in deliberating government proposals and monitoring the administration in adherence with sophisticated rules and conventions. Still, law-making power is not confined to the power to formulate or generate legislative proposals, but also includes the power to amend or veto bills. Further, in modern political systems, legislatures can perform functions other than legislation, such as representation, deliberation, information attainment and the exercise of checks. The emergence of an autonomous Legco and the executive-led governing philosophy adopted by the government has sharpened the competition between the executive and legislative branches in Hong Kong. However, as Professor Anthony King points out, the term 'executive-legislative relations' may be highly misleading because there are a number of distinct political relationships in each political system. The distinctive feature of Hong Kong's political structure is the interaction of multiple actors, including the Central People's Government (CPG), the Chief Executive (CE) and Legco. This core feature exerts great influence on the level of autonomy that Legco enjoys and on shaping the real impact of Legco within the HKSAR's political system.

## Level of Autonomy

### *External Environment*

As discussed in Chapter 1, the indicators of Legco's autonomy in the external environment dimension include the separate existence of the legislature, the constraints imposed upon it by external institutions, the constitutional powers it enjoys and role it places, its representation function and general public support.

 | DOI 10.1163/9789004276284_009

1. An institution separate from the executive

An overlap between the legislative and executive branches appears when a legislator is appointed a member of Exco. A member sitting in Legco and Exco concurrently has the obligation to cast a vote in the former that is in accordance with the government's position. However, even when this member is a party leader, his or her colleagues in Legco will still follow the party line rather than the party leader's position. In addition, although members of the major political parties have occasionally been appointed principal officials, these members are generally considered to be primarily cabinet officers rather than party members. Nonetheless, a seat in Exco is attractive to Legco members, as it offers them an opportunity to participate in an earlier stage of the policy-making process, namely, to become involved in the formulation of public policy.

2. Constraints from external institution

The Hong Kong's courts have gradually established their jurisdiction to determine not only the constitutional validity of the Rules of Procedure of Legco (RoP) and laws enacted by Legco, but also the existence of powers, privileges or immunities of Legco and its President. In its landmark decision on *Leung Kwok Hung v The President of the Legislative Council of the Hong Kong Special Administrative Region* [2014] HKEC 1604, the CFA recognised Legco's exclusive authority to determine its internal processes, the legislative process in particular, and refused to review the occasion or the manner of exercising the powers by Legco and its President. Following such a non-intervention principle, the CFA left Legco to exclusively manage and resolve its own internal affairs. Furthermore, the CFA declined to invalidate an enacted law on the basis of procedural regularity in which the Basic Law remains ambiguous on such issues. It is clear that the CFA has refrained from intervening in not only the post-enactment but also the pre-enactment stage in the legislative process. Hence, inviting judicial intervention is no longer a practical option to Legco members who are dissatisfied with the internal procedures and rulings made by the Legco President and committee chairs. The decision has narrowed the space for Legco members continue using unusual procedural manoeuvre on one hand, and consolidated the autonomy of Legco in the external dimension on the other.

3. Constitutional powers and role

Legco's power to initiate public policy through the introduction of private members' bills is diminished by Article 74 of the Basic Law. However, Legco secured the power to amend bills by rejecting Article 74's application to committee stage amendments (CSAs). It seems that Legco is unwilling to give up its role as scrutiniser of the legislative process within the system of 'checks and balances'. As current Legco President Jasper Tsang wrote in his ruling on a piece of subsidiary legislation, 'Legco must have effective oversight of the exercise of all legislative power and relevant legislation governing the exercise of law-making powers'.[1] However, generally speaking, Legco has failed to develop effective means of holding the executive accountable, whether by no-confidence motions or through the investigative reports of select committees.

4. Representation of social stratification

Since 1998, Functional Constituencies (FCs) have held at least half the seats in Legco, despite the limited franchise. The dominance of the pro-Beijing and pro-business camps in Legco has handicapped the legislature's ability to promote social welfare and civil liberties on many occasions. The flaws in the existing system of representation were highlighted by a case study of the legislative process surrounding the proposed legislation on Article 23 of the Basic Law in 2003 and the Interception of Communications and Surveillance Bill in 2006. When the debates and deliberations in Legco do not reflect the wishes or meet the demands of the general public, it is unsurprising that people employ other methods such as street politics, social movements and unusual procedural manoeuvres in the Legco chamber. Without a system of adequate representation, Legco will continue to find it difficult to become a genuine forum for public debate and dialogue, which will undermine its public mandate and weaken its role as a representative organ.

5. General public support and Channels for communication with the public

The malfunction of a system of representation has weakened the public support for Legco and impeded the communication between legislators and the public. The people have changed their tactics for demanding policy changes due to their powerlessness in using the conventional methods, such as attending public hearing and pressing the political parties in Legco. According to Lam, in recent years, 'people have become more willing to break the conventional standards of social peace and order, and employ physical tactics to catch public attention. One example is the Anti-Express Rail Protest in 2009 and 2010'.[2] An angry protest

1 President's Ruling on Proposed Resolution to Repeal the Country Parks (Designation) (Consolidation) (Amendment) Order 2010 Proposed by Hon Tanya Chan (7 October 2010).

2 Wai-Man Lam, 'Political Identity, Culture, and Participation', in Wai-Man Lam, Percy Luen-Tim Lui, and Wilson Wong (eds.), *Contemporary Hong Kong Government and Politics* (Expanded 2nd edn., Hong Kong: Hong Kong University Press, 2012), 207.

against the development plan in the north eastern New Territories further displays the tendency to increasingly employ radical tactics. On 13 June 2014, during the deliberation on funding request relating to the north eastern New Territories development plan in the Finance Committee, hundreds of protestors tried to storm into the Legco building and caused some damage to the building, with 21 people arrested.[3] Given the further intensified social fragmentation and disintegration after the 2012 CE election, it is difficult to rectify the situation that Legco has been losing respect and trust of the public.

### *Internal Characteristics*

In terms of the internal characteristics of autonomy, Legco has developed administrative and financial autonomy through the Legco Commission, and it enjoys stable, albeit perhaps insufficient, research support for the work of legislators and committees. Other aspects of internal autonomy, in contrast, are more complicated.

1. Exclusive authority over internal rules and procedures

The first question is whether Legco follows its own rules and conventions without interference from outside in its internal operations and proceedings. Chapters 3 and 5 discuss the way in which the Legco President makes final decisions on procedural affairs in accordance with the RoP. Moreover, Presidents have adhered to the fundamental principles underpinning the reasoning for those decisions. These principles have become constitutional conventions. Legco's autonomy to determine its own rules and norms also gained support from the cross-party unanimity regarding the disputes over Legco's frontiers of powers when the RoP were drafted in 1998.[4] Legco also maintained control over subsidiary legislation in the Tseung Kwan O landfill dispute in 2010.[5]

There have indeed been attempts to amend the RoP with the aim of restricting the behaviour of activists within Legco. For instance, an amendment in 2011 proposed extending the power of committee chairs, and the same year saw discussion of the need to develop a mechanism to shut down filibusters. It is clear that Legco has both the autonomy and an obligation to improve its own procedural rules occasionally to ensure

3 Jeffie Lam, 'Legco Storming "May Be a Trial Run"', *South China Morning Post*, 15 June 2014, EDT1.

4 See 'Dispute on the Application of Article 74 to Members' CSAs' in Chapter 4.

5 See 'Scrutiny of Subsidiary Legislation' in Chapter 4.

that its internal business proceeds in smoother fashion. However, given the executive's insistent condemnation of object throwing and filibuster manoeuvres by members, it is difficult to conclude that these discussions and proposed amendments originate solely in internal pressure. Before any decision is taken to restrict the rights of Legco members, legislators, regardless of their political orientation, need to consider carefully the double-edged nature of such restrictions.

2. Agenda control

This indicator examines whether Legco and its committees can determine the agenda of internal business. It is the House Committee that actually assumes responsibility for determining Legco's agenda, and it is unsurprising that owing to a lack of initiation power Legco plays virtually no role in determining the legislative programme, financial proposals or any other government business put before it. However, Legco and its committees do have the final say over the priority accorded the items they deal with and over how long the deliberation on a specific item will last. That right to a final say can exert considerable pressure on the executive when Legco and its committees prolong the deliberation on an item accorded the highest priority by the executive, as we saw in our study of the Bills Committees in Chapter 3. The role of the committee chair is therefore rather vital, and filibusters have become an important means by which legislators compete with the executive for control over the agenda.

3. Committee organisation and jurisdiction

The institutional legacy of the colonial era has seen Legco develop a complete and specialised committee organisation. As Chapters 3 and 4 reveal,[6] Legco panels, which are parallel to government departments, have become forums in which the executive tests legislators' reactions to policies and bills at the embryonic stage,[7] with legislators then conducting a follow-up and review of the implementation of government policy at the final stage of the policy cycle. Correspondingly, the major political groups often assign their members to various panels dealing with distinct policy areas.[8] Bills Committees and the Finance Committee, along with its two subcommittees, are arenas for detailed deliberation on legislative and financial proposals. As Chapter 7 makes clear, in terms of

6 See case study on Bills Committee on the Interception of Communications and Surveillance Bill in Chapter 4, and discussions on examination of other financial proposals in Chapter 5.

7 Interview with President Jasper Tsang on 22 July 2011.

8 Ibid.

information acquisition by committees, the most effective channel of information access may be the power to summon witnesses, given its deterrent effect on the officials or other individuals concerned. However, given the corresponding distribution of the major political forces in committees and panels, that power cannot be activated without the support of the majority political parties in Legco.

In observing committee work, partisan factors have thus become an important force, exerting various effects on the operation of committees or panels. With respect to the Public Accounts Committee (PAC), for example, its authority stems partly from its non-partisan and non-policy character, as we saw in Chapter 4. With regard to other committees or panels, although a cross-party coalition can exert considerable pressure on the executive, the legislative process concerning Article 23 indicates that the majority parties can push or accelerate the deliberation process. In contrast to the pro-democracy camp, the pro-Beijing camp finds it considerably easier to obtain 'exclusive' concessions from the executive behind the scenes of open committee meetings, which diminishes the importance of committee deliberation.

4. Leadership selection

The party affiliation or political orientation of the President and of committee chairs has changed over time. President Jasper Tsang, the first President with a party political affiliation, has manifested his intention to be a neutral presiding officer in his rulings on members' CSAs and private members' bills. However, President Tsang has been confronted with severer political cleavage than that his predecessor President Rita Fan faced. His ruling on 'cut cloth' was reviewed by the CFA, and the outcome has finally established the threshold of judicial intervention in Legco Presidents' rulings. What is more noteworthy is the pro-Beijing camp's nearly full control over committee chairmanships and the decline in the level of committee chairs' parliamentary experience as a whole since 2012. The adverse effects of these political dynamics can be seen in the 2012 dispute over Old Age Living Allowance funding amongst then-Chairman Tommy Cheung and other committee members and the more recent chaos in the Finance Committee concerning the northeast New Territories development plan.[9] In both cases, the Finance Committee chairs have

9 The Finance Committee Chairman Tommy Cheung waived the five-day notice required for the government to hold another special meeting after the Finance Committee passed a motion to defer the deliberation on Old Age Living Allowance funding, see '劉慧卿斥張宇人破壞規矩 (Emily Lau Criticised of Tommy Cheung for Breaking Convention)', *Hong Kong*

been questioned over their role as participants with clear policy objectives rather than neutral presiding officers.

### *Autonomy of Legco*

Legco has structured its institutional framework to underscore its legislative autonomy. Former Legco President Rita Fan and her successor, President Jasper Tsang, have both played a crucial role in developing and retaining an autonomous legislature. An autonomous Legco inevitably competes for various powers more actively, although the continued existence of FCs constitutes a fundamental flaw in the HKSAR's system of representation. There has been no evident improvement in the situation even 17 years after the return of sovereignty to China. Furthermore, the political dynamics in the external dimension of Legco autonomy, particularly the deeper political cleavage seen in recent years, have affected the internal dimension in terms of leadership, rules, committee autonomy and control of the legislative agenda. The corresponding adjustments in the internal dimension in fact seem opposed to an autonomous Legco, particularly the new restrictions on members' activities and the growing policy role of committee leaders. Therefore, it is doubtful whether Legco will be able to play its intended role as a check on executive branch power if the major pro-Beijing political groups therein remain determined to develop more collaborative relations with the executive.

## Actual Impact of Legco

The preceding analysis assesses Legco's level of autonomy in playing its constitutional role and performing various functions, which provides a basic framework for measuring the actual impact of Legco. It is obvious that Legco members have little proactive power such as the power to propose bills, and are even undergoing a shift towards reactive if not passive functions. However, the constitutional power and institutional capacity of Legco are not equal to its real impact, as demonstrated by the relatively small impact exerted by the Separate Voting Mechanism on the results of members' CSAs and motions elucidated in Chapter 3.

---

*Economic Journal*, 30 October 2012, A14. On recent chaos in the Finance Committee concerning the northeast New Territories development plan, see Beatrice Siu, 'We Won't Back Down', *The Standard*, 16 June 2014, P01.

### *Interaction Pattern*

There are several modes of executive-legislative interaction in which Legco performs various functions with particular legal consequences. For example, the bargaining mode, which is based on anticipated reactions, has been particularly effective in exercising functions with binding power, including law-making and financial control, whilst functions without legislative effects, including motion debates and questions, have served a supportive, albeit necessary, role in facilitating Legco's access to information and in consensus-building and conditioning public opinion.

Having the final say on bills has allowed Legco members to squeeze concessions from the government even if they rarely use their veto power. They tend to force the executive to proactively move amendments, withdraw proposals or offer more assurances in response to members' requirements concerning bills.[10] Policy panels and Bills Committees have therefore become the major arenas in which most amendments or concessions from the executive are formulated, with voting at the later Committee Stage of the Whole Council merely reflecting the consequences of earlier committee discussions and bargaining.

Legco's control over public finances faces a major challenge that members lack the capacity to allocate resources to policy areas to which the government is reluctant to distribute funds. However, relative to bills, financial proposals with few political implications are more likely to gain consensus support across the political spectrum. Party cooperation in committees, including panels and the Finance Committee and its subcommittees, has led to Legco's wide-ranging spectrum of scrutiny in the financial arena, which stems largely from its veto power over budgets and other financial proposals, becoming arguably its most powerful function.

By contrast, the pattern of interplay in anticipated reactions is difficult to apply to functions without legislative effects. PAC reports and decisions, which have persuasive power alone, have limited impact on improving government efficiency. Successful motions cannot effect direct and immediate policy changes, despite the positive written responses the executive makes in most cases. During Legco's question time, the executive branch provides the information sought by legislators, with officials charged with answering the questions raised at Legco meetings. This procedure allows Legco members to bring originally unavailable materials and information 'into the public domain'.[11] At the same time, informed members of the public, whether acting as individuals or groups, are able to discover the details of the policies under discussion so as

10 See 'Scrutiny of Bills: Bills Committees' in Chapter 3.

11 Ibid.

to voice informed views in hearings or submissions. In the event that the executive branch refuses to provide information or rectify its conduct, the most effective weapon at Legco's disposal is its ability to mobilise members of the public to press for government action. It can also invoke the Legislative Council (Power and Privilege) Ordinance to summon witness to give evidence and produce documents. However, it is usual practice for members to employ multiple methods, including motions, questions and panel discussions, to keep issues under review and seek public support.

Legco has shifted its focus towards squeezing concessions out of the government and scrutinising the conduct of the executive branch on a case-by-case basis through extensive committee work and inter-party cooperation. This shift was originally a reluctant move on Legco members' part in response to their lack of initiation power, but it has proved an effective means of extending Legco's real impact. Legco has also managed to serve additional information- and representation-orientated functions beyond their lawmaking role.

### *Trends in Legco's Actual Impact*

There was a visible change in government strategy under the rule of Mr Donald Tsang, the HKSAR's previous CE. As we saw in Chapter 3, since Legco's third term, the 2005–2006 session in particular, the executive has strengthened its control over agenda-setting and adopted a more defensive stance on members' proposals by curtailing the number of bills introduced and adjusting or narrowing long titles of bills.[12] Hence, the restriction of 'subject matter' under Rule 57(4)(a) has become more influential.[13] Prior to Legco's third term, members' CSAs, amendments and repeals of resolutions to subsidiary legislation were passed on some occasions, but there have been few successful such cases in the years since. In addition, our case study of the Interception of Communications and Surveillance Bill enacted in 2006 reveals that the government would rather incorporate members' proposals than allow them to propose CSAs to adhere to its position on Article 74.[14] The complete defeat of members' proposals in recent years suggests that, in view of the critical impact of the government's position on pro-Beijing members' voting behaviour, the government has adopted a barely tolerable stance on such proposals since Legco's third term.

Nonetheless, the government's stricter control over agenda setting has produced an unexpected outcome. Relief from the burden of bill deliberation

12 See 'Bills under Scrutiny of Bills Committees' in Chapter 3.

13 See 'Restrictions on the Introduction of Members' CSAs' in Chapter 3.

14 See case study on Bills Committee on the Interception of Communications and Surveillance Bill in Chapter 3.

since the 2005–06 session has allowed legislators to spend considerably more time on each bill or proposal, thereby enhancing the efficiency and effectiveness of committee work. As Chapter 3 reveals, on the one hand, the proportion of government bills scrutinised by the Bills Committees increased gradually from 1998 to 2012 whilst, on the other, the establishment of Bills Committees appears to have a positive correlation with the introduction of government CSAs.[15] Chapter 4 also shows a steady increase in the amount of time spent on deliberation over budget proposals and on members' questions concerning budget proposals over the years.[16] Hence, government bills and financial proposals have, in recent years, been subject to more extensive and careful scrutiny by both the Bills Committees and Finance Committee.

## Strategy Shift and New Rule after 2012

### *Beijing's New Strategy and Its Impact*

It was pointed out earlier in this book that the HKSAR has failed in its objective to achieve an executive-led government in the absence of sufficient capacity and a public mandate. Intervention by the CPG and its representatives in Hong Kong, particularly the Liaison Office of the CPG (LOCPG), may be invited by the executive and the pro-Beijing camp to realise a more powerful CE and executive dominance over the legislature. There has been a clear shift in CPG strategy towards Hong Kong from 'laissez faire' to 'a new policy' of deeper engagement and involvement in Hong Kong's political development.[17] Mr Danny Gittings finds that the LOCPG has become 'a key player in this more interventionist approach' and 'direct intervention' by the LOCPG has been extended to 'an increasing range of issues'.[18] The LOCPG's role in local elections is an open secret, with Professor Joseph Cheng's research showing that it 'has been conducting campaign activities and coordinating work for the pro-Beijing candidates in both the Legco direct elections and District Councils elections'.[19] As a result, 'in recent years, more and more protest rallies related to political reforms have chosen to approach the Central Liaison Office', rather than government headquarters.[20]

15 See 'Scrutiny of Bills: Bills Committees' in Chapter 3.

16 See 'Examination of Budget Proposals' in Chapter 4.

17 Cheng, 'The Story of a New Policy'.

18 Danny Gittings, *Introduction to the Hong Kong Basic Law* (Hong Kong: Hong Kong University Press, 2013), 70.

19 Lo, *The Dynamics of Beijing-Hong Kong Relations: A Model for Taiwan?* 154.

20 Joseph Y.S. Cheng, 'Has He Got the Job Done? An Evaluation of Donald Tsang Administration', in Joseph Y.S. Cheng (ed.), *The Second Chief Executive of Hong Kong*

The more interventionist approach adopted by both the CPG and LOCPG has become the most influential external factor in Legco's autonomy by affecting the distribution of political forces and Legco leadership, as well as supervising the voting behaviour of members (whether directly or indirectly). The CPG has also exerted an impact on agenda setting in Hong Kong. The most prominent examples of this are the legislation concerning Article 23 of the Basic Law, the Guangzhou-Hong Kong Express Rail Link project and North East New Territories Development Plan, which are considered to herald greater convergence between Hong Kong and the Mainland. Related policy matters, which are accorded high priority on the executive's agenda, have effected a serious split in the community.

It is arguable whether the CPG's more interventionist approach has enhanced executive dominance over the legislature. However, it has certainly effected a number of gradual changes in executive-legislative interactions. For example, the executive has gradually abandoned its earlier practice of negotiating with as many political groups in Legco as possible, not only to secure enough votes for its policies but also to garner popularity with the populace and obtain a public mandate. One pro-democracy legislator expressed the view that Financial Secretary Mr John Tsang cares less about the 'scores' of the annual budget than his predecessor but is focused more on the secure passage of that budget.[21] Furthermore, the executive and the major pro-Beijing political groups have reached tacit agreement that the pro-Beijing camp should avoid allying itself with the pro-democracy camp in return for more opportunities for negotiation and a range of concessions.[22] Such a tactic has served to marginalise pro-democracy legislators and enhance the importance of their pro-Beijing counterparts in the policymaking process. At the same time, as it emphasises vote calculation at the expense of consensus-building within the community, the tactic runs the risk of attracting public opposition to the government. The recent transformation in government strategy may be considered an extension of Beijing's post-2003 strategy, which openly stresses the need for executive-led government and seeks to counter the influence of the pro-democracy forces within Legco. In conjunction with the proportional representation voting system in Legco elections, the government's new strategy has led to the gradual disintegration of Legco, deepened the growing fragmentation therein and weakened the potential of political groups within Legco to operate as a collective actor

*Sar—Evaluating the Tsang Years 2005–2012* (Hong Kong: City University of Hong Kong Press, 2013), 24.

21 Interview with Councillor Lee Cheuk Yan on 11 February 2009.

22 Interview with Councillor Jasper Tsang on 22 July 2011.

in proposing alternative policies. As a result, cross-party concensus has gradually declined since 2002.[23]

Accompanying these political dynamics is 'the people's growing use of radical tactics', and, inside Legco, 'politicians' strategies are also increasingly deviating from the traditional manner of lobbying and politicking'.[24] The pro-democracy camp has made adjustments in response to the executive's more aggressive approach and to growing public impatience with the lack of universal suffrage. The external means employed by democrats within Legco include seeking judicial intervention in Legco's internal business and mobilising members of the public, as seen, for instance, in the 'five-constituency resignation' incident and de-facto referendum of 2010. The non-traditional or unusual manoeuvres within Legco include throwing objects during Legco meetings and filibusters in the Finance Committee and in plenary meetings. These manoeuvres seemingly have a double-edged effect on Legco autonomy. For instance, inviting judicial invention in Legco's internal business constitutes an essential external constraint on the legislature's autonomy. Given the growing tensions surrounding political development, such non-traditional means may become increasingly common and perhaps even unavoidable, even if the majority of legislators, moderate democrats in particular, are generally reluctant to support them. The powerlessness of the pro-democracy camp may lead to a lower level of public administration given its role as a provider of checks and balances against the executive branch. More importantly, in view of the pro-democracy camp's firm position on the protection of civil liberties and the rule of law, its growing weakness in Hong Kong's political structure is clearly not conducive to the pursuit of more transparent government and a more democratic political system.

### *Rule of Leung Chun Ying*

Mr Leung Chun Ying's win in the 2012 CE election and the subsequent redistribution of political resources within the pro-Beijing camp have shed light on the impact of Beijing's strategy shift. The extensive involvement of the LOCPG in the election was evidenced by the high-profile visit of the then CE-elect to the LOCPG on the day following the election. Furthermore, during the fierce election campaign, 'very damaging divisions' appeared within the pro-Beijing camp.[25]

23 See 'The Short-Lived Cross-Party Coalition' in Chapter 5.

24 For political activism, see Lam (n 2), 207.

25 Joseph Yu-Shek Cheng, 'The 2012 Chief Executive Election in Hong Kong and the Challenges for the Chinese Authorities', *East Asian Policy*, 05 (2013), 100.

After the failure of any 'grand reconciliation',[26] more political power became concentrated in Leung's hands.

Under Hong Kong's new rulers, the traditional professional, political and business elites from the colonial era have gradually been removed from the political centre and replaced by Leung's active supporters and allies in various public bodies. Of the current non-official Exco members, apart from representatives of the major pro-Beijing political groups, most are loyal Leung supporters who played an important role in his election campaign despite some of them either having a controversial track record in public service or lacking relevant experience.[27] After the 2012 Legco elections, Leung strengthened executive control over FCs for the removal of a number of long-term FC legislators, including representatives of the Finance, Commercial and several professional sectors. At the same time, the professional and business forces within Legco have been integrated into a new political group called the Business and Professionals Alliance for Hong Kong (HKBPA), which no longer constitutes the loose grouping of its predecessor organisation, the Alliance or Professional Forum. The HKBPA has become a more influential political group than the Liberal Party which was previously the sole political party representing the business sector in Legco as well as Leung's political adversary within the pro-Beijing camp. The leader of HKBPA Jeffrey Lam is currently serving in Exco. In addition to this redistribution of political power, Leung has named his allies as the chairs of several politically or economically important advisory and statutory bodies, such as the Independent Police Complaints Council (IPCC),

26 Ibid.

27 For example, in 2007, Mr Arthur Li and Ms Fanny Law were alleged to have interfered in academic freedom and institutional autonomy of the Hong Kong Institute of Education during their respective tenure of Secretary for Education and Manpower and of Permanent Secretary for Education and Manpower. The government set up a Commission of Inquiry to investigate the incident. Mr Fanny Law resigned from the civil service after the Inquiry Commission delivered a report which found that 'the allegation on Mrs Law's demand to sack academics was "partially established" in relation to two case'. The allegation against Professor Arthur Li was not established in the Report. See Polly Hui, Liz Gooch and Albert Wong, 'Fanny Law Quits over "Interference"', *South China Morning Post*, 21 June 2007, EDT. After Leung Chun Ying won the 2012 CE election, Ms Fanny Law and Mr Arthur Li were appointed Executive Councillors, probably because of their core roles in Leung's election campaign. See Ng Kang-chung and Colleen Lee, 'Several Old Faces to Stay on in Exco under Leung', *South China Morning Post*, 22 June 2012, CITY5. In addition, Mr Chi Kong, former executive director of the One Country Two Systems Research Institute, was appointed as Executive Councillor in spite of his lack of relevant experience in the public service.

Airport Authority Hong Kong (AAHK), Hong Kong Trade Development Council (HKTDC) and Hong Kong Science and Technology Parks Corporation. Leung has also created new advisory bodies to push forward a policy agenda focusing on housing and economic cooperation with the Mainland. They include the Long Term Housing Strategy Steering Committee, Consultative Committee on Economic and Trade Co-operation between Hong Kong and the Mainland, Financial Services Development Council, Lantau Development Advisory Committee and Economic Development Commission.

However, these moves have not been without controversy. For example, few of Leung's loyal supporters (the so called 'Leung Fans') are on a par with their predecessors in terms of reputation and long experience in public service. Since July 2012, one principal official and two Exco members have resigned in the wake of various scandals.[28] Leung's appointment of the IPCC chair was also considered contrary to the convention of appointing a Senior Counsel to this position.[29] In addition, the intricate transfer arrangements for senior staff members of the AAHK and HKTDC have also given rise to criticism.[30] Even after the Audit Commission's disclosure of the Mega Events Fund scandal, Leung still reappointed members of the Assessment Committee, and HKBPA leader Jeffrey Lam has continued to hold the chairmanship.[31] The government has faced ongoing criticism over its inability to attract competent candidates to fill vacant positions in government and public bodies.[32]

The Central Policy Unit (CPU) has reportedly played a vital role in recruiting and selecting people for the government and public bodies, with the CPU head promising that the unit will 'strengthen its capability in policy research in the areas of public opinion and cultivation of a reserve of talents'.[33] Other attempts

28 They are Secretary for Development, Mr Mak Chai-kwong, and members of the Executive Council, Mr Barry Cheung and Franklin Lam. Mr Mak resigned after involving a housing allowance scandal. Mr Barry Cheung was involved in the controversy over Hong Kong Mercantile Exchange. Mr Franklin Lam stepped down in 2013 after nine months' leave of absence prompted by alleged misconduct in public office and offering illicit advantage. *See* Editorial, 'Impartiality Key in HKMEx Case', *South China Morning Post*, 23 May 2013, EDT.

29 Stuart Lau, 'Unknown Face Is Police Watchdog's New Chairman', *South China Morning Post*, 31 May 2014, City.

30 Hansard HK (25 June 2014), 130.

31 Phila Siu, 'Mega Events Fund Criticised for Overstating Attendances and Expenditure "Irregularities"', *South China Morning Post*, 17 April 2014, EDT3.

32 Jolie Ho, 'Exco Loss Sparks Talent Pool Fears', *South China Morning Post*, 3 August 2013, CITY3.

33 'Minutes of Panel on Public Service of the Legco' (LC Paper No. CB(4)312/12-13, 2012), 5.

to tighten control over the political structure include the frequent mobilisation of patriotic members of the public to counteract the greater mobilisation ability of the pro-democracy camp.[34]

The preceding analysis seems to suggest that the consensus-seeking and coalition-building approaches of the HKSAR's early years have given way to a desire for the concentration of power and full control over the political system on the part of the government. The result may be damage to the efficiency of public administration and increase political polarisation, given the decline of moderate forces in both the pro-Beijing and pro-democracy camps.

On 10 June 2014, the Information Office of the State Council of the PRC issued a *White Paper on the Practice of the 'One Country, Two Systems' Policy in the Hong Kong Special Administrative Region* (White Paper hereafter). According to the White Paper, 'loving the country is the basic political requirement for Hong Kong's administrators',[35] who also have a responsibility to safeguard 'the country's sovereignty, security and development interests and [to ensure] the long-term prosperity and stability of Hong Kong'.[36] The White Paper also sheds light on the necessity 'to stay alert to the attempt of outside forces to use Hong Kong to interfere in China's domestic affairs, and prevent and repel the attempt made by a very small number of people who act in collusion with outside forces to interfere with the implementation of "one country, two systems" in Hong Kong'.[37]

This was the first time that the State Council comprehensively elucidated Beijing's current policy towards Hong Kong in a white paper. The overwhelming dominance of 'one country' over 'two systems' will inevitably increase the CE's dependence on the CPG and its representatives in Hong Kong, despite the CE's dual accountability to the CPG and Legco. The aforementioned White Paper statements clearly convey the message that the people of Hong Kong need to look at the 'bigger' picture of 'the country's sovereignty, security and development interests' when considering their rights and the autonomy their city enjoys. In this sense, the democrats of Hong Kong, as dissidents and the severest of the CPG's critics, will find it increasingly difficult to enter the 'administrator' class owing to their embrace of universal values and

34 In recent years, a lot of patriotic organisations have sprung up, including for example The Voice of Loving Hong Kong and Caring Hong Kong Power.

35 See The State Council Information Office, 'The Practice of the "One Country, Two Systems" Policy in the Hong Kong Special Administrative Region' (2014) <http://news.xinhuanet.com/english/china/2014-06/10/c_133396891.htm> accessed 15 June 2014.

36 Ibid.

37 Ibid.

connection with 'outside forces' (whether that connection is accurate or not). Furthermore, despite Mr Leung's continued low popularity rating, the ideology of his team is seemingly much closer to the message conveyed by the White Paper than that of his predecessors. Hence, there is a predicable impasse in Hong Kong's political structure and in the coming constitutional reform.

Under the overwhelming influence of the 'one country' policy, Legco members may continue to perform a vital role in checking executive power and shaping public policy provided that they are able to build effective communication with and mobilise the citizenry. Normally, an autonomous legislative branch that serves as a popular and effective body for checking the executive branch and as a forum for public debate is in the best interests of all political parties. Ironically, in Hong Kong, it seems that political forces from both the pro-Beijing and pro-democracy camps have been working to diminish Legco's autonomy, whether intentionally or not. The current situation is disappointing for many because a weak legislature 'undermines horizontal accountability as well as vertical accountability'.[38]

38 M. Steven Fish, 'Stronger Legislatures, Stronger Democracies', *Journal of Democracy*, 17/1 (2006) 12.

# Bibliography

## Articles and Books


Blackburn, Robert and Kennon, Andrew (2001), *Griffith & Ryle on Parliament: Functions, Practice and Procedures*. (2nd edn.; London: Sweet & Maxwell).

Blondel, J. (1973), *Comparative Legislatures* (Englewood Cliffs, N.J.: Prentice-Hall).

Carey, John M. (2006), 'Legislative Organization', in Rhodes, R.A.W., Binder, Sarah A., and Rockman, Bert A. (eds.), *The Oxford Handbook of Political Institutions* (Oxford; New York: Oxford University Press).

Carey, John M., Formanek, Frantisek, and Karpowicz, Ewa (1999), 'Legislative Autonomy in New Regimes: The Czech and Polish Cases', *Legislative Studies Quarterly*, 24, 569.

Cheek-Milby, Kathleen (1995), *A Legislature Comes of Age: Hong Kong's Search for Influence and Identity* (Hong Kong: Oxford University Press).

Chen, Albert H.Y. (1997), 'The Provisional Legislative Council of the SAR', *Hong Kong Law Journal*, 27/1, 1.

——. (2002), 'Hong Kong's Legal System in the New Constitutional Order: The Experience of 1997–2000', in Chen, Jianfu, Li, Yuwen, and Otto, Jan Michiel (eds.), *Implementation of Law in the People's Republic of China* (The Hague: Kluwer Law International).

——. (2004), 'The Constitutional Controversy of Spring 2004', *Hong Kong Law Journal*, 34, 215.

——. (2007), 'The Basic Law and the Development of the Political System in Hong Kong', *Asia Pacific Law Review*, 15/1, 19.

——. (2009), 'Constitutional Developments in Autumn 2009', *Hong Kong Law Journal*, 39, 751.

——. (2010a), 'An Unexpected Breakthrough in Hong Kong's Constitutional Reform', *Hong Kong Law Journal*, 40, 259.

——. (2010b), 一國兩制下香港的法治探索 (*Hong Kong's Explorations in the Rule of Law under One Country Two Systems*) (Hong Kong: Zhonghua Shu Ju).

Cheng, Jie (2009a), 'The Story of A New Policy', *Hong Kong Journal*, 15/July <http://web.archive.org/web/20120107011853/http://www.hkjournal.org/archive/2009_fall/1.htm>, accessed 2 January 2015.

——. (2009b), '香港宪制发展与行政主导体制 (*Constitutional Development and the Executive-Dominated System in Hong Kong*)', 法学(*Legal Science*), 1, 45–56.

Cheng, Joseph Y.S. (2013a), 'Has He Got the Job Done? An Evaluation of Donald Tsang Administration', in Cheng, Joseph Y.S. (ed.), *The Second Chief Executive of Hong Kong SAR—Evaluating the Tsang Years 2005–2012* (Hong Kong: City University of Hong Kong Press).

——. (2013b), 'The 2012 Chief Executive Election in Hong Kong and the Challenges for the Chinese Authorities', *East Asian Policy*, 05.

Cheung, Anne S.Y. and Chen, Albert H.Y. (2004), 'The Search for the Rule of Law in the Hong Kong Special Administrative Region, 1997–2003', in Yiu-Chung, Wong (ed.), *'One Country, Two Systems' in Crisis: Hong Kong's Transformation since the Handover* (Lanham: Lexington Books).

Cheung, Anthony B.L. (2007), 'Executive-Led Governance or Executive Power "Hollowed-Out" – The Political Quagmire of Hong Kong', *Asian Journal of Political Science*, 15, 17.

——. (2010), 'Restoring Governability in Hong Kong: Managing Plurality and Joining up Governance', in Tao, Julia Lai Po-Wah et al. (eds.), *Governance for Harmony in Asia and beyond* (New York: Routledge), 158–185.

Choy, Chi-keung and Lau, Sai-leung (1996), '九七回歸前的行政立法關係 (*The Executive-Legislative Relations in Hong Kong before 1997*)', *Hong Kong Journal of Social Sciences*, 8, 237.

Cooray, M.J.A. (1999), 'Hong Kong's Ombudsman: The First Decade', in Institutional Ombudsman Institute and Reif, L.C. (eds.), *The International Ombudsman Yearbook*, Vol. 3 (The Hague: Kluwer Law International), 71–88.

Cox, Gary W. and Morgenstern, Scott (2001), 'Latin America's Reactive Assemblies and Proactive Presidents', *Comparative Politics*, 33, 171.

Cullen, Richard and Simmons, Richard (2008), 'Tax Reform and Democratic Reform in Hong Kong: What Do the People Think?' *British Tax Review*, 6, 667–690.

Cullen, Richard, Wong, Antonietta, and Civic Exchange (2008), *The Foundations of the Hong Kong Revenue Regime* (Hong Kong: Civic Exchange).

Endacott, G.B. (1964), *Government and People in Hong Kong 1841–1962: A Constitutional History* (Hong Kong: Hong Kong University Press).

Fish, M. Steven (2006), 'Stronger Legislatures, Stronger Democracies', *Journal of Democracy*, 17/1, 5.

Ghai, Yash (1999), *Hong Kong's New Constitutional Order: The Resumption of Chinese Sovereignty and the Basic Law* (2nd edn.; Hong Kong: Hong Kong University Press).

Gittings, Danny (2013), *Introduction to the Hong Kong Basic Law* (Hong Kong: Hong Kong University Press).

Hong Kong Government (1984), 'Green Paper: The Further Development of Representative Government in Hong Kong'.

——. (1987), 'Green Paper: The 1987 Review of Developments in Representative Government'.

Johnson, Nevil (1971), 'Financial Accountability to Parliament', in Smith, Bruce L.R. and Hague, Douglas Chalmers (eds.), *The Dilemma of Accountability in Modern Government: Independence versus Control* (London: Macmillan).

Kellogg, Tom (2004), 'Legislating Rights: Basic Law Article 23, National Security, and Human Rights in Hong Kong', *Columbia Journal of Asian Law*, 17/2, 307.

King, Ambrose (1975), 'Administrative Absorption of Politics in Hong Kong: Emphasis on the Grass Roots Level', *Asian Survey*, 15/5, 422.

Kwok, Rowena Y.F. and Chow, Chiu Tak (2006), 'The Dynamics of Social Policy Making in Hong Kong: The Role of Functional Representatives (1998–2004)', in Loh, Christine and Exchange, Civic (eds.), *Functional Constituencies: A Unique Feature of the Hong Kong Legislative Council* (Hong Kong: Hong Kong University Press).

Lam, Jermain T.M. (2004), 'Ministerial System in Hong Kong: A Strengthening of the Executive Leadership', *Asian Perspective*, 28, 183.

Lam, Wai-man (2012), 'Political Identity, Culture, and Participation', in Lam, Wai-man, Lui, Percy Luen-tim, and Wong, Wilson (eds.), *Contemporary Hong Kong Government and Politics* (Expanded 2nd edn.; Hong Kong: Hong Kong University Press).

Lau, Siu Kai (2007), 'In Search of a New Political Order', in Yeung, Yue Man (ed.), *The First Decade: The Hong Kong SAR in Retrospective and Introspective Perspectives* (Hong Kong: Chinese University Press).

Lau, Siu-kai and Kuan, Hsin-chi (2000), 'Partial Democratization, "Foundation Moment" and Political Parties in Hong Kong', *The China Quarterly*, 163, 705.

Lo, P.Y. (2012), 'Lai Bo and Other 'Procedural Kills: A Study of Discontent in the Legislative Council', *Hong Kong Law Journal*, 42, 287.

Lo, Sonny Shiu Hing (1997), 'Hong Kong's Legislative Council as a Symbol of Political Development', *Hong Kong Law Journal*, 27/2, 271.

——. (2007), 'The Mainlandization and Recolonization of Hong Kong: A Triumph of Convergence over Divergence with Mainland China', in Cheng, Joseph Y.S. (ed.), *The Hong Kong Special Administrative Region in Its First Decade* (Hong Kong: City University of Hong Kong Press).

——. (2008), *The Dynamics of Beijing-Hong Kong Relations: A Model for Taiwan?* (Hong Kong: Hong Kong University Press).

Loh, Christine and Civic Exchange (2006), *Functional Constituencies: A Unique Feature of the Hong Kong Legislative Council* (Hong Kong: Hong Kong University Press).

Louie, Kin-shuen and Shum, Kwok Cheung (eds.) (1995), 香港選舉資料彙編 *1982 年–1994 年(Hong Kong Electorate Facts: 1982–1994)* (Hong Kong: Hong Kong Institute of Asia-Pacific Studies, The Chinese University of Hong Kong).

Lui, Percy Luen-tim (2007), 'The Legislature', in Lam Wai-man et al. (eds.), *Contemporary Hong Kong Politics: Governance in the Post-1997 Era* (Hong Kong: Hong Kong University Press).

Ma, Ngok (2002), 'Executive-Legislative Relations: Assessing Legislative Influence in an Executive-Dominant System', in Lau, Siu Kai (ed.), *The First Tung Chee-hwa Administration: The First Five Years of the Hong Kong Special Administrative Region* (Hong Kong: The Chinese University Press).

——. (2007a), 'Democratic Development in Hong Kong: A Decade of Lost Opportunities', in Cheng, Joseph Y.S. (ed.), *The Hong Kong Special Administrative Region in Its First Decade* (Hong Kong: City University of Hong Kong Press).

——. (2007b), *Political Development in Hong Kong: State, Political Society, and Civil Society* (Hong Kong: Hong Kong University Press).

——. (2010), 香港政治: 發展歷程與核心課題 (*Hong Kong Politics: Development Process and Key Issues*) (Hong Kong: Hong Kong Institute of Asia-Pacific Studies).

Ma, Ngok and Chan, Kin-man (2008), 'Asian Barometer – Hong Kong Report: The State of Democratic Governance in Hong Kong', *The Asian Barometer Conference on 'The State of Democratic Governance in Asia'* (Taipei, 20–21 June 2008).

Mattson, Ingvar and Strom, Kaare (1995), 'Parliamentary Committees', in Döring, Herbert (ed.), *Parliaments and Majority Rule in Western Europe* (Frankfurt/Main; Campus Verlag; New York: St. Martin's Press).

May, Thomas Erskine, McKay, W.R., and Cranmer, Frank (2004), *Erskine May's Treatise on the Law, Privileges, Proceedings, and Usage of Parliament* (23rd edn.; London: LexisNexis UK).

McGee, David (2007), 'Strengthening Financial Scrutiny', *53rd Commonwealth Parliamentary Conference* (New Delhi, India, 21–30 September 2007).

Mezey, Michael L. (1979), *Comparative Legislatures* (Durham, N.C.: Duke University Press).

Miners, Norman John (1994), 'The Transformation of the Hong Kong Legislative Council 1970–1994: From Consensus to Confrontation', *Asian Journal of Public Administration*, 16, 224.

Miners, Norman John and Tang, Tuck-hang James (1998), *The Government and Politics of Hong Kong* (5th edn.; Hong Kong: Oxford University Press).

Norton, Philip (1984), 'Parliament and Policy in Britain: The House of Commons as a Policy Influencer', *Teaching Politics*, 13/2, 198.

——. (1993), 'Questions and the Role of Parliament', in Franklin, Mark N., Norton, Philip, and Study of Parliament Group (eds.), *Parliamentary Questions* (Oxford: Clarendon Press).

——. (2005), *Parliament in British Politics* (Contemporary political studies series; Houndmills, Basingstoke, Hampshire; New York: Palgrave Macmillan).

Olson, David M. (1994), *Democratic Legislative Institutions: A Comparative View* (Armonk, N.Y.: M.E. Sharpe).

Olson, David M. and Norton, Philip (1996), 'Legislatures in Democratic Transition', in Olson, David M. and Norton, Philip (eds.), *The New Parliaments of Central and Eastern Europe* (London; Portland, Ore.: Frank Cass).

Packenham, Robert A. (1970), 'Legislatures and Political Development', in Kornberg, Allan, Musolf, Lloyd D., and American Society for Public Administration Comparative Administration Group (eds.), *Legislatures in Developmental Perspective* (Comparative Administration Group Series; Durham, N.C.,: Duke University Press).

Peabody, Robert L. (1984), 'Leadership in Legislatures: Evolution, Selection, Functions', *Legislative Studies Quarterly*, 9/3, 441.

Pelizzo, Riccardo and Stapenhurst, Rick (2008), 'Tools for Legislative Oversight: An Empirical Investigation', in Stapenhurst, Rick et al. (eds.), *Legislative Oversight and Budgeting: A World Perspective* (WBI Development Studies; Washington DC: World Bank).

Petersen, Carole J. (2005), 'Hong Kong's Spring of Discontent: The Rise and Fall of the National Security Bill in 2003', in Fu, Hualing, Petersen, Carole J., and Young, Simon N.M. (eds.), *National Security and Fundamental Freedoms Hong Kong's Article 23 under Scrutiny* (Hong Kong: Hong Kong University Press).

Premchand, Arigapudi (1999), 'Public Financial Accountability', in Schiavo-Campo, Salvatore (ed.), *Governance, Corruption, and Public Financial Management* (Manila: Asian Development Bank).

Sisson, Richard (1973), 'Comparative Legislative Institutionalization: A Theoretical Exploration', in Kornberg, Allen (ed.), *Legislatures in Comparative Perspective* (New York: David McKay Company, Inc.).

Tang, Shu Hung (2006), 'A Critical Review of the 2006 Consultation Document on Broadening the Tax Base in Hong Kong', *Asia-Pacific Journal of Taxation*, 10, 37.

Wang, Shucheng and Gu, Minkang (2010), '香港立法会调查权界限分析 (*An Analysis of the Investigation Power of the Legislative Council of Hong Kong*)', *Global Law Review*, 6, 140–151.

Wang, Yu (2008), "一国两制" 宪法精神研究 (*A Study of the Spirit of the Constitution Concerning "One Country Two Systems"*) (Guangzhou: Guangdong People's Press).

Wehner, Joachim (2003), 'Principles and Patterns of Financial Scrutiny: Public Accounts Committees in the Commonwealth', *Commonwealth & Comparative Politics*, 41, 16.

——. (2004), *Back from the Sidelines? Redefining the Contribution of Legislatures to the Budget Cycle* (Series on Contemporary Issues in Parliamentary Development; Washington, DC: World Bank Institute).

——. (2006), 'Assessing the Power of the Purse: An Index of Legislative Budget Institutions', *Political Studies*, 54, 767.

Wehner, Joachim and Byanyima, Winnie (2004), 'Parliament, the Budget and Gender' (Inter-Parliamentary Union, United Nations Development Programme, World Bank Institute, and United Nations Fund for Women) <http://www.ipu.org/PDF/publications/budget_en.pdf>, accessed 20 October 2011.

Wesley-Smith, Peter (1994), *Constitutional and Administrative Law in Hong Kong* (Hong Kong: Longman Asia Ltd).

Wong, Max Wai-lun (1998), 'The Meaning of "Charge": Private Member's Bills in the Legislative Council', *Hong Kong Law Journal*, 28, 230.

Wong, Timothy Ka-ying and Wan, Shirley Po-san (2007), 'Citizen's Evaluations of Legitimacy in Post-colonial Hong Kong: Results of a Longitudinal Study', in Cheng, Joseph Yu-shek (ed.), *The Hong Kong Special Administrative Region in Its First Decade* (Hong Kong: City University of Hong Kong Press).

Xiao, Weiyun (2005), '关于香港特别行政区基本法的几个问题 (*Three Problems about the Basic Law of Hong Kong Special Administrative Region*)', 法学杂志(*Law Science Magazine*), 2, 4.

## Selected Committee Minutes, Reports and Factsheets of Legco and Government Documents

Advisory Committee on New Broad-based Taxes (2002), 'Report of the Advisory Committee on New Broad-Based Taxes', <http://www.fstb.gov.hk/tb/en/docs/btreport.pdf>, accessed 20 October 2011.

Bills Committee on National Security (Legislative Provisions) Bill (2003a), 'Minutes of Meeting Held on 6 March 2003' (LC Paper No. CB(2) 1612/02-03).

——. (2003b), 'Minutes of Meeting Held on 10 June 2003' (LC Paper No. CB(2) 2838/02-03).

——. (2003c), 'Minutes of Meeting Held on 14 June 2003' (LC Paper No. CB(2) 2848/02-03).

——. (2003d), 'Minutes of Meeting Held on 14 June 2003' (LC Paper No. CB(2) 2847/02-03).

——. (2003e), 'Minutes of Meeting Held on 17 June 2003' (LC Paper No. CB(2) 2962/02-03).

——. (2003f), 'Minutes of Meeting Held on 26 June 2003' (LC Paper No. CB(2) 2893/02-03).

——. (2003g), 'Paper No. 111', <http://www.legco.gov.hk/yr02-03/english/bc/bc55/papers/bc55-111-e.pdf>, accessed 21 September 2008.

Committee on Rules of Procedure (1998), 'Procedure in Dealing with the Introduction of Members' Bills as provided in Article 74 of the Basic Law and the interpretation of Article 48(10) of the Basic Law' (LC Paper No. CB(1) 45/98-99).

Constitutional and Mainland Affairs Bureau (2012), 'Legislative Council Brief on the Legislative Council (Amendment) Bill 2012' (CMAB C1/30/5).

Department of Justice (2010a), 'Legal Implications Concerning Repeal of the Country Parks (Designation) (Consolidation) (Amendment) Order 2010' (CB(1)2976/09-10(01)).

——. (2010b), 'Summary of the Advice Given by Mr Michael Thomas, Q.C., S.C. on the Power of LegCo to Repeal the Country Parks (Designation) (Consolidation) (Amendment) Order 2010' (CB(1)2988/09-10(01)).

Development Bureau (2010), 'Legislative Council Brief on Land (Compulsory Sale for Redevelopment) (Specification of Lower Percentage) Notice' (DEVB(PL-UR) 70/41/85).

Environmental Protection Department and Agriculture, Fisheries and Conservation Department (2010), 'Legislative Brief on Country Parks (Designation) (Consolidation) (Amendment) Order 2010' (EP CR 9/25/15).

Finance Committee (1999a), 'Minutes of Meeting Held on 12 March 1999' (LC Paper No. FC156/98-99).

——. (1999b), 'Minutes of Meeting Held on 15 January 1999' (LC Paper No. FC119/98-99).

——. (2003), 'Minutes of Meeting Held on 16 May 2003' (LC Paper No. FC136/02-03).

——. (2011a), 'Minutes of Meeting Held on 14 January 2011' (LC Paper No. FC116/10-11).

——. (2011b), 'Minutes of Meeting Held on 9 December 2011' (LC Paper No. FC87/11-12).

First Report and Second Report of the Select Committee on Building Problems of Public Housing Units.

House Committee of the Legislative Council (2003), 'Minutes of the 31st Meeting Held on 27 June 2003' (LC Paper No. CB(2) 2979/02-03).

Legislative Council (2004), 'The Legislative Council Annual Report, 2003-04', <http://www.legco.gov.hk/general/english/sec/reports/a_0304.pdf> accessed 21 September 2008.

Legislative Council Commission (2013), 'Report on the Activities of The Legislative Council Commission 2012–2013', <http://www.legco.gov.hk/general/english/sec/reports/c_1213.pdf>, accessed 1 June 2014.

Legislative Council Library (2011), 'LegCo InfoPack 2011–2012', *HKSAR Legislative Council* [web document] (October 2011) <http://www.legco.gov.hk/general/english/library/infopacks/yr11-12/1112infopacks-lc-01-e.pdf>, accessed 1 June 2014.

Legislative Council Secretariat (1998), 'Information Paper for the House Committee: Committee on Rules of Procedure Voting Procedures' (LC Paper No. CB(1) 72/98-99).

——. (2003a), 'Legal Service Division Report on National Security (Legislative Provisions) Bill' (LC Paper No. LS61/02-03).

——. (2003b), 'Report of the Bills Committee on National Security (Legislative Provisions) Bill' (LC Paper No. CB(2)2646/02-03).

——. (2003c), 'Summary of Concerns and Queries Raised by Members at the Joint Meetings on 26 September 2002, 21 October 2002, 19 December 2002 and 7 January 2003' (LC Paper No. CB(2) 1082/02-03(01)).

——. (2006a), 'Background Brief (for Regulation of Surveillance and the Interception of Communications)' (LC Paper No. CB(2)1423/05-06(05)).

——. (2006b), 'Issues Undertaken by the Administration to Be Incorporated in the Code of Practice to Be Issued by the Secretary for Security under the Bill' (LC Paper No. CB(2)2829/05-06(01)).

——. (2006c), 'Legal Service Division Report on Interception of Communications and Surveillance Bill' (LC Paper No. LS44/05-06).

——. (2006d), 'Report of the Bills Committee on Interception of Communications and Surveillance Bill' (LC Paper No. CB(2)2837/05-06).

——. (2008a), 'Report of the Bills Committee on Race Discrimination Bill' (LC Paper No. CB(2)2478/07-08).

——. (2008b), 'Legislative Council Procedures on Members' Bills', [web document] (3 January 2008) <http://www.legco.gov.hk/general/english/bills/mem-bill.pdf>, accessed 2 January 2015.

——. (2010a), 'Report of the Subcommittee on Country Parks (Designation) (Consolidation) (Amendment) Order 2010' (LC Paper No. CB(1)3017/09-10).

——. (2010b), 'Report of the Subcommittee on Land (Compulsory Sale for Redevelopment) (Specification of Lower Percentage) Notice' (LC Paper No. CB(1)1362/09-10).

Panel on Public Service (2012), 'Minutes of Panel on Public Service of the Legco' (LC Paper No. CB(4)312/12-13).

Panel on Security and Panel on Administration of Justice and Legal Services (2003), 'Minutes of Joint Meeting Held on 15 February 2003' (LC Paper No. CB(2)2035/02-03).

Public Accounts Committee (1999), 'PAC Report No. 31'.

——. (2000), 'PAC Report No. 33'.

——. (2001), 'PAC Report No. 36'.

——. (2002) 'PAC Report No. 37'.

——. (2003), 'PAC Report No. 39'.

——. (2004), 'PAC Report No. 41'.

——. (2005), 'PAC Report No. 45'.

Report of the Legislative Council Select Committee to Inquire into the Circumstances Leading to the Problems Surrounding the Commencement of the Operation of the New Hong Kong International Airport at Chek Lap Kok since 6 July 1998 and related issues (2004).

Report of the Select Committee to inquire into the handling of the Severe Acute Respiratory Syndrome outbreak by the Government and the Hospital Authority (2004).

Report of the Select Committee to Inquire into Matters Relating to the Post-service Work of Mr LEUNG Chin-man (2010).

Report of the Subcommittee to Study Issues Arising from Lehman Brothers-related Minibonds and Structured Financial Products (2012).

Report of the Select Committee to Study Mr LEUNG Chun-ying's Involvement as a Member of the Jury in the West Kowloon Reclamation Concept Plan Competition and Related Issues (2012).

Security Bureau (2002a), 'Legislative Council Brief: National Security (Legislative Provisions) Bill' (SBCR 2/1162/97).

——. (2002b), 'Proposals to Implement Article 23 of the Basic Law Consultation Document', <http://www.info.gov.hk/archive/consult/2002/bl23-e.pdf>, accessed 21 September 2008.

Subcommittee on Country Parks (Designation) (Consolidation) (Amendment) Order 2010 (2010), 'Minutes of the Fourth Meeting Held on 27 September 2010' (LC Paper No. CB(1)38/10-11).

The HKSAR Government (2003), 'Government Further Clarifies Legislative Proposals to Implement BL 23' (LC Paper No. CB(2)1069/02-03(02)).

## Internet Sources

Catholic Monitors on Legislative Councillors <http://www.legco-monitors.org>, accessed 10 September 2011.

Chan, Kin-man and Chung, Robert Ting-Yiu (2003), 'Redress for the Public Voice', *HKU POP Site* <http://hkupop.hku.hk/english/columns/columns20.html>, accessed 2 January 2015.

Legislative Council, 'Research Office', [web page], <http://www.legco.gov.hk/general/english/sec/corg_ser/research.htm>, accessed 1 June 2014.

——. (2010) 'Council Meeting (Voting Result) 17 March 2010', [web page], <http://www.legco.gov.hk/yr09-10/english/counmtg/voting/v201003172.htm>, accessed 2 January 2015.

Lienert, Ian (2005), 'Who Controls the Budget: The Legislature or the Executive?' (IMP WP/05/115, International Monetary Fund) <https://www.imf.org/external/pubs/ft/wp/2005/wp05115.pdf>, accessed 2 January 2015.

Maskell, Jack and Beth, Richard S. (2007), '"No Confidence" Votes and Other Forms of Congressional Censure of Public Officials' (Congrssional Research Service) <https://www.hsdl.org/?view&did=739550>, accessed 2 January 2015.

SynergyNet (2010), 'Review of the Governance Performance of the HKSAR Government 2010', <http://www.synergynet.org.hk/pdf/201012122320_en.pdf>, accessed 20 October 2011.

The Article 23 Concern Group (2003), 'Article 23 Legislation–what needs to be done' (8 July 2003), <http://www.article23.org.hk/english/main.htm>, accessed 10 September 2014.

The Chinese University of Hong Kong Institute of Asia-Pacific Studies (2009a), '市民對立法會表現評價意見調查結果摘要 (*Survey Results on Citizens' Opinions towards the Legislative Council's Performance*)', *CUHK* [web document] (29 July 2009) <http://www.cuhk.edu.hk/cpr/pressrelease/090729_survey.pdf>, accessed 2 January 2015.

——. (2009b), '表一:對特區政府各項施政的滿意度 (*Table 1: Satisfaction with Various Policies of the HKSAR Government*)', CUHK [web document] (20 April 2009) <http://www.cpr.cuhk.edu.hk/resources/press/pdf/4c43c7d775479.pdf>, accessed 2 January.

The Commissioner on Interception of Communications and Surveillance (2008), 'Annual Report 2008 to the Chief Executive', <http://www.info.gov.hk/info/sciocs/eng/pdf/Annual_Report_2008.pdf>, accessed 20 October 2011.

The Committee of Public Accounts of the House of Commons (2007), 'Holding Government to Account: 150 Years of the Committee of Public Accounts' (House of Commons) <http://www.parliament.uk/documents/commons-committees/public-accounts/pac-history-booklet-pdf-version-p1.pdf>, accessed 2 January 2015.

The CPA Parliamentary Financial Scrutiny Workshop (2006), 'Parliamentary Financial Scrutiny: the Role of Public Accounts Committees (PACS)' (Commonwealth Parliamentary Association, World Bank Institute, and La Trobe University) <http://www.agora-parl.org/sites/default/files/pacs.pdf > accessed 20 October 2011.

The HKSAR Government (2003a), 'Chief Executive's Transcript on Basic Law Article 23', [web page] (5 July 2003) <http://www.info.gov.hk/gia/general/200307/05/0705158.htm>, accessed 2 January 2015.

——. (2003b) 'List of Submissions', <http://www.basiclaw23.gov.hk/english/download/forward-e.pdf>, accessed 2 January 2015.

——. (2003c) 'Foreword (to the Conpendium of Submissions)', <http://www.basiclaw23.gov.hk/english/download/forward-e.pdf>, accessed 2 January 2015.

The Hong Kong Transition Project (2002), 'Accountability & Article 23: Freedoms, Fairness and Accountability in Hong Kong', <http://hktp.hkbu.edu.hk/article23/article23.pdf> accessed 21 September 2008.

The State Council Information Office (2014), 'The Practice of the "One Country, Two Systems" Policy in the Hong Kong Special Administrative Region', <http://news.xinhuanet.com/english/china/2014-06/10/c_133396891.htm>, accessed 15 June 2014.

The University of Hong Kong Public Opinion Programme (2011), '你對特區立法會成員既整體表現滿唔滿意?(*Are you satisfied with the overall performance of the members of HKSAR Legislative Council?*)', *HKU POP Site* [web page] <http://hkupop.hku.hk/chinese/popexpress/sargperf/fourthlc/poll/datatables.html#lc4>, accessed 2 January 2015.

# Index


accountability
  financial 25, 110
  of the government to Legco 4, 18, 24–25
    *see also* Article 64 of the Basic Law
advisory bodies 227–228
agenda control 12, 14, 15, 55, 219
annual Draft Estimates of Expenditure 112
anticipated reactions 9, 109, 133, 152, 222
Appropriation Bill 112
  amendment to 119–120
  deliberation on 116–119
  *see also* annual Draft Estimates of Expenditure
Article 23 Concern Group 94
Audit Commission 134, 136–137
autonomy
  administrative 5, 12, 34–35, 218
  committee 19, 35, 38–41, 219–220
  external environment for 12–13, 23–34, 215–218
  financial 5, 12, 34–35, 218
  institutional 4–5, 10–11
  internal characteristics for 12, 14–15, 34–41, 218–221
  legislative 5–12
  managerial 18
  of HKSAR 14, 158

Basic Law
  amendment to 27
  Annex II 7, 24, 36
  Article 8 98
  Article 23 34, 55, 88–96
  Article 39 59
  Article 48(11) 200
  Article 50 25, 25n39
  Article 64 24
  Article 73 23–24, 112
  Article 74 6–7, 37, 46–51, 68–69, 114–115, 216, 223
  Article 113 149
  Article 159 3n11
  interpretation of 15, 33, 68, 115, 180, 210, 210n51, 211–213
Basic Law Consultative Committee (BLCC) 34
Basic Law Drafting Committee 212n72
Bills Committee 19, 52–58, 219, 222, 224
  on National Security (Legislative Provisions) Bill 93–95
  *see also* Interception of Communications and Surveillance Bill; National Security (Legislative Provisions) Bill
Breakfast Group 80–81, 122, 126
British government 4
British parliament 39, 43, 111, 170, 185–186
Business and Professionals Alliance for Hong Kong (HKBPA) 227

Central Authorities 1, 15
Central People's Government (CPG) 2, 24–25, 29, 34, 88, 153, 155, 157–159, 171, 177–178, 205,
  representative of
    *see* LOCPG
  strategy shift of 224–225
Central Policy Unit 2, 228
Chan, Albert Wai Yip 83
Chan, Tanya 105–107, 175
Chan Yuen Han 97
Chen, Albert 52n38, 89n169, 159, 212
charging effect 24, 49, 69–70, 114, 154
  *see also* Rule 57(6) of the RoP
checks and balances 1, 4, 23, 69, 147, 214, 217
Chief Executive 59
  election of 3, 27, 33, 34, 176, 204–205, 218, 226
  impeachment of 1, 25, 25n38, 178
  no confidence in 172, 175–177
    *see also* no confidence motion
  powers of 1, 3–4
  question-and-answer session 193–195
  written consent of 33, 67, 114, 154
    *see also* charging effect
Chief Justice 24
Chinese People's Political Consultative Conference (CPPCC) 173
Constitution 1
Civic Party 37, 89n173

Civil Service 209
Code on Access to Information 22
Commissioner on Interception of Communications and Surveillance 64–65
committee
  leadership of 38, 40, 137–138, 220–221
  parliamentary 10
  system of 12
  *see also* Bills Committee; Committee on Members' Interests; Election Committee; ESC; Finance Committee; House Committee; PAC; PWSC; RoPC;
Committee on Members' Interests 38, 197
Committee on Rules of Procedure of Legco (RoPC) 68–69
Committee Stage Amendment (CSA) 58, 66
  determinants of members' 73–80
  restrictions on members' 66–68
Common Law 26, 98
constitution of the PRC 1
consultation 60, 89, 170, 198
Cooperative Resource Centre (CRC) 20
  *see also* Liberal Party
Court of Appeal 84, 132
Court of Final Appeal (CFA) 23, 24, 26, 60, 84–85, 87
Court of First Instance 59, 83, 115

democracy 3, 7, 17, 33
Democratic Alliance for the Betterment and Progress of Hong Kong (DAB) 20, 34, 57n55, 81, 91–97, 107, 121, 122, 131, 132, 162, 204
Democratic Party (DP) 20, 37, 59, 81, 94, 119, 121, 131
direct election 7, 224
  *see also* universal suffrage
District Councils 107, 164, 224

Economic Synergy 34, 81
eight-party coalition 34, 101, 121–126, 133
Election Committee 14, 27
electoral system 13–14
emergency power 3
Equal Opportunities Commission 22
Establishment Subcommittee (ESC) 111, 113, 129,
Eu, Audrey 83
Exchange Fund 148–149
  Advisory Committee for 149
Executive and Legislative Councils (Members) Bill 19
Executive Council 3, 18–19, 23, 73, 126, 136, 143–144, 205, 216
executive-led 2–6, 69, 177, 179, 179n69, 215, 224–225

Fan, Mrs Rita 46, 48, 67–69, 159, 159n20, 181–182, 221
  see *also* President of Legco
Federation of Hong Kong and Kowloon Labour Unions (FLU) 80–81, 88, 97
filibuster 82–87, 117, 218–219
Finance Committee 20, 38, 86, 111, 116–119, 127–129, 219, 222, 224, 226
  Chairmanship of 39, 220–221, 220n9
Financial Secretary (FS) 112, 120, 150–151
fiscal reserves 148
five-constituency resignation 83
Functional Constituencies (FCs) 1, 7, 27–30, 34, 162, 217
  democrats in 72
  election by 14, 18, 21, 27
  voting behaviour of 77–78

Geographical Constituencies (GCs) 14, 162–164, 204
  election by 14, 18, 21
  voting behaviour of 79–80, 166
Ghai, Yash 1

Heung Yee Kuk 29
Ho, Albert Chun Yan 53, 53n43, 69, 71, 71n120, 156, 157, 159n20, 180
Hong Kong and Macau Affairs Office of the State Council 29
Hong Kong Association for Democracy and People's Livelihood (ADPL) 20, 80–81, 94, 122
Hong Kong Confederation of Trade Unions (CTU) 81, 127
Hong Kong Federation of Trade Unions (FTU) 34, 80–81, 88, 93, 96, 97, 103, 107, 121, 122, 127
Hong Kong Monetary Authority 149–151
Hong Kong Progressive Alliance (HKPA) 20, 57, 93, 122, 131

House Committee (HC) 19, 20, 35, 38, 52, 53, 135, 180, 204, 219
 chairmanship of 39

information acquisition 14, 220
Interception of Communications and Surveillance Bill 59–65
Interpretation and General Clauses Ordinance (IGCO)
 section 34 99, 100–104
  *see also* negative vetting procedure
 section 35 99, 100–104
  *see also* positive vetting procedure
Ip Kwok Him 57, 93
Ip, Regina 80, 132

judiciary 1
 *see also* Chief Justice; Court of Appeal; Court of Final Appeal; Court of First Instance

Lau, Emily 39, 73, 116n40, 119, 121, 220n9
Lau Kong Wah 131
Lau, Miriam 61
Lau Siu Kai 2, 32
League of Social Democrats (LSD) 81, 83, 117
Lee Cheuk Yan 46, 127, 156, 225n21
Lee, Martin 94, 156, 157
legislative capacity 16
Legislative Council
 commission of 19, 34–35
 constitutional role of 23, 26, 206, 208, 212
 CE's power to dissolve
  *see* Article 50 of the Basic Law
 secretariat of 35
 *see also* Provisional Legislative Council
Legislative Council (Powers and Privileges)
 Ordinance (PPO) 20, 140–141, 197
 application of 200–205
 drafting history of 197–200
legislative viscosity 43n1
Letters Patent 1
Leung Chin Man 141, 202, 209
Leung Chun Ying 40, 85, 171, 176, 203, 226–229
 *see also* Chief Executive
Leung, Elsie 172–173
Leung Kwok Hung 83, 86, 115, 181–182
Liaison Office of the Central People's Government (LOCPG) 15, 158, 228
Liberal Party (LP) 20, 33–34, 79, 80–81, 92–96, 107, 121, 122, 162, 227
Li Fung Ying 97
Lo, Sonny
 *see* mainlandization

mainlandization 32
Meeting Point 20
Miners, Norman 30, 98
motion
 debates 155–156
 for adjournment 179–183
 of no confidence 170–178

National People's Congress (NPC) 3n11
 Decision of the National People's Congress on the Method for the Formation of the First Government and the First Legislative Council of the Hong Kong Special Administrative Region 22n35
 Standing Committee of (NPCSC) 2–3, 33, 153–159, 172, 180, 183
National Security (Legislative Provisions)
 Bill 88–98
 *see also* Article 23 of the Basic Law
negative vetting procedure 101–102
 *see also* section 34 of IGCO
New People's Party (NPP) 80–81,
Ng, Margaret 26, 39, 57, 64, 90n179, 96, 172, 175, 195

Office of the Unofficial Members of the Executive and Legislative Council (UMELCO) 18–19
One country, Two systems (OCTS) 2, 15, 32, 131n87, 158–159, 229–230
 *see also* White Paper

parliamentary privilege 84
Patten, Christopher Francis 18–19, 185
People Power 80–81, 83, 117
political party 14, 20–22, 30, 39, 81, 121–122, 131, 180, 199n7, 216, 220
 *see also* ADPL; Breakfast Group; Civic Party; CTU; DAB; DP; Economic Synergy; FLU; FTU; HKBPA; HKPA; LP;

LSD; NPP; People Power; Professional Forum; The Alliance; UDHK
positive vetting procedure 104
  *see also* section 35 of IGCO
President of Legco
  ruling amenable to judicial review 26, 84
  ruling on adjournment motion 180–183
  ruling on member's CSA 66–71
  ruling on motions 154–159
  ruling on private member's bill 46–51
  *see also* Fan, Mrs Rita; Tsang, Jasper Yok Sing
Principal Officials Accountability System (POAS) 175
private member's bills 21, 43–52
  introduction of 44
pro-Beijing camp 21, 28, 29, 33, 39, 40, 109, 119–120, 126, 217
  CSAs introduced by 72–73
  division of 34, 80–82
  motion moved by 160
  voting behaviour of 75–77
pro-business camp 33, 76, 77, 121, 217
pro-democracy camp 21, 28, 33, 39, 40, 109
  CSAs introduced by 71–73
  voting behaviour of 75–77
pro-grassroots camp 33, 76, 77, 97, 121
Professional Forum 80–81, 127, 162
proportional representation voting system 225
Provisional Legislative Council (PLC) 23, 104
Public Accounts Committee (PAC) 25, 113, 134–136, 222
  access to information of 143
  composition of 137–138
  non-partisan of 148, 220
  non-policy of 111, 220
  impartiality of 111
  summons power of 197, 202, 205
Public Opinion Programme of the University of Hong Kong 30, 31n64, 131n89
Public Works Subcommittee (PWSC) 111, 113, 129

Qiao Xiaoyang 29

representation 8, 10, 11–14, 22, 27, 30, 32, 217
Royal Instructions 49
  Clause XXIV 21
    *see also* charging effect
Rules of Procedure of the Legislative Council (RoP) 14, 36–37, 218
  amendments to 218–219
  Rule 16(2) 181
  Rule 16(4) 180
  Rules 51(3) and (4) 44
  Rule 57(4)(a) 70–71
    *see also* subject matter of a bill or a clause
  Rule 57(6) 115
    *see also* charging effect

Secretary for State for Foreign and Commonwealth Affairs 17
Separate Voting Mechanism (SVM) 7, 14, 36, 66, 74–77, 87, 97, 101, 103–104, 116, 164–166, 168
  *see also* Annex II of the Basic Law
separation of powers 1, 5, 84, 215
Sin Chung Kai 71, 79, 92, 189
Sino-British Declaration of the Government of the United Kingdom of Great Britain and Northern Ireland and the Government of the People's Republic of China on the Question of Hong Kong (Joint Declaration) 4n16, 17, 18
Standing Orders of Legco 20, 36, 198
subject matter of a bill or a clause 67, 70–71, 223
subsidiary legislation 98
  *see also* negative vetting procedure; positive vetting procedure
summons power
    *see* PPO

Tam, Maria 199
Tam Yiu Chung 151
The Alliance 80, 97–98
Tien, James Pei Chun 34, 95, 122, 126
To, James Kun Sun 51–52, 59, 62, 103–104, 119, 189, 193
Tsang, Donald 33, 55, 65, 175, 193n25, 204, 223
  *see also* Chief Executive
Tsang, Jasper Yok Sing 46, 62, 68, 83–87, 103, 106, 181–182
  *see also* President of Legco

Tsang, John 225
see also Financial Secretary
Tung Chee Hwa 33, 174, 175, 179n69
see also Chief Executive

United Democrats of Hong Kong (UDHK) 20
universal suffrage 3, 29–30, 33, 156

Value for Money(VFM) 135–136

Wesley-Smith, Peter 98
White Paper on the Practice of the 'One Country, Two Systems' Policy in the Hong Kong Special Administrative Region (White Paper) 229
Wong, Andrew 49, 189
Wong, Philip 39, 83, 137, 162
Wong Yuk Man 83, 172
Wu Bangguo 2

Xiao Weiyun 177

Yeung Sum 70, 119, 130, 175

Zhang Xiaoming 29

www.ingramcontent.com/pod-product-compliance
Lightning Source LLC
LaVergne TN
LVHW010626300926
849162LV00001B/72